✔ KU-714-724

REEDS MARINA GUIDE 2007

The source directory for all sail & power boat owners

© Adlard Coles Nautical 2006

Adlard Coles Nautical,
38 Soho Square, London W1D 3HB
Tel: 0207 758 0200
Fax: 0207 758 0222/0333
e-mail: info@reedsalmanac.co.uk
www.reedsalmanac.co.uk

Cover photo: Dean & Reddyhoff Ltd
Tel: 023 9260 1201
www.deanreddyhoff.co.uk

Section 1

The Marinas and Services Section has been fully updated for the 2007 season. These useful pages provide chartlets and facility details for over 170 marinas around the shores of the UK and Ireland, including the Channel Islands, the perfect complement to any *Reeds Nautical Almanac*.

Section 2

The Marine Supplies & Services section lists more than 500 services at coastal and other locations around the British Isles. It provides a quick and easy reference to manufacturers and retailers of equipment, services and supplies both nationally and locally together with emergency services.

Advertisement Sales

Enquiries about advertising space should be addressed to:

**MS Publications, 2nd Floor
Ewer House, 44-46 Crouch Street
Colchester, Essex, CO3 3HH
Tel: +44(0)1206 506223
Fax: +44 (0)1206 500228**

Section 1

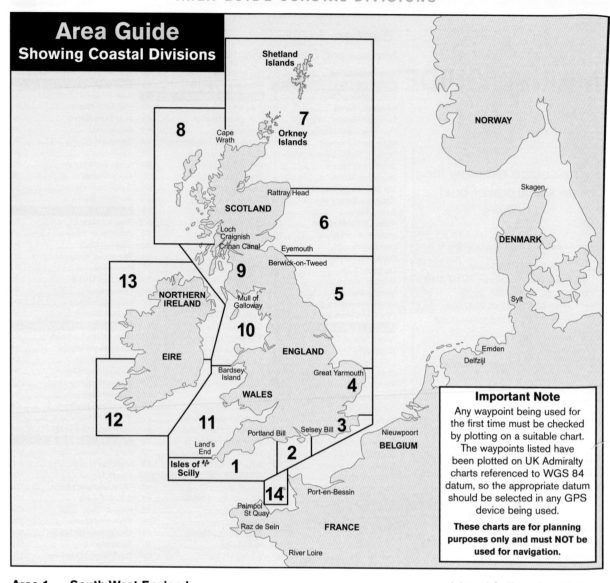

Area Guide
Showing Coastal Divisions

Important Note
Any waypoint being used for the first time must be checked by plotting on a suitable chart. The waypoints listed have been plotted on UK Admiralty charts referenced to WGS 84 datum, so the appropriate datum should be selected in any GPS device being used.

These charts are for planning purposes only and must NOT be used for navigation.

Area 1	**South West England**	Isles of Scilly to Anvil Point
Area 2	**Central Southern England**	Anvil Point to Selsey Bill
Area 3	**South East England**	Selsey Bill to North Foreland
Area 4	**East England**	North Foreland to Great Yarmouth
Area 5	**North East England**	Great Yarmouth to Berwick-upon-Tweed
Area 6	**South East Scotland**	Eyemouth to Rattray Head
Area 7	**North East Scotland**	Rattray Head to Cape Wrath including Orkney & Shetland Is
Area 8	**North West Scotland**	Cape Wrath to Crinan Canal
Area 9	**South West Scotland**	Crinan Canal to Mull of Galloway
Area 10	**North West England**	Isle of Man & N Wales, Mull of Galloway to Bardsey Is
Area 11	**South Wales & Bristol Channel**	Bardsey Island to Land's End
Area 12	**South Ireland**	Malahide, south to Liscanor Bay
Area 13	**North Ireland**	Lambay Island, north to Liscanor Bay
Area 14	**Channel Islands**	Guernsey, Jersey & Alderney

SOUTH WEST ENGLAND - Isles of Scilly to Anvil Point

ADLARD COLES NAUTICAL
WEATHER FORECASTS
BY FAX & TELEPHONE

Coastal/Inshore	2-day by Fax	5-day by Phone
Bristol	09065 222 349	09068 969 649
South West	09065 222 348	09068 969 648
Mid Channel	09065 222 347	09068 969 647
Channel Islands	–	09068 969 656
National (3-5 day)	09065 222 340	09068 969 640

Offshore	2-5 day by Fax	2-5 day by Phone
English Channel	09065 222 357	09068 969 657
Southern North Sea	09065 222 358	09068 969 658
Irish Sea	09065 222 359	09068 969 659
Biscay	09065 222 360	09068 969 660

09068 CALLS COST 60P PER MIN. 09065 CALLS COST £1.50 PER MIN.

Key to Marina Plans symbols

Calor Gas		Parking
Chandler		Pub/Restaurant
Disabled facilities		Pump out
Electrical supply		Rigging service
Electrical repairs		Sail repairs
Engine repairs		Shipwright
First Aid		Shop/Supermarket
Fresh Water		Showers
Fuel - Diesel		Slipway
Fuel - Petrol		Toilets
Hardstanding/boatyard		Telephone
Internet Café		Trolleys
Laundry facilities		Visitors berths
Lift-out facilities		Wi-Fi

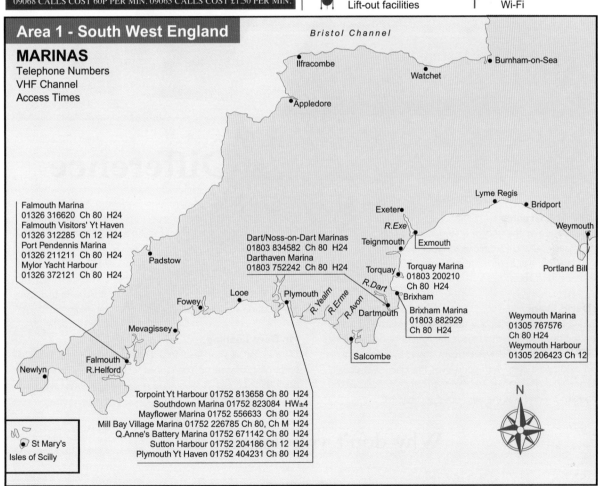

Area 1 - South West England

MARINAS
Telephone Numbers
VHF Channel
Access Times

Bristol Channel

Ilfracombe
Watchet
Burnham-on-Sea
Appledore

Falmouth Marina
01326 316620 Ch 80 H24
Falmouth Visitors' Yt Haven
01326 312285 Ch 12 H24
Port Pendennis Marina
01326 211211 Ch 80 H24
Mylor Yacht Harbour
01326 372121 Ch 80 H24

Padstow

Dart/Noss-on-Dart Marinas
01803 834582 Ch 80 H24
Darthaven Marina
01803 752242 Ch 80 H24

Exeter
R.Exe
Teignmouth
Exmouth
Torquay
R.Dart
Brixham

Lyme Regis
Bridport
Weymouth

Torquay Marina
01803 200210
Ch 80 H24

Portland Bill

Looe
Plymouth
R.Yealm
R.Erme
R.Avon
Dartmouth

Brixham Marina
01803 882929
Ch 80 H24

Weymouth Marina
01305 767576
Ch 80 H24
Weymouth Harbour
01305 206423 Ch 12

Fowey
Mevagissey

Salcombe

Falmouth
R.Helford

Newlyn

Torpoint Yt Harbour 01752 813658 Ch 80 H24
Southdown Marina 01752 823084 HW±4
Mayflower Marina 01752 556633 Ch 80 H24
Mill Bay Village Marina 01752 226785 Ch 80, Ch M H24
Q.Anne's Battery Marina 01752 671142 Ch 80 H24
Sutton Harbour 01752 204186 Ch 12 H24
Plymouth Yt Haven 01752 404231 Ch 80 H24

St Mary's
Isles of Scilly

N

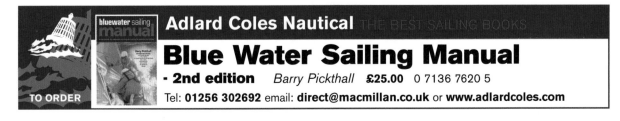

bluewater sailing manual

Adlard Coles Nautical
THE BEST SAILING BOOKS

Blue Water Sailing Manual
- 2nd edition *Barry Pickthall* **£25.00** 0 7136 7620 5

Tel: **01256 302692** email: **direct@macmillan.co.uk** or **www.adlardcoles.com**

TO ORDER

We Discovered the Difference

Sir Anthony Greener

"I hope we are at the end of a very long road and I would like to thank you and Pantaenius for your outstanding service and support. It has been an exemplary (and very unusual) experience for a client."

Mr. David Evans

"Why would I ever try to buy the cheapest insurance? I now have a self-satisfied glow that I made the right decision by buying the BEST insurance. This was brought about by listening to a friend who had a claim with yourselves. His claim was equally well handled by Pantaenius and that experience persuaded me that what I needed was the best, not the cheapest!"

Dr. H. Chadwick

"I would like to thank Pantaenius and especially yourself for the way in which you have dealt with things, as losing one's boat, especially in such dangerous circumstances is quite a traumatic event. I was very grateful for both the immediate help and advice that I received and the subsequent help with managing the situation and the rapid settlement of the insurance issues."

Mr. Dave Leaning

"Thanks for all your help throughout this claim, one reads all sorts of insurance horror stories in the yachting press but I don't think I could possibly have received any better service. It made a difficult process painless."

Why don't you contact us

PANTAENIUS
Yacht Insurance

Hamburg · Plymouth · Monaco · Skive · Vienna · Palma de Mallorca · Zagreb · New York

Marine Building · Victoria Wharf · Plymouth · Devon PL4 0RF · Phone +44-1752 22 36 56 · Fax +44-1752 22 36 37
Authorised and regulated by the Financial Services Authority

www.pantaenius.com

2007/NC10/e

1

FALMOUTH MARINA

Falmouth Marina
North Parade, Falmouth, Cornwall, TR11 2TD
Tel: 01326 316620 Fax: 01326 313939
Email: falmouth@premiermarinas.com
www.premiermarinas.com

VHF Ch 80, 37
ACCESS H24

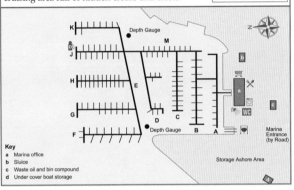

Falmouth Marina lies tucked away in sheltered waters at the southern end of the Fal Estuary. Welcoming to both visiting and residential yachts, its comprehensive facilities include a restaurant, convenience store and hairdresser, while just a 15-minute walk away is Falmouth's town centre where you will find no shortage of shops and eating places. Comprising more than 70 sq miles of navigable water, the Fal Estuary is an intriguing cruising area full of hidden creeks and inlets.

FACILITIES AT A GLANCE

Key
a Marina office
b Sluice
c Waste oil and bin compound
d Under cover boat storage

Performance Sails & Service

PENROSE SAILMAKERS

▼ Computer aided sail design
▼ Yacht Covers

▼ Sail servicing
▼ 24 hour repair service
▼ Collection service

01326 312705
50 Church Street, Upton Slip. Falmouth, Cornwall
www.penrosesails.co.uk
2007/M&WC81/z

When responding to adverts please mention Marina & Waypoint Guide 2007

FALMOUTH MARINA
North Parade, Falmouth, Cornwall TR11 2TD
Tel: (01326) 316620
Fax: (01326) 313939
e-mail: falmouth@premiermarinas.co.uk
www.permiermarinas.com
Ideal for West country cruising, Falmouth Marina boats fully servied berths and an onsite boatyard.
2007/M&WL1/e

Visitors Yacht Haven Falmouth

2007/NC67/e

Fresh water & electricity on pontoons.
Close proximity to town centre.
Toilets, showers & laundry.
Fuel barge dispensing diesel & petrol.

"NEW FOR 2006 WiFi internet hotspot"

Berthing now available ALL YEAR

FALMOUTH HARBOUR COMMISSIONERS
44 Arwenack Street,
Falmouth TR11 3JQ
Tel: 01326 312285/310991
Fax: 01326 211352
www.falmouthport.co.uk

FALMOUTH VISITORS' YACHT HAVEN

Falmouth Visitors Yacht Haven
44 Arwenack Street
Tel: 01326 312285 Fax: 01326 211352
Email: admin@falmouthport.co.uk

VHF Ch 12
ACCESS H24

Run by Falmouth Harbour Commissioners (FHC), Falmouth Visitors' Yacht Haven has become increasingly popular since its opening in 1982, enjoying close proximity to the amenities and entertainments of Falmouth town centre. Sheltered by a breakwater, the Haven caters for 100 boats and offers petrol and diesel supplies as well as good shower and laundry facilities.

Falmouth Harbour is considered by some to be the cruising capital of Cornwall and its deep water combined with easily navigable entrance – even in the severest conditions – makes it a favoured destination for visiting yachtsmen.

FACILITIES AT A GLANCE

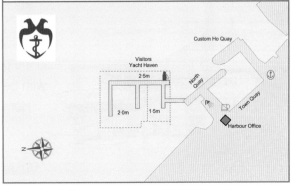

PORT PENDENNIS MARINA

Port Pendennis Marina
Challenger Quay, Falmouth, Cornwall, TR11 3YL
Tel: 01326 211211 Fax: 01326 311116
www.portpendennis.com

VHF	Ch 80
ACCESS	H24

Easily identified by the tower of the National Maritime Museum, Port Pendennis Marina is a convenient arrival or departure point for trans-Atlantic or Mediterranean voyages. Lying adjacent to the town centre, Port Pendennis is divided into an outer marina, with full tidal access, and inner marina, accessible three hours either side of HW. Among its impressive array of marine services is Pendennis Shipyard, one of Britain's most prestigious yacht builders, while other amenities on site include car hire, tennis courts and a yachtsman's lounge, from where you can send faxes or e-mails.

FACILITIES AT A GLANCE

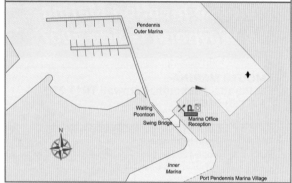

MYLOR YACHT HARBOUR

Mylor Yacht Harbour Marina
Mylor, Falmouth, Cornwall, TR11 5UF
Tel: 01326 372121 Fax: 01326 372120
Email: djones@mylor.com

VHF	Ch 37, 80
ACCESS	H24

Situated on the western shore of Carrick Roads in the beautiful Fal Estuary, Mylor Yacht Harbour has been improved and expanded in recent years, now comprising two substantial breakwaters, three inner pontoons and approximately 250 moorings. With 24 hour access, good shelter and excellent facilities, it ranks among the most popular marinas on the SW Coast of England.

Formerly the Navy's smallest dockyard, established in 1805, Mylor is today a thriving yachting centre as well as home to the world's only remaining sailing oyster fishing fleet. With Falmouth just 10 mins away, local attractions include the Eden Project in St Austell and the National Maritime Museum next to Pendennis Marina.

FACILITIES AT A GLANCE

Key
a Harbour cafe and shops
b Showers/toilets/laundry
c Kingsmoor Cottage and Castaways Wine Bar
d Club
e Rigging pontoon
f New public slipway
g Fueling pontoon
h Marine services and Harbour office
i Water taxi pick up

Not Dredged

Dredged to 2m below CD

Pendennis Outer Marina

Waiting Pontoon
Swing Bridge
Marina Office Reception

Inner Marina

Port Pendennis Marina Village

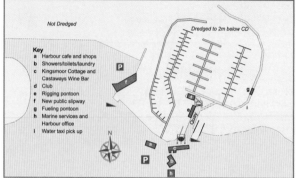

port pendennis

**CHALLENGER QUAY • FALMOUTH
CORNWALL • TR11 3YL
Tel: 01326 211211 • Fax: 01326 311116
E-mail: marina@portpendennis.com**

A friendly marina, adjacent to the centre of Falmouth, bounded by areas of outstanding beauty.
The ideal centre for cruising the West Country, the Isles of Scilly, Brittany, the Channel Islands and south coast of Ireland.
All facilities available for the discerning yachtsman & family.
Also the perfect stopover for Transatlantic & Biscay passages with berthing for yachts to over 70m l.o.a. & 4m + draft.
Home to the new NATIONAL MARITIME MUSEUM

PLEASE VISIT OUR WEBSITE
www.portpendennis.com

2007/M&WC17/z

MYLOR CHANDLERY & RIGGING SERVICES
Mylor Yacht Harbour, Mylor Church Town, Falmouth, Cornwall. TR11 5UF
Tel: (01326) 375482
Email: info@mylorchandlery.co.uk
Website: www.mylorchandlery.co.uk
The best Stocked Chandlery & Rigging company in the South West.

2007/M&Wext14/z

CHALLENGER MARINE LTD
Freemans Wharf, Falmouth Road, Penryn, Cornwall TR10 8AD
Tel: (01326) 377222 Fax: (01326) 377800
e-mail: challengermarine@yahoo.co.uk
www.challengermarine.co.uk
Volvo Penta, Mercruiser, Tomatsu pontoons, storage, chandlery, brokerage, shipwrights, engineers. M&WL20

ARMADA SUPPLIES
Unit 3, Brickland Industrial Park, Falmouth, Cornwall TR11 4TA
Tel: (01326) 375566
Fax: (01326) 375588
www.armadasupplies.co.uk
Hydraulic & pneumatic engineering & supplies. UK & European coverage.

2007/M&WL21/z

R. PEARCE AND CO
St. Mary's House, Commercial Road, Penryn, Cornwall TR10 8AG
Tel: (01326) 375500 Fax: (01326) 374777
e-mail: admin@rpearce.co.uk
www.rpearce.co.uk
Marine surveyors & consulting engineers, UK & international services provided. M&WL21

SOUTHDOWN MARINA

Southdown Marina
Southdown Quay, Millbrook, Cornwall, PL10 1HG
Tel: 01752 823084 Fax: 01752 823084
www.southdownmarina.co.uk

VHF
ACCESS HW±4

Set in peaceful, rural surroundings, Southdown Marina lies in a picturesque inlet on the western bank of the River Tamar, some quarter of a mile from its mouth in Plymouth Sound. It is situated in the shallow inlet of Millbrooke Lake, which stretches westward for a mile or so to the small village of Millbrook.

Ideally suited for yachts that can take the ground, the marina is accessible four hours either side of high water and dries out at low tide onto soft mud. Its boatyard sits on a site which in the 1700s was occupied by the King's Brewhouse to provide ale for the Navy: over 20,000 gallons a week were allegedly ferried across the water to the fleet at Devonport.

The River Tamar and its numerous creeks provide a safe cruising ground in all weathers. Alternatively Plymouth affords a convenient stopover if heading slightly further afield to Dartmouth, Falmouth, Salcombe and the Scilly Isles.

FACILITIES AT A GLANCE

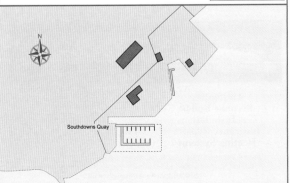

Southdowns Quay

TORPOINT YACHT HARBOUR

Tollesbury Marina
The Yacht Harbour, Tollesbury, Essex, CM9 8SE
Tel: 01621 869204 Fax: 01621 868489
email: marina@woodrolfe.com

VHF Ch M, 80
ACCESS HW-2

Torpoint Yacht Harbour is situated on the western bank of the River Tamar, virtually opposite the well-established shipyard, Devonport Management Ltd (DML). It lies within the old Ballast Pound, built in 1783 to protect and load the barges that ferried rock ballast out to ships that were light on cargo.

Enclosed within four 20ft-thick walls, the Yacht Harbour is dredged to 2m and comprises 80 pontoon berths that are accessible at all states of the tide. There are also drying berths alongside the quay walls which can be reached approximately three hours either side of high water.

Just a few minutes walk from the Yacht Harbour, adjacent to which is the welcoming Torpoint Mosquito Sailing Club, is Torpoint's town centre, where there are enough shops and restaurants to suit most yachtsmen's needs.

FACILITIES AT A GLANCE

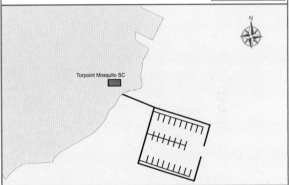

Torpoint Mosquito SC

PADSTOW HARBOUR COMMISSIONERS
Tel: 01841 532239 Fax: 01841 533346
E-mail: info@padstowharbour.fsnet.co.uk
Services include showers, toilets, diesel, water and ice, CCTV security.
Inner harbour controlled by tidal gate – open HW ±2hours – minimum depth 3 metres
Harbour Office, Padstow, Cornwall PL28 8AQ.
Website: www.padstow-harbour.co.uk

2007/M&WMD8/z

MULTIHULL CENTRE
Foss Quay, Millbrook, Torpoint, Cornwall PL10 1EN
Tel: 1752 823900
Fax: 01752 823200
Email: info@multihullcentre.co.uk
www.multihullcentre.co.uk
Catamaran & shoal craft boatyard with pontoon moorings, chandlery & repairs. 2007/M&WL23/e

OCEAN ENGINEERING (FIRE) LTD
Unit 8A, Kernick Industrial Estate, Penryn, Cornwall TR10 9EP
Tel: 01326 378878
Fax: 01326 378870
Mob: 07870 155996
Email: errolhopkins@oceanengineering.co.uk
www.oceanengineering.co.uk
Lloyds approved marine fire engineers. Design, supply, installation and servicing of fire suppression systems, Co2, FM200, Pyrogen etc and portables throughout the south west.

2007/M&WL25/e

MAYFLOWER MARINA

Mayflower International Marina
Ocean Quay, Richmond Walk, Plymouth, PL1 4LS
Tel: 01752 556633 Fax: 01752 606896
Email: mayflower@mayflower.co.uk

VHF	Ch 80
ACCESS	H24

Sitting on the famous Plymouth Hoe, with the Devon coast to the left and the Cornish coast to the right, Mayflower Marina is a friendly, well-run marina, exemplified by its Five Gold Anchor award. Facilities include 24 hour access to fuel, gas and a launderette, full repair and maintenance services as well as an on site bar and brasserie. The marina is located only a short distance from Plymouth's town centre, where there are regular train services to and from several major towns and cities.

FACILITIES AT A GLANCE

Key
a Marina office, surveyors office
b Brokerage, charter office, chandlery
c Cafe
d Bar
e Brasserie
f Berth holders toilets and showers
g Harbour Master's office
h Riggers shop
i Engineers shop
j Picnic/BBQ area
k Tourist information booth

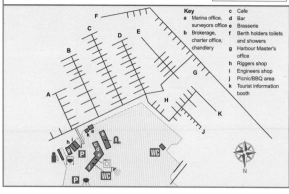

Mayflower Marina . . .

Located in the centre of the South West's superb cruising area. Mayflower Marina is an independant marina has a reputation for its service and standard of facilities.

⚓ Competitive rates

⚓ Impressive facilities

⚓ Warm, friendly atmosphere

⚓ Proven safety and security–24hours.

⚓ Excellent road, rail air &ferry links

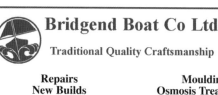

MAYFLOWER
MARINA · PLYMOUTH

Ocean Quay · Richmond Walk · Plymouth Marina
Plymouth · Devon · PL1 4LS
Telephone: (01752) 556633 · Facsimile: (01752) 606896
E-mail: info@mayflowermarina.co.uk
www.mayflowermarina.co.uk

2007/NC34/e

Ultra Marine Systems

Marine Electrical and Electronic Services

Radar / GPS / DSC / Charging systems and much more

For honest helpful advice, give your on-site engineer a ring

Raymarine approved installer   Adverc dealer specialist

Mobile: 07989 941020
email:
ultramarine.adasail@blueyonder.co.uk

2007/M&WC23/z

Bridgend Boat Co Ltd

Traditional Quality Craftsmanship

Repairs	**Moulding**
New Builds	**Osmosis Treatments**
Refits	**Teak Decks**
Engineering	**FirePro Installations**

Major Refit and Fit Out Specialists
Professional Project Management
Any Size Boat Up To 100 Foot
Maximum of 60 Tons Lifting Capacity
Wood/GRP/Steel

Antifouling	**Electronics**
Bespoke Builds	**Painting**
Gas Installations	**Air Conditioning**
Insurance Repairs	**Propulsion Control Systems**
Heating Systems	**Boat Restoration**

Western Hangar, Lawrence Road, Mount Batten, Plymouth PL9 9SJ
Tel: 01752 404082 Fax: 01752 403405 Email: Bboatsco@aol.com
www.bridgendboatcompany.co.uk

2007/M&WC137/e

MILL BAY VILLAGE MARINA

Mill Bay Village Marina
Great Western Road
Mill Bay Docks, Plymouth, Devon, PL1 3TG
Tel: 01752 226785 Fax: 01752 226785

| VHF | Ch M, 80 |
| ACCESS | H24 |

Just west of Plymouth Hoe lies Millbay Docks, encompassing the RoRo terminal from where ferries ply to and from Roscoff and Santander. The entrance to Mill Bay Village Marina, accessible at all states of the tide, can be found on the starboard side of the docks. Offering few facilities for visiting yachtsmen, it is primarily geared up for resident berth holders, although berthing can be made available subject to prior arrangement.

Nearby is the city of Plymouth, where the main shopping precinct is situated around the Royal Parade. Flattened during WWII, this area was rebuilt in a modern, unimaginative way, contrasting sharply with the picturesque, historic Barbican from where the Pilgrim Fathers reputedly boarded the *Mayflower* to sail to the New World in 1620. The latter's ancient streets are full of bars and restaurants, while other attractions include the Mayflower Visitor Centre, the Elizabethan House and Garden and the Plymouth Gin Distillery.

FACILITIES AT A GLANCE

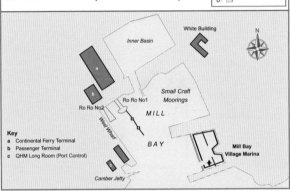

Key
a Continental Ferry Terminal
b Passenger Terminal
c QHM Long Room (Port Control)

QUEEN ANNE'S BATTERY MARINA

Queen Anne's Battery
Plymouth, PL4 OLP
Tel: 01752 671142 Fax: 01752 266297
www.marinas.co.uk Email: qab@mdlmarinas.co.uk

| VHF | Ch 80 |
| ACCESS | H24 |

At the centre of Plymouth lies Queen Anne's Battery, comprising 280 resident berths as well as a visitor's basin with alongside pontoon berthing. All berths are well protected by a breakwater and double wavescreen.

As Plymouth Sound frequently provides the starting point for many prestigious international yacht races as well as the finish of the Fastnet Race, the marina is often crowded with racers during the height of the season and its vibrant atmosphere can at times resemble a mini 'Cowes'.

FACILITIES AT A GLANCE

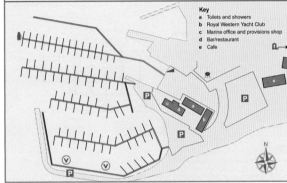

Key
a Toilets and showers
b Royal Western Yacht Club
c Marina office and provisions shop
d Bar/restaurant
e Cafe

SUTTON HARBOUR

Sutton Harbour
North Quay House, Sutton Harbour, Plymouth, PL4 0RA
Tel: 01752 204186 Fax: 01752 205403
Email: marina@sutton-harbour.co.uk
www.sutton-harbour.co.uk

| VHF | Ch 12 |
| ACCESS | H24 |

Boasting a superb location alongside Plymouth's famous Barbican centre, Sutton Harbour lies just north of Queen Anne's Battery Marina. The harbour can be entered 24 hours a day via a lock which is marked by green and red chevrons. Affording good shelter in 3.5m of water, it offers a comprehensive range of marine services, including a fuel berth that opens from 0800 to 1800.

Situated within a minute's walk from the marina is a Tourist Information Centre, providing all the necessary details of how best to explore the surrounding Devon countryside.

FACILITIES AT A GLANCE

Key
a Fish market
b National Marine Aquarium
c Customs House
d The Cove
e Marina office
f Lock tower

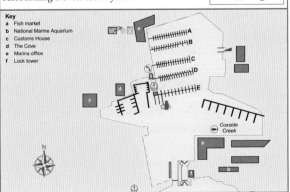

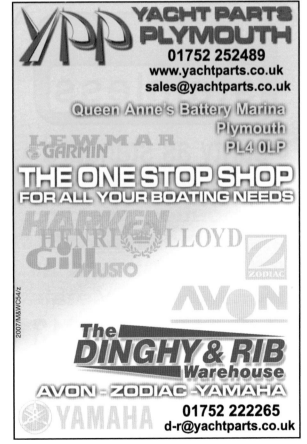

YACHT PARTS PLYMOUTH
01752 252489
www.yachtparts.co.uk
sales@yachtparts.co.uk

Queen Anne's Battery Marina
Plymouth
PL4 0LP

THE ONE STOP SHOP
FOR ALL YOUR BOATING NEEDS

LEWMAR
GARMIN
HARKEN
HENRI LLOYD
Gill
MUSTO
ZODIAC
AVON

The DINGHY & RIB Warehouse
AVON - ZODIAC - YAMAHA
01752 222265
d-r@yachtparts.co.uk
YAMAHA

2007/M&WC54/z

PLYMOUTH YACHT HAVEN

Plymouth Yacht Haven Ltd
Shaw Way, Mount Batten, Plymouth, PL9 9XH
Tel: 01752 404231 Fax: 01752 484177
www.yachthavens.com Email: plymouth@yachthavens.com

VHF	Ch 37, 80
ACCESS	H24

Situated in Clovelly Bay at the mouth of the Cattewater, Plymouth Yacht Haven offers good protection from the prevailing winds and is within close proximity to Plymouth Sound from where you can enjoy a day's sail to Fowey, Salcombe, Torquay or Dartmouth. Boasting 450 berths, the marina has the capacity to accommodate vessels up to 45m in length and 7m in draught.

Within easy access are several coastal walks, a golf course and a fitness centre with heated swimming pool. A water taxi is also on hand to take yachtsmen across the water to the historic Barbican, incorporating a plethora of shops, restaurants and bars amongst its attractive cobbled streets.

FACILITIES AT A GLANCE

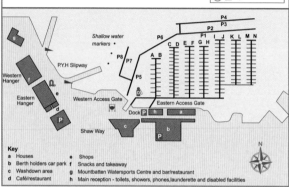

Key
a Houses
b Berth holders car park
c Washdown area
d Café/restaurant
e Shops
f Snacks and takeaway
g Mountbatten Watersports Centre and bar/restaurant
h Main reception - toilets, showers, phones,launderette and disabled facilities

NOSS-ON-DART MARINA

Noss-on-Dart Marina
Noss Quay, Dartmouth, Devon, TQ6 0EA
Tel: 01803 833351 Fax: 01803 835150
Email: marinas@dartmarina.com
www.dartmarina.com

VHF	Ch 80
ACCESS	H24

Upstream of Dartmouth on the east shore of the River Dart is Noss-on-Dart Marina. Enjoying a peaceful rural setting, this marina is well suited to those who prefer a quieter atmosphere. Besides 180 fully serviced berths, 50 fore-and-aft moorings in the middle reaches of the river are also run by the marina, with mooring holders entitled to use all the facilities available to berth holders. During summer, a passenger ferry service runs regularly between Noss-on-Dart and Dartmouth, while a grocery service to your boat can be provided on request.

FACILITIES AT A GLANCE

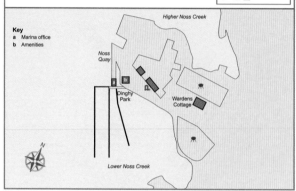

Key
a Marina office
b Amenities

100% stainless ™

• purity as standard •

Specialist in the Fabrication, Welding and Polishing of Stainless Steel & all Non Ferrous Metals

Tel: 01752 401213

www.100percentstainless.co.uk
100% Stainless Ltd
Unit 2, Chittleburn Business Park,
Brixton, Plymouth PL8 2PH

2007/M&WC80/z

Marine Engineering Looe

VOLVO PENTA
MARINE CENTRE

Unit 1 & 2, The Maypool Building, Dartside Quay, Galmpton Creek, Brixham, Devon. TQ5 0GL

Telephone No: 01803 844777
Fax No: 01803 845684
email: torbay@marine-engineering-looe.co.uk

Also at: Looe 01503 263009
Q.A.B. Plymouth 01752 226143

2007/M&WC8/z

MARINE BAZAAR

SUTTON ROAD, PLYMOUTH
5 MINS WALK FROM QUEEN ANNE'S BATTERY MARINA

NEW LOCATION MEGASTORE WITH AMPLE FREE PARKING
YOU WILL NEED TO USE OUR TROLLIES WHEN YOU SEE THE HUGE SELECTION OF MARINE GOODS ON ONE LEVEL!

PALLET LOADS OF ANTI-FOULING

- Display of Dinghies, Canoes & Outboard Motors
- Parts - Service - Repair
- All Your Boat Requirements

2007/M&WC152/z

OPEN 7 DAYS

SUZUKI   TOHATSU

MARINE

Main Shop
Tel: 01752 201023

Outboard Motors
Tel: 01752 201003

www.marinebazaar.co.uk

MAIL ORDER

DART MARINA

**Dart Marina
Sandquay Road, Dartmouth
Devon, TQ6 9PH
Tel: 01803 832580 Fax: 01803 835040
Email: yachtharbour@dartmarina.com www.dartmarina.com**

VHF	Ch 80
ACCESS	H24

Annual berth holders enjoy the finest marina location in the West Country, with the atmosphere and facilities of an exclusive club. The Yacht Harbour on the River Dart is a perfect retreat for simply relaxing and an ideal base for local boating and more ambitious cruising further afield. During the season there are a limited number of visitors' berths available and a waiting list for the 110 annual berths. The berths are accessible at any tide and are located in peaceful surroundings, just a short walk along the riverfront from Dartmouth's historic centre.

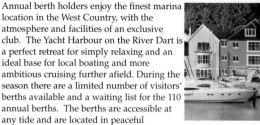

The showers and bathrooms are of high quality and some first class facilities are conveniently onsite - the Wildfire Bistro, Health Spa, River Restaurant and quayside dining.

FACILITIES AT A GLANCE

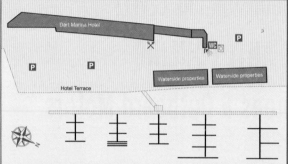

DARTHAVEN MARINA

**Darthaven Marina
Brixham Road, Kingswear, Devon, TQ6 0SG
Tel: 01803 752545 Fax: 01803 752722
Email: darthaven@darthaven.co.uk
www.darthaven.co.uk**

VHF	Ch 80
ACCESS	H24

Darthaven Marina is a family run business situated in the village of Kingswear on the east side of the River Dart. Within half a mile from Start Bay and the mouth of the river, it is the first marina you come to from seaward and is accessible at all states of the tide. Darthaven prides itself on being more than just a marina, offering a high standard of marine services with both electronic and engineering experts plus wood and GRP repairs on site. A shop, post office and five pubs are within a walking distance of the marina, while a frequent ferry service takes passengers across the river to Dartmouth.

FACILITIES AT A GLANCE

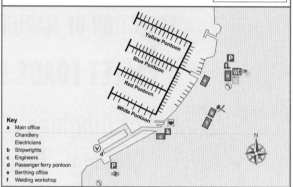

Key
a   Main office
    Chandlery
    Electricians
b   Shipwrights
c   Engineers
d   Passenger ferry pontoon
e   Berthing office
f   Welding workshop

DARTSIDE QUAY

**Dartside Quay
Galmpton Creek, Brixham, Devon, TQ5 0QH
Tel: 01803 845445 Fax: 01803 843558
Email: dartsidequay@mdlmarinas.co.uk**

VHF	Ch 80
ACCESS	H24

Located at the head of Galmpton Creek, Dartside Quay lies three miles up river from Dartmouth.

In a sheltered position and with beautiful views across to Dittisham, it offers extensive boatyard facilities. The 7-acre dry boat storage area has space for over 300 boats and is serviced by a 65-ton hoist operating from a purpose-built dock, a 16-ton trailer hoist and 25-ton crane.

There are also a number of summer mud moorings available and a well stocked chandlery, in fact if the item you want is not in stock we can order it in for you.

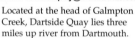

FACILITIES AT A GLANCE

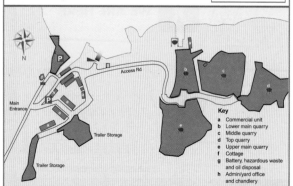

Key
a   Commercial unit
b   Lower main quarry
c   Middle quarry
d   Top quarry
e   Upper main quarry
f   Cottage
g   Battery, hazardous waste and oil disposal
h   Admin/yard office and dockyard

Total Service, Total Darthaven...

- VOLVO PENTA Marine Centre
- YANMAR Engines Dealer
- Mobile Engine Service Units
- All Engine Types Serviced
- Raymarine Installer/Dealer
- System Software Updates
- First Class Spares Service
- Comprehensive Chandlery
- Scheduled Servicing Plans
- Engine Management Systems
- Pre-Passage Checks and Preparation
- Turbo Set-Up and Replacement
- 35 Tonne Hoist Working 7 days per week
- Shipwright Services on Site
- Colourmatched GRP Repairs
- Visitor Pontoons (Call channel 80)
- Express Lube Fuel Cleaning

Darthaven Marina Limited
Brixham Road, Kingswear, Devon. TQ6 0SG
General Office Tel:01803 752242
Chandlery Tel:01803 752733
www.darthaven.co.uk

Electronics Mobiles:07767 250787 and 07887 726093
Engineering Mobile:07973 280584.

EMERGENCY CALL-OUT 24 x 7 x 365:

2007M&WC39A/e

Darthaven   VOLVO PENTA Marine Centre   YANMAR Main Dealer

TORBAY'S NUMBER ONE

CHANDLERY

Bayside Marine

Towable Inflatables

Mooring Lines / Fenders / Hardware

Clothing and accesories

Blakes Paint / Teamac / Jotun
International

TELEPHONE: 01803 856771

HIGHER FURZEHAM RD   BRIXHAM

BRIXHAM MARINA

Brixham Marina
Berry Head Road, Brixham
Devon, TQ5 9BW
Tel: 01803 882929 Fax: 01803 882737
www.marinas.co.uk Email: n.salter@mdlmarinas.co.uk

| VHF | Ch 80 |
| ACCESS | H24 |

Home to one of Britain's largest fishing fleets, Brixham Harbour is located on the southern shore of Tor Bay, which is well sheltered from westerly winds and where tidal streams are weak. Brixham Marina, housed in a separate basin to the work boats, provides easy access in all weather conditions and at all states of the tide. Established in 1989, it has become increasingly popular with locals and visitors alike, enjoying an idyllic setting right on the town's quayside.

Local attractions include a walk out to Berry Head Nature Reserve and a visit to the replica of Sir Francis Drake's ship, the *Golden Hind*.

FACILITIES AT A GLANCE

Key
a   Dock manager's office
b   Information centre
c   Boat sales and Sea School

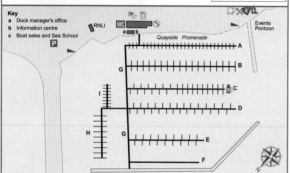

Bay Rigging

Yacht rigging services

From a rig inspection to a full re-rig - consider it done!

t/f 01803 846333   m 07816 925666
www.bay-rigging.co.uk
Unit 1 & 2 Dartside Quay Galmpton

2007/M&WC30/e0

HARRIS RIGGING

**Baltic Wharf Boatyard,
St Peters Quay, Totnes TQ9 5EW
Phone/fax: Graeme on
01803 840160
Mobile: 07970 712877**

Standing and running rigging, Masts, Booms, Jib reefing systems, Rig inspections, Braided rope, Spectra, Splicing, Hydraulic Swaging and talurit splicing, Lewmar, Profurl, Hood, Harken, Schaeffer, Rotostay, Frederiksen

Impartial advice and sensible prices!

2007/M&WC37/e

BASED AT DARTHAVEN MARINA

Dart Harbour
SEA SCHOOL

OUR SCHOOL BOAT - FAIRLINE 40   OUR SCHOOL BOAT - ZODIAC 6.5M

THE SOUTH WEST'S PREMIER MOTOR CRUISING AND POWER-BOATING SCHOOL

- All the RYA courses for motor cruising and power boating from novice to advanced
- Special holiday refresher or beginners courses organised at short notice on school boat or your own
- RYA shorebased courses all year round

RYA Training Centre

2007/M&WC116/e

Tel: 01803 839339
E-mail: info@dartharbourseaschool.co.uk
www.dartharbourseaschool.co.uk
24 South Town, Dartmouth, Devon TQ6 9BX

1

TORQUAY MARINA

Torquay Marina
Torquay, Devon, TQ2 5EQ
Tel: 01803 200210 Fax: 01803 200225
www.marinas.co.uk

VHF Ch 80
ACCESS H24

Tucked away in the north east corner of Tor Bay, Torquay Marina is well sheltered from the prevailing SW'ly winds, providing safe entry in all conditions and at any state of the tide. Located in the centre of Torquay, the marina enjoys easy access to the town's numerous shops, bars and restaurants. Torquay is ideally situated for either exploring Tor Bay itself, with its many delightful anchorages, or else for heading further west to experience several other scenic harbours such as Dartmouth and Salcombe. It also provides a good starting point for crossing to Brittany, Normandy or the Channel Islands.

FACILITIES AT A GLANCE

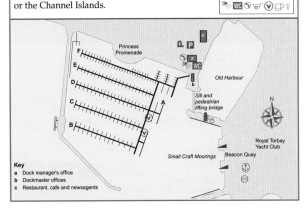

Key
a Dock manager's office
b Dockmaster offices
c Restaurant, cafe and newsagents

WEYMOUTH MARINA

Weymouth Marina
70 Commercial Road, Dorset, DT4 8NA
Tel: 01305 767576 Fax: 01305 767575
www.weymouth-marina.co.uk
Email: russl@deanreddyhoff.co.uk

VHF Ch 80
ACCESS H24

With more than 280 permanent and visitors' berths, Weymouth is a modern, purpose-built marina ideally situated for yachtsmen cruising between the West Country and the Solent. It is also conveniently placed for sailing to France or the Channel Islands.
Accessed via the town's historic lifting bridge, which opens every even hour 0800–2000 (plus 2100 Jun–Aug), the marina is dredged to 2.5m below chart datum. It provides easy access to the town centre, with its abundance of shops, pubs and restaurants, as well as to the traditional seafront where an impressive sandy beach is overlooked by an esplanade of hotels. More details can be found at ww.weymouth.gov.uk/harbour.

FACILITIES AT A GLANCE

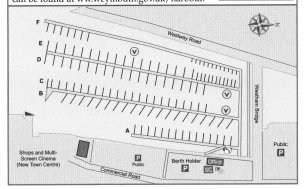

UPPER DECK MARINE/OUTRIGGERS

Chandlery, fastenings, paints, cords, fenders, anchors, compasses, lifejackets, Gaz. Leading names in waterproofs and marine casuals.
Albert Quay, Fowey, Cornwall PL23 1AQ
Tel: 01726 832287 and 833233 Fax: 01726 833265
Website www.upper-deck.co.uk

2007/M&WMD6/e

SEAFIT MARINE SERVICES LTD
Falmouth Marina, North Parade, Falmouth,
Cornwall TR11 2TD
Tel: (01326) 313713   Fax: (01326) 313713
Mob: 07971 196175
e-mail: marytownshend@tiscali.co.uk
For installation maintenance and repair work - electrical, plumbing, hulls, rigs etc.

M&WL24/e

SHIPMATES Chandlers Ltd

Telephone: +44 (0)1803 839292
Fax: +44 (0)1803 832538

We stock a huge range of Chandlery, Paint Rope, Safety Equipment, Electronics etc. and Marine Clothing, Footwear, Books & Charts

Friendly Expert Advice - Open 7 days a week
2, Newcomen Road, DARTMOUTH

SHOP ONLINE NOW AT
www.chandlery.co.uk

2007/M&WC136/f

Bussells
Yacht Chandlers

SUPPLIERS OF ALL MARINE EQUIPMENT

30 Hope Street, Weymouth, Dorset DT4 8TU

Tel: (01305) 785633

2007/M&WC44/e

When responding to adverts please mention Marina & Waypoint Guide 2007

DEAN & REDDYHOFF LTD - WEYMOUTH MARINA
Commercial Rd, Weymouth, Dorset DT4 8NA
Tel: (01305) 767576 Fax: (01305) 767575
e-mail: sales@weymouthmarina.co.uk
www.deanreddyhoff.co.uk
Located in the centre of town only minutes from local pubs & restaurants, the marina has proven a great success with berth holders and visitors alike. Weymouth's recent regeneration programme has been a complete success, making Weymouth a must visit port, whilst cruising the South Coast.
See our full page advert at the end of Area 1.   2007/M&WEXT12/eb

WEYMOUTH HARBOUR

Weymouth & Portland Borough Council
North Quay, Weymouth, Dorset, DT4 8TA
Tel: 01305 206423 Fax: 01305 767927
Email: berthingoffice@weymouth.gov.uk

VHF	Ch 12
ACCESS	H24

Weymouth Harbour, which lies to the NE of Portland in the protected waters of Weymouth Bay, benefits from deep water at all states of the tide. If wishing to moor up in the old Georgian outer harbour, you should contact the harbour authority, which also controls several municipal pontoons above the bridge. In recent years the facilities have been significantly improved and now include electricity and fresh water on both quays, as well as free showers and a coin-operated launderette. Visiting yachtsmen are very welcome both at the Royal Dorset Yacht Club, situated on Customs House Quay in the inner harbour, and the Weymouth Sailing Club, on the south pier of the outer harbour.

FACILITIES AT A GLANCE

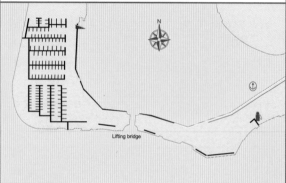

Lifting bridge

2007/NC37/j

QUAYSIDE FUEL

MOBILE MARINE FUEL SERVICE
You call and we deliver
Call ANDY on
077 4718 2181 or 079 7073 7620
VHF Channel 60
Pre-booking welcome

A. D. GORDON
MODERN & TRADITIONAL YACHT RIGGING

Hand Splicing in Wire & Rope

Talurit Splicing

Roll Swaging

N.D.T. Rigging Terminal Testing

Tel/Fax: 01305 821569
Mobile: 07774 633419

Units 8,9&10 St. Georges Centre,
Reeforne, Portland, Dorset DT5 2HN

AGENT FOR

SELDÉN
Masts, Spars & Fittings

2007/M&WC101/f

KINGFISHER
MARINE

51 Commercial Road,
Weymouth, Dorset DT4 8AQ

E-mail: sales@kingfishermarine.co.uk
Website: www.kingfishermarine.co.uk

2007/NC77/e

Tel: 01305 766595

Fax: 01305 766502

24hour Call Out 07836 713219

Browse through our extensive ranges of clothing, electronics, safety equipment and boat maintenance products. Marine engineering with top brand names including Mercury, Mercruiser and Yanmer. Rigging jobs large and small. Boat building, repairs and lifting complete our range of services. Whatever your boating needs you are sure of a warm welcome at Kingfisher Marine.

Yacht Management,
Maintenance and Support Services

MCA Code Compliance Consultancy

Pre-purchase, Condition
and Valuation Surveys

Yacht Deliveries

Agency Agreements

Yacht Valet
and Provisioning Services

devonmarine

26 Foss Street ○Dartmouth ○Devon ○TQ6 9DR
e: info@devonmarine.com
t: 01803 832323
f: 01803 833615
m: 07958 203965

www.devonmarine.com

2007/M&WC157/z

1

KELVIN HUGHES

BOOKHARBOUR.COM

SOUTHAMPTON ☎ 023 8063 4911

Kilgraston House, Southampton Street
Southampton SO15 2ED
southampton@kelvinhughes.co.uk

GLASGOW ☎ 0141 429 6462

Unit 5, 22 St Luke's Place
Glasgow G5 0TS
glasgow@kelvinhughes.co.uk

For the widest range of nautical books, charts, software and videos in Europe

DUFOUR 44

A new era, a new Dufour design

The Dufour 40 has been central to the new era in Dufour design. Boat of the year in Paris, the Dufour 40 is renowned as a thoroughbred comfortable and fast cruising yacht.

DUFOUR 40:
2005 World Champion IMS 670
Winner of the Copa Del Rey

World championship honours confirm the success of the new Dufour era after the victory of the Dufour 34 QUUM in last year's Copa Del Rey.

DUFOUR 44

DUFOUR
YACHTS

2007/M&WC72/z

Portway
Yacht Sales

SOUTH COAST MAIN DEALER

www.portway.co.uk

PORTWAY YACHT SALES
Hayling Island, Hants
+44 (0) 2392 466 330 - hayling@portway.co.uk

PORTWAY YACHT SALES
Torquay, Devon
+44 (0) 1803 380 518 - torquay@portway.co.uk

PORTWAY YACHT SERVICES
Galmpton, Devon
+44 (0) 1803 845 045 - services@portway.co.uk

International Dealer Network available on
www.dufour-yachts.com

DUFOUR
NETWORK BROKERAGE

BUREAU VERITAS

CENTRAL SOUTHERN ENGLAND - Anvil Point to Selsey Bill

ADLARD COLES NAUTICAL
WEATHER FORECASTS
BY FAX & TELEPHONE

Coastal/Inshore	2-day by Fax	5-day by Phone
South West	09065 222 348	09068 969 648
Mid Channel	09065 222 347	09068 969 647
Channel East	09065 222 346	09068 969 646
Channel Islands	–	09068 969 656
National (3-5 day)	09065 222 340	09068 969 640

Offshore	2-5 day by Fax	2-5 day by Phone
English Channel	09065 222 357	09068 969 657
Southern North Sea	09065 222 358	09068 969 658
Irish Sea	09065 222 359	09068 969 659
Biscay	09065 222 360	09068 969 660

09068 CALLS COST 60P PER MIN. 09065 CALLS COST £1.50 PER MIN.

Key to Marina Plans symbols

Calor Gas		P	Parking
Chandler		✗	Pub/Restaurant
Disabled facilities			Pump out
Electrical supply			Rigging service
Electrical repairs			Sail repairs
Engine repairs		✗	Shipwright
First Aid			Shop/Supermarket
Fresh Water			Showers
Fuel - Diesel			Slipway
Fuel - Petrol		WC	Toilets
Hardstanding/boatyard			Telephone
Internet Café			Trolleys
Laundry facilities		V	Visitors berths
Lift-out facilities			Wi-Fi

Area 2 - Central Southern England

MARINAS
Telephone Numbers
VHF Channel
Access Times

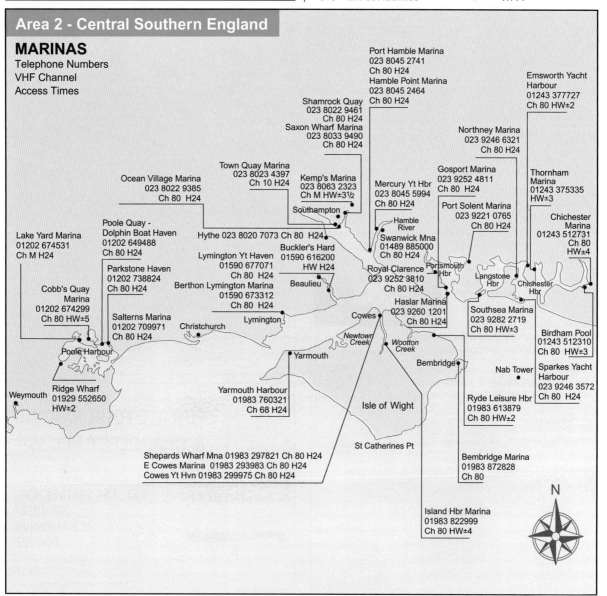

Port Hamble Marina
023 8045 2741
Ch 80 H24
Hamble Point Marina
023 8045 2464
Ch 80 H24

Emsworth Yacht Harbour
01243 377727
Ch 80 HW±2

Shamrock Quay
023 8022 9461
Ch 80 H24
Saxon Wharf Marina
023 8033 9490
Ch 80 H24

Northney Marina
023 9246 6321
Ch 80 H24

Town Quay Marina
023 8023 4397
Ch 10 H24

Kemp's Marina
023 8063 2323
Ch M HW±3½

Mercury Yt Hbr
023 8045 5994
Ch 80 H24

Gosport Marina
023 9252 4811
Ch 80 H24

Thornham Marina
01243 375335
HW±3

Ocean Village Marina
023 8022 9385
Ch 80 H24

Southampton

Port Solent Marina
023 9221 0765
Ch 80 H24

Chichester Marina
01243 512731
Ch 80 HW±4

Lake Yard Marina
01202 674531
Ch M H24

Poole Quay - Dolphin Boat Haven
01202 649488
Ch 80 H24

Hythe 023 8020 7073 Ch 80 H24

Hamble River

Swanwick Mna
01489 885000
Ch 80 H24

Buckler's Hard
01590 616200
HW H24

Parkstone Haven
01202 738824
Ch 80 H24

Lymington Yt Haven
01590 677071
Ch 80 H24

Beaulieu

Royal Clarence
023 9252 3810
Ch 80 H24

Portsmouth Hbr

Langstone Hbr

Chichester Hbr

Cobb's Quay Marina
01202 674299
Ch 80 HW±5

Berthon Lymington Marina
01590 673312
Ch 80 H24

Haslar Marina
023 9260 1201
Ch 80 H24

Salterns Marina
01202 709971
Ch 80 H24

Christchurch

Lymington

Cowes

Southsea Marina
023 9282 2719
Ch 80 HW±3

Birdham Pool
01243 512310
Ch 80 HW±3

Poole Harbour

Newtown Creek

Wootton Creek

Bembridge

Nab Tower

Sparkes Yacht Harbour
023 9246 3572
Ch 80 H24

Weymouth

Ridge Wharf
01929 552650
HW±2

Yarmouth

Yarmouth Harbour
01983 760321
Ch 68 H24

Isle of Wight

Ryde Leisure Hbr
01983 613879
Ch 80 HW±2

St Catherines Pt

Shepards Wharf Mna 01983 297821 Ch 80 H24
E Cowes Marina 01983 293983 Ch 80 H24
Cowes Yt Hvn 01983 299975 Ch 80 H24

Bembridge Marina
01983 872828
Ch 80

Island Hbr Marina
01983 822999
Ch 80 HW±4

N

RIDGE WHARF YACHT CENTRE

Ridge Wharf Yacht Centre
Ridge, Wareham, Dorset, BH20 5BG
Tel: 01929 552650 Fax: 01929 554434
Email: office@ridgewharf.co.uk

VHF	
ACCESS	HW±2

On the south bank of the River Frome, which acts as the boundary to the North of the Isle of Purbeck, is Ridge Wharf Yacht Centre. Access for a 1.5m draught is between one and two hours either side of HW, with berths drying out to soft mud. The Yacht Centre cannot be contacted on VHF, so it is best to phone up ahead of time to inquire about berthing availability.

A trip upstream to the ancient market town of Wareham is well worth while, although owners of deep-draughted yachts may prefer to go by dinghy. Tucked between the Rivers Frome and Trent, it is packed full of cafés, restaurants and shops.

FACILITIES AT A GLANCE

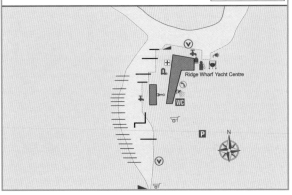

LAKE YARD MARINA

Lake Yard Marina
Lake Drive, Hamworthy, Poole, Dorset BH15 4DT
Tel: 01202 674531 Fax: 01202 677518
Email: yard@bostonwhaler.co.uk www.lakeyard.co.uk

VHF	Ch M
ACCESS	H24

Lake Yard is situated towards the NW end of Poole Harbour, just beyond the SHM No 73. The entrance can be easily identified by 2FR (vert) and 2FG (vert) lights. Enjoying 24 hour access, the marina has no designated visitors' berths, but will accommodate visiting yachtsmen if resident berth holders are away. Its on site facilities include full maintenance and repair services as well as hard standing and a 50 ton boat hoist, although for the nearest fuel go to Corralls (Tel 01202 674551), opposite the Town Quay. Lake Yard's Waterfront Club, offering spectacular views across the harbour, opens seven days a week for lunchtime and evening meals.

FACILITIES AT A GLANCE

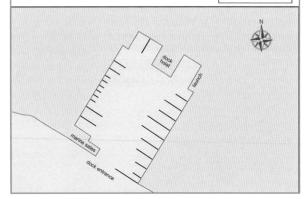

COBB'S QUAY MARINA

Cobb's Quay
Hamworthy, Poole, Dorset, BH15 4EL
Tel: 01202 674299 Fax: 01202 665217
Email: cobbsquay@mdlmarinas.co.uk www.marinas.co.uk

VHF	Ch 80
ACCESS	HW±5

Lying on the west side of Holes Bay in Poole Harbour, Cobb's Quay is accessed via the lifting bridge at Poole Quay. With fully serviced pontoons for yachts up to 25m LOA, the marina can be entered five hours either side of high water and is normally able to accommodate visiting yachts. On site is Cobb's Quay Yacht Club, which welcomes visitors to its bar and restaurant.

Poole is one of the largest natural harbours in the world and is considered by many to be among the finest. Its N side incorporates several modern marinas in close proximity to a multitude of shops and restaurants, while its S side boasts tranquil anchorages set within unspoilt nature reserves.

FACILITIES AT A GLANCE

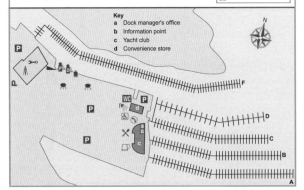

Key
a Dock manager's office
b Information point
c Yacht club
d Convenience store

For all your marine and auto valeting requirements

Tel/Fax: 01258 456190

www.mdmarineservices.com

- Full Valeting Service
- Hot pressure wash
- Teak clean and refurbishment
- Machine Polishing
- Upholstery and carpet cleaning
- Anti Fouling
- Gel coat repairs/
- Weekly/Monthly cleaning contracts

2007/M&WC78/z

"FOR ALL YOUR RIGGING & CHANDLERY NEEDS"

CHRIS HORNSEY
(Chandlery) Ltd

152 -154 EASTNEY ROAD
SOUTHSEA
HAMPSHIRE
PO4 8DY

Tel: 02392 734728
Fax: 02392 611500
E-mail: sales@chishornsey.com

2007/M&WC145/f

2

POOLE QUAY BOAT HAVEN

Poole Quay Boat Haven
20 Newquay Road, Hamworthy, Poole, Dorset, BH15 4AF
Tel: 01202 649488 Fax: 01202 649488
Email: poolequayboathaven@phc.co.uk

VHF Ch 80
ACCESS H24

Once inside Poole Harbour entrance, small yachts heading for Dolphin Haven should use the Boat Channel running parallel south of the dredged Middle Ship Channel, which is primarily used by ferries sailing to and from the Hamworthy terminal. The marina, benefiting from deep water at all states of the tide, is then accessed via the Little Channel and can be easily identified by its large breakwater. Although 100 berths are designated entirely to visitors, due to its central location, the marina can get very crowded in season so it is best to reserve a berth ahead of time. A stone's throw away is Poole Quay where, besides a multitude of bars and restaurants, there are several places of interest, including the well-known Poole Pottery and the Waterfront Museum in Old High Street.

FACILITIES AT A GLANCE

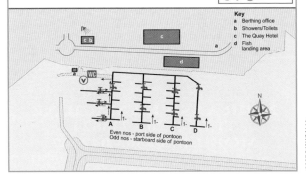

Key
a Berthing office
b Showers/Toilets
c The Quay Hotel
d Fish landing area

Even nos - port side of pontoon
Odd nos - starboard side of pontoon

Piplers of Poole

FOR ALL YOUR BOATING NEEDS
THE QUAY, POOLE, DORSET BH15 1HF
Tel. 01202 673056 Fax. 01202 683065
Email. orders@piplers.co.uk
Website. www.piplers.co.uk
OPEN 7 DAYS A WEEK ALL YEAR ROUND

Rossiter Yachts
Moorings in Christchurch town centre
Repairs & Restorations in wood and GRP
Osmosure Treatment Centre
Marine engineering & servicing
Rigging Service + Marine Diesel + Chandlery

Builders of **Curlew** & **Pintail II**

Rossiter's Quay, Bridge Street, Christchurch, Dorset, BH23 1DZ.
t: 01202 483250   f: 01202 490164
rossiteryachts@hotmail.com   www.rossiteryachts.co.uk

POOLE QUAY BOAT HAVEN

The Haven is a modern purpose built marina comprising of 125 serviced pontoon berths, dedicated to visitors for the Poole area. We are able to accommodate vessels up to 30mtrs in length. We are situated at the eastern end of the Poole Town Quay and we have easy access to a variety of shops, restaurants and bars. It is approximately a 10–15 minute walk to the railway and a short taxi ride to Bournemouth airport.

PHONE +44(0) 1202 649488
FAX +44 (0) 1202 649488
EMAIL: poolequayboathaven@phc.co.uk
VHF Ch80 call sign "Poole Quay Boat Haven"

Formerly know as Dolphin Haven.

2007/M&WM18/z

PARKSTONE YACHT HAVEN

Parkstone Yacht Club
Pearce Avenue, Parkstone, Poole, Dorset, BH14 8EH
Tel: 01202 738824 Fax: 01202 716394
Email: haven@parkstoneyachtclub.co.uk

VHF	Ch 37,80
ACCESS	H24

Situated on the north side of Poole Harbour between Salterns Marina and Dolphin Boat Haven, Parkstone Yacht Haven can be entered at all states of the tides. Its approach channel has been dredged to 2.0m and is clearly marked by buoys. Run by the Parkstone Yacht Club, the Haven provides 200 deep water berths for members and visitors' berths. Other facilities include a bar, restaurant, new shower/changing rooms and wi-fi. With a busy sailing programme for over 2,500 members, the Yacht Club plays host to a variety of events including Poole Week, which is held towards the end of August.

FACILITIES AT A GLANCE

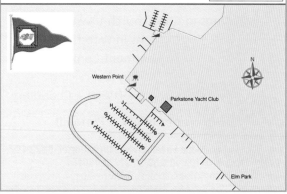

YARD SERVICES

THE FOLLOWING RANGE OF SERVICES ARE CURRENTLY AVAILABLE

MOORING LINES
BOAT VALETING
HULL POLISHING
LIFERAFT HIRE
HIGH PRESSURE CLEANING
G.R.P & GENERAL REPAIRS
PAINTING - ANTIFOULING
VARNISHNG
MARINE ENGINEERING
SERVICES
HAUL OUT AND SCRUB
WI-FI

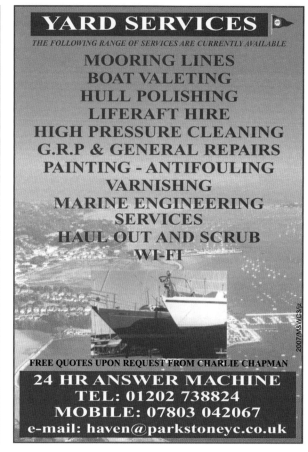

FREE QUOTES UPON REQUEST FROM CHARLIE CHAPMAN

24 HR ANSWER MACHINE
TEL: 01202 738824
MOBILE: 07803 042067
e-mail: haven@parkstoneyc.co.uk

SALTERNS MARINA

Salterns Marina
40 Salterns Way, Lilliput, Poole
Dorset, BH14 8JR
Tel: 01202 709971 Fax: 01202 700398
Email: marina@salterns.co.uk www.salterns.co.uk

VHF	Ch 37, 80
ACCESS	H24

Holding both the Blue Flag and Five Gold Anchor awards, Salterns Marina provides a service which is second to none. Located off the North Channel, it is approached from the No 31 SHM and benefits from deep water at all states of the tide. Facilities include 220 alongside pontoon berths as well as 75 swinging moorings with a free launch service. However, with very few designated visitors' berths, it is best to contact the marina ahead of time for availability. Fuel, diesel and gas can all be obtained 24 hours a day and the well-stocked chandlery, incorporating a coffee shop, stays open seven days a week.

FACILITIES AT A GLANCE

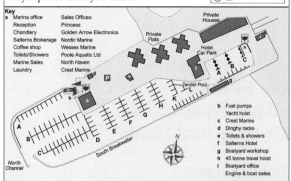

SALTERNS
·CHANDLERY·

Full Chandlery Facilities Incl:
24Hr Diesel/Petrol
International Paints
Anti-Fouling
HENRI-LLOYD,
MUSTO & SPLASHDOWN
CLOTHING,
SEBAGO DOCKSIDE SHOES
OAKLEY SUNGLASSES
OPEN 7 DAYS A WEEK
COFFEE SHOP
OVERLOOKING MARINA

01202-701556

SALTERNS WAY, LILLIPUT, POOLE, DORSET

YARMOUTH HARBOUR

Yarmouth Harbour
Yarmouth, Isle of Wight, PO41 0NT
Tel: 01983 760321 Fax: 01983 761192
info@yar-iow-harbour.demon.co.uk
www.yarmouth-harbour.co.uk

VHF Ch 68
ACCESS H24

The most western harbour on the Isle of Wight, Yarmouth is not only a convenient passage stopover but has become a very desirable destination in its own right, with virtually all weather and tidal access, although strong N to NE'ly winds can produce a considerable swell. The HM launch patrols the harbour entrance and will direct visiting yachtsmen to a pontoon berth or pile. With the exception of the town quay, the way ashore is by dinghy or water taxi (VHF Ch 15). The pretty harbour and town offer plenty of fine restaurants and amenities as well as being within easy reach of many of the Isle of Wight tourist attractions. One of its primary features is the castle, constructed in 1547 by order of Henry VIII.

FACILITIES AT A GLANCE

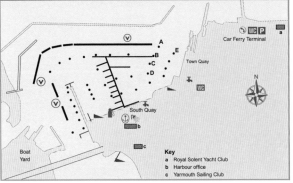

Key
a Royal Solent Yacht Club
b Harbour office
c Yarmouth Sailing Club

LYMINGTON YACHT HAVEN

Lymington Yacht Haven
King's Saltern Road, Lymington, S041 3QD
Tel: 01590 677071 Fax: 01590 678186
www.yachthavens.com email: lymington@yachthavens.com

VHF Ch 80
ACCESS H24

The attractive old market town of Lymington lies at the western end of the Solent, just three miles from the Needles Channel. Despite the numerous ferries plying to and from the Isle of Wight, the river is well sheltered and navigable at all states of the tide, proving a popular destination with visiting yachtsmen. LPG has been added to the available fuel.

Lymington Yacht Haven is the first of the two marinas from seaward, situated on the port hand side. Offering easy access to the Solent, it is a 10-minute walk to the town centre and supermarkets.

FACILITIES AT A GLANCE

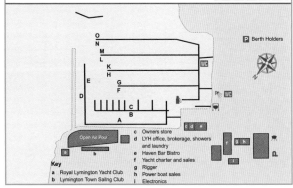

c Owners store
d LYH office, brokerage, showers and laundry
e Haven Bar Bistro
f Yacht charter and sales
g Rigger
h Power boat sales
i Electronics

Key
a Royal Lymington Yacht Club
b Lymington Town Sailng Club

harold hayles LTD.

THE HARBOUR BOATYARD FOR ALL MARINE SERVICES AND MOORINGS

RESERVE YOUR VISITING PONTOON BERTH WALK-A-SHORE INC POWER AND WATER

Five Slipways to 65 Tons • 10 Ton Crane • Repairs, Refurbishing & Refits • Rigging • Service Talurit & Swage Cordage • Chandlery • Paints & Antifoulings • Calor & Camping Gaz • Moorings • Yacht Brokerage & Insurance • C.A. Boatman • Liferaft Servicing

SPECIALIST MARINE ENGINEERS

VOLVO PENTA DEALER

Sales, Servicing & Repairs, Installation & Commissioning, Parts & Accessories held in stock, Warranty work.

SPURS

THE ORIGINAL PROPELLER PROTECTORS

In production now for 25 years enabling thousands of vessels inc. RNLI to enjoy safety and protection against prop fouling.

Whilst in Yarmouth we can haul you out & fit while you wait!

harold hayles LTD.

THE QUAY, YARMOUTH, IOW. PO41 0RS
TEL: (01983) 760373 FAX: (01983) 760666
Email: info@spurscutters.co.uk
website: www.spurscutters.co.uk

2007/M&WMD11/b

Tel: (01590) 677071
Fax: (01590) 678186
email: lymington@yachthavens.com

LYMINGTON YACHT HAVEN

King's Saltern Rd, Lymington, Hampshire SO41 3QD

Perfectly situated at the mouth of the Lymington river giving instant access to the western Solent. Full marina services, boatyard, brokerage, diesel, petrol and LPG.

SPECIAL WINTER RATE NOV-FEB (INCLUSIVE)

When responding to adverts please mention Marina & Waypoint Guide 2007

Charlie Sailing Ltd.

Lilac Cottage, Brickfield Lane, Lymington SQ41 5RD

RYA Training Centre

• RYA Courses
• Skippered Charter
• Cross Channel Passages
• Mile Building
• Coperate Adventures
• Yacht Deliveries
• Holiday Cruises
• Assisted Passages
• Own Boat Tuition

Tel: (01590) 688 328
e-mail: charliesailing@yahoo.com
www.charliesailing.co.uk

2007/M&WG124/f

BERTHON LYMINGTON MARINA

Berthon Lymington Marina Ltd
The Shipyard, Lymington, Hampshire, SO41 3YL
Tel: 01590 647405 Fax: 01590 676353
www.berthon.co.uk Email: marina@berthon.co.uk

VHF Ch 80
ACCESS H24

Situated approximately half a mile up river of Lymington Yacht Haven, on the port hand side, is Lymington Marina. Easily accessible at all states of the tide, it offers between 60 to 70 visitors' berths, although its close proximity to the town centre and first rate services mean that it can get very crowded in summer.

Besides the numerous attractions and activities to be found in the town itself, Lymington also benefits from having the New Forest, with its wild ponies and picturesque scenery, literally on its doorstep. Alternatively, the Solent Way footpath provides an invigorating walk to and from Hurst Castle.

FACILITIES AT A GLANCE

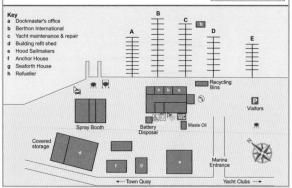

Key
a Dockmaster's office
b Berthon International
c Yacht maintenance & repair
d Building refit shed
e Hood Sailmakers
f Anchor House
g Seaforth House
h Refueller

BUCKLER'S HARD MARINA

Buckler's Hard
Beaulieu, Brockenhurst, Hampshire, SO42 7XB
Tel: 01590 616200 Fax: 01590 616211
www.bucklershard.co.uk Email: river@beaulieu.co.uk

VHF
ACCESS H24

Meandering through the New Forest, the Beaulieu River is considered by many to be one of the most attractive harbours on the mainland side of the Solent. A few miles upstream from the mouth of the river lies Buckler's Hard, an historic 18th century village where shipwrights skilfully constructed warships for Nelson's fleet.

The marina, which offers deep water at all states of the tide (although note that the river's entrance bar can only be crossed approximately three and half hours either side of HW), is manned 24 hours a day. It's comprehensive facilities range from boat and rigging repairs to a fuel pump and chandlery.

FACILITIES AT A GLANCE

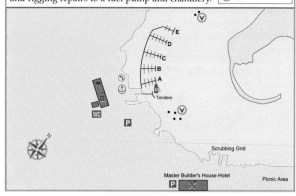

COWES YACHT HAVEN

Cowes Yacht Haven
Vectis Yard, Cowes, Isle of Wight, PO31 7BD
Tel: 01983 299975 Fax: 01983 200332
www.cowesyachthaven.com
Email: info@cowesyachthaven.com

VHF Ch 80
ACCESS H24

Situated virtually at the centre of the Solent, Cowes is best known as Britain's premier yachting centre and offers all types of facilities to yachtsmen. Cowes Yacht Haven, operating 24 hours a day, has very few permanent moorings and is dedicated to catering for visitors and events. At peak times it can become very crowded and for occasions such as Skandia Cowes Week you need to book up in advance.

FACILITIES AT A GLANCE

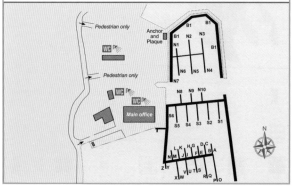

COWES YACHT HAVEN
the home of international boating since 1800

The Reputation The Location The People

Boatyard Facilities Include...
- 250 fully serviced berths
- 30 ton hoist & 15 ton mobile crane
- Free Wireless Broadband Internet access
- Seasonal packages for winter berthing & dry sailing

Shoreside Activities Include...
- Haven Events Centre for all your Hospitality & Events needs
- Conferences
- Seminars & Meetings
- Product Launches
- Exhibitions
- Parties & Weddings
- Boatshed Bar & Terrace

For more information visit:
www.cowesyachthaven.com
Tel: +44 (0) 1983 299975 or
Email: info@cowesyachthaven.com

2007/M&WC19/e

2

BUCKLERS HARD
BOAT BUILDERS LIMITED
The Agamemnoon Boat Yard,
Beaulieu, Hampshire SO42 7XB
Tel: +44 (0) 1590 616214/616336
Fax: +44 (0) 1590 616267
E-mail: info@bucklers.co.uk
Web Site: www.bucklers.co.uk

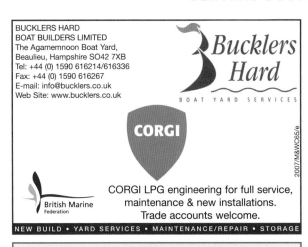

Bucklers Hard
BOAT YARD SERVICES

CORGI

British Marine Federation

2007/M&WC65/e

CORGI LPG engineering for full service,
maintenance & new installations.
Trade accounts welcome.

NEW BUILD • YARD SERVICES • MAINTENANCE/REPAIR • STORAGE

TRAFALGAR YACHT SERVICES

SPECIALIST BROKERAGE FOR WESTERLY YACHTS
·············
SPARE PARTS FOR WESTERLY YACHTS (and other makes)
·············
GENERAL CHANDLERY - OPEN 7 DAYS
·············
MAIL ORDER WORLDWIDE

Lower Quay, Fareham, Hants PO16 0RA. Tel: 01329 823577 Fax: 01329 221565
Website: www.westerly-yachts.co.uk E-mail: info@westerly-yachts.co.uk

2007/M&WC24/e

MARINE HEADLININGS

INTERIOR BOAT REURBISHMENT SERVICE
WORLDWIDE SERVICE

WESTERLY / SUNSEEKER /
BENETEAU / JEANEAU etc.
LININGS SUPPLIED / FITTED

01202 849339
Mobile 07970 440794
Roger Nantais

2007/M&WC125/a

EAST COWES MARINA

East Cowes Marina
Britannia Way, East Cowes, Isle of Wight, PO32 6UB
Tel: 01983 293983 Fax: 01983 299276
www.eastcowesmarina.co.uk

VHF Ch 80

Accommodating around 230 residential yachts and 160 visiting boats, East Cowes Marina is situated on the quiet and protected east bank of the Medina River, about a quarter mile above the chain ferry. The on-site chandlery stocks essential marine equipment and a small convenience store is just five minutes walk away. The brand new *club style* centrally heated shower and toilet facilities ensure the visitor a warm welcome at any time of the year, as does the on-site bar and restaurant. Several water taxis provide a return service to Cowes, ensuring a quick and easy way of getting to the town centre.

FACILITIES AT A GLANCE

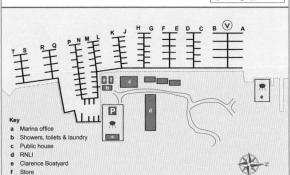

Key
a Marina office
b Showers, toilets & laundry
c Public house
d RNLI
e Clarence Boatyard
f Store

KEVIN MOLE
Marine Excellence

Powered by
YAMAHA

**Outboards, RIBs & Inflatable Dinghy Sales, Chandlery
Including Safety Equipment, Clothing & Outboards Spares
Fully Equipped Workshops for Outboard Service & Repair.**

**MEDINA COURT, ARCTIC ROAD, COWES, ISLE OF WIGHT
01983 289699**

2007/M&WC75/b

**DEAN & REDDYHOFF LTD -
EAST COWES MARINA
Britannia Way, East Cowes,
Isle of Wight PO32 6HA
Tel: (01983) 293983
Fax: (01983) 299276
e-mail: sales@eastcowesmarina.co.uk
www.deanreddyhoff.co.uk**

Perfectly situated up stream of Cowes town centre, the marina has undergone a complete refurbishment in 2003/04 both in and out of the water. New features include pontoons and services, luxurious washroom facilities, marquee and children's grass play area, public house, landscaping and much more. All visitors more than welcome.
See our full page advert at the end of Area 1.   2007/M&WEXT12/ebe

SHEPARDS WHARF MARINA

Shepards Wharf Boatyard
Medina Road, Cowes, Isle of Wight, PO31 7HT
Tel: 01983 297821 Fax: 01983 294814
www.shephards.co.uk

VHF Ch 80
ACCESS H24

A cable upstream of Cowes Yacht Haven, still on the starboard side, is Shepards Wharf. Incorporating several visitor pontoon berths, its facilities include water as well as full boatyard services ranging from a chandler and sailmaker to a 20-ton boat hoist. Fuel can be obtained from Lallows Boatyard (Tel 01983 292111) or Cowes Yacht Haven. For berthing availability, visiting yachtsmen should contact Cowes Harbour Control on VHF Ch 69 or Tel 01983 293952.

Shepards Wharf is within easy walking distance of Cowes town centre, where among the restaurants to be highly recommended are the Red Duster and Murrays Seafoods on the High Street and Tonino's on Shooters Hill. Also worth visiting are the Maritime Museum, exhibiting the Uffa Fox boats *Avenger* and *Coweslip*, and the Sir Max Aitken Museum. Sir Max contributed enormously to ocean yacht racing and the museum is dedicated to his collection of nautical instruments, paintings and maritime artefacts.

FACILITIES AT A GLANCE

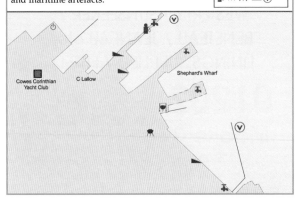

ISLAND HARBOUR MARINA

Island Harbour Marina
Mill Lane, Binfield, Newport, Isle of Wight, PO30 2LA
Tel: 01983 822999 Fax: 01983 526020
Email: pafharbour@aol.com

VHF Ch 80
ACCESS HW±4

Situated in beautiful rolling farmland about half a mile south of Folly Inn, Island Harbour Marina provides around 200 visitors' berths. Protected by a lock that is operated daily from 0700 – 2100 during the summer and from 0800 – 1730 during the winter, the marina is accessible for about four hours either side of HW for draughts of 1.5m.

Due to its remote setting, the marina's on site restaurant also sells essential provisions and newspapers. A half hour walk along the river brings you to Newport, the capital and county town of the Isle of Wight.

FACILITIES AT A GLANCE

Key
a Control tower
b Bin store
c Chandlery
d Restaurant

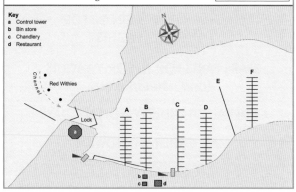

HYTHE MARINA

Hythe Marina Village
Shamrock Way, Hythe, Southampton, SO45 6DY
Tel: 023 8020 7073 Fax: 023 8084 2424
www.marinas.co.uk Email: d.wilson@mdlmarinas.co.uk

VHF Ch 80
ACCESS H24

Situated on the western shores of Southampton Water, Hythe Marina Village is approached by a dredged channel leading to a lock basin. The lock gates are controlled 24 hours a day throughout the year, with a waiting pontoon to the south of the approach basin.

Hythe Marina Village incorporates full marine services as well as on site restaurants and shops. Forming an integral part of the New Forest Waterside, Hythe is the perfect base from which to explore Hampshire's pretty inland villages and towns, or alternatively you can catch the ferry to Southampton's Town Quay.

FACILITIES AT A GLANCE

Key
a Salt Bar and Kitchen
b Lock building
c Boat storage and Trailer park

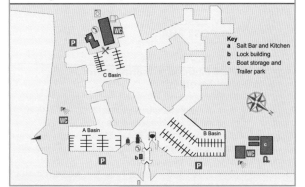

OCEAN VILLAGE MARINA

Ocean Village Marina
2 Channel Way, Southampton, SO14 3TG
Tel: 023 8022 9385 Fax: 023 8023 3515
www.marinas.co.uk Email: oceanvillage@mdlmarinas.co.uk

VHF Ch 80
ACCESS H24

The entrance to Ocean Village Marina lies on the port side of the River Itchen, just before the Itchen Bridge. With the capacity to accommodate large yachts and tall ships, the marina, accessible 24 hours a day, is renowned for hosting the starts of the Volvo and BT Global Challenge races. Situated at the heart of a waterside development incorporating shops, cinemas, restaurants and housing as well as The Royal Southampton Yacht Club, Ocean Village offers a vibrant atmosphere along with high quality service.

FACILITIES AT A GLANCE

Key
a Marina manager's office
b RSYC
c Dock manager's office
d Dock office
e Harbour Lights Cinema

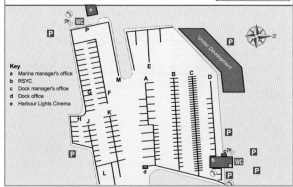

2

SHAMROCK QUAY MARINA

Shamrock Quay Marina
William Street, Northam, Southampton, Hants, SO14 5QL
Tel: 023 8022 9461 Fax: 023 8021 3808
Email: r.fogerty@mdlmarinas.co.uk

VHF Ch 80
ACCESS H24

Shamrock Quay, lying upstream of the Itchen Bridge on the port hand side, offers excellent facilities to yachtsmen. It also benefits from being accessible 24 hours a day, although the inside berths can get quite shallow at LWS. Note that it is best to arrive at slack water as the cross tide can be tricky when close quarter manoeuvring.

The city centre is about two miles away, where among the numerous attractions are the Maritime Museum at Town Quay, the Medieval Merchant's House in French Street and the Southampton City Art Gallery in the Civic Centre.

FACILITIES AT A GLANCE

Key
a Office, bar and restaurant
b Marina office
c Cafe

GREENHAM REGIS

Means a Great Deal in
marine electronics

WWW.GREENHAM-REGIS.COM

SALES * SERVICE * INSTALLATION

MAIN SALES OFFICES

KINGS SALTERN ROAD **LYMINGTON** HANTS. SO41 3QD TEL: 01590 671144 FAX: 01590 679517	SHAMROCK QUAY **SOUTHAMPTON** HANTS. SO14 5QL TEL: 023 8063 6555 FAX: 023 8023 1426

ALSO AT

EMSWORTH YACHT HARBOUR **EMSWORTH** HAMPSHIRE PO10 8BP TEL: 01243 378314 FAX: 01243 379120	UNIT 3, WEST QUAY ROAD **POOLE** DORSET BH15 1HX TEL: 01202 676363 FAX: 01202 671651	ITCHENOR SHIPYARD **CHICHESTER** WEST SUSSEX PO20 7AE TEL: 01243 511070 FAX: 01243 511070

MAIN AGENTS FOR ALL THE LEADING MANUFACTURERS :-
INCLUDING

Raymarine   **FURUNO**   **SIMRAD**

ICOM   **B&G**   **tacktick**

British Marine Federation

MEMBERS OF BOTH THE BRITISH MARINE ELETRONICS ASSOCIATION AND THE BRITISH MARINE FEDERATION

BMEA

2007/M&WC110/e

KEMP'S SHIPYARD

Kemp's Shipyard Ltd
Quayside Road, Southampton, SO18 1BZ
Tel: 023 8063 2323 Fax: 023 8022 6002
Email: bel@kempsquay.com

VHF
ACCESS HW±3.5

At the head of the River Itchen on the starboard side is Kemp's Marina, a family-run business with a friendly, old-fashioned feel. Accessible only 3½ hrs either side of HW, it has a limited number of deep water berths, the rest being half tide, drying out to soft mud. Its restricted access is, however, reflected in the lower prices.

Although situated on the outskirts of Southampton, a short bus or taxi ride will soon get you to the city centre. Besides a nearby BP Garage selling bread and milk, the closest supermarkets can be found in Bitterne Shopping Centre, which is five minutes away by bus.

FACILITIES AT A GLANCE

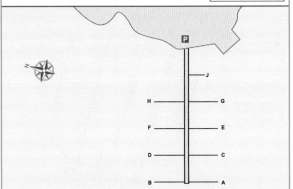

SAXON WHARF MARINA

Saxon Wharf Marina
Lower York Street, Northam
Southampton, SO14 5QF
Tel: 023 8033 9490 Fax: 023 8033 5215
www.marinas.co.uk Email: m.leigh@mdlmarinas.co.uk

VHF Ch 80
ACCESS H24

Saxon Wharf is a relatively new development which is situated towards the top of the River Itchen at the head of Southampton Water. Equipped with 50-metre marina berths and heavy duty pontoons, it is intended to accommodate superyachts and larger vessels. Boasting a 200-ton boat hoist and several marine specialists, including Southampton Yacht Services, it is the ideal place for the refit and restoration of big boats, whether it be a quick liftout or a large scale project. Located close to Southampton city centre and airport, Saxon Wharf is easily accessible by road, rail or air.

FACILITIES AT A GLANCE

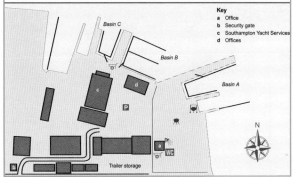

Key
a Office
b Security gate
c Southampton Yacht Services
d Offices

HAMBLE POINT MARINA

Hamble Point Marina
School Lane, Hamble, Southampton, SO31 4NB
Tel: 023 8045 2464 Fax: 023 8045 6440
Email: hamblepoint@mdlmarinas.co.uk

VHF	Ch 80
ACCESS	H24

Situated virtually opposite Warsash, this is the first marina you will come to on the western bank of the Hamble. Accommodating yachts up to 20m and power boats to 25m in length, it offers easy access to the Solent.

As with all the berths in the Hamble, be careful when manoeuvring at certain states of the tide and if possible try to avoid berthing when the tide is ebbing strongly. Boasting extensive facilities, the marina is within a 15-minute walk of Hamble Village, where services include a plethora of pubs and restaurants as well as a post office, bank and general store.

FACILITIES AT A GLANCE

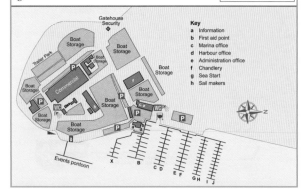

Key
a Information
b First aid point
c Marina office
d Harbour office
e Administration office
f Chandlery
g Sea Start
h Sail makers

VETUS DEN OUDEN LTD
5 Compass Point, Ensign Business Park, Hamble, Southampton SO31 4RA
FOR VETUS BOAT EQUIPMENT INCLUDING DIESEL EQUIPMENT, HYDRAULIC STEERING, BOW THRUSTERS AND HUNDREDS OF OTHER PRODUCTS - ASK FOR FREE COLOUR CATALOGUE
TEL: 023 8045 4507   FAX: 023 8045 4508
E-mail: sales@vetus.co.uk   Website: www.vetus.co.uk

Parker & Kay Sailmakers (South)
Hamble Point Marina, School Lane, Hamble, Southampton, Hampshire SO31 4JD
Tel: 023 8045 8213 Fax: 023 8045 8228
Parker & Kay Sailmakers (East)
Suffolk Yacht Harbour, Levington, Ipswich, Suffolk IP10 0LN
Tel: 01473 659878 Fax: 01473 659197
PARTNERS IN THE QUANTUM SAIL DESIGN GROUP

Hamble Sailing Services in association with **Hamble Cover Services Ltd**

Upholstery Boat Covers

Tel: 023 8045 5868
Tel: 023 8045 6354

sales@hamblesailingservices.co.uk
Mercury Yacht Harbour, Satchell Lane, Hamble, SO31 4HQ
www.hamblesailingservices.co.uk

PORT HAMBLE MARINA

Port Hamble Marina
Satchell Lane, Hamble, Southampton, SO31 4QD
Tel: 023 8045 2741 Fax: 023 8045 5206
www.marinas.co.uk

VHF	Ch 80
ACCESS	H24

On the west bank of the River Hamble, Port Hamble is the closest marina to the picturesque Hamble Village, therefore proving extremely popular with visiting yachtsmen. However, with no dedicated places for visitors, berthing availability is often scarce in the summer and it is best to contact the marina ahead of time.

Besides exploring the River Hamble, renowned for its maritime history which began as far back as the ninth century when King Alfred's men sank as many as 20 Viking long ships at Bursledon, other nearby places of interest include the 13th century Netley Abbey, allegedly haunted by Blind Peter the monk, and the Royal Victoria Country Park.

FACILITIES AT A GLANCE

Key
a Dock manager's office
b Boat sales
c Royal Air Force YC
d Hamble yacht services

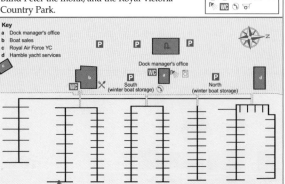

MERCURY YACHT HARBOUR

Mercury Yacht Harbour
Satchell Lane, Hamble, Southampton, SO31 4HQ
Tel: 023 8045 5994 Fax: 023 8045 7369
www.marinas.co.uk Email: mercury@mdlmarinas.co.uk

VHF	Ch 80
ACCESS	H24

Mercury Yacht Harbour is the third marina from seaward on the western bank of the River Hamble, tucked away in a picturesque, wooded site adjacent to Badnam Creek. Enjoying deep water at all states of water, it accommodates yachts up to 24m LOA and boasts an extensive array of facilities.

Hamble Village is at least a 20-minute walk away, although the on site chandlery does stock a small amount of essential items, and for a good meal you need look no further than the Oyster Quay bar and restaurant whose balcony offers striking views of the water.

FACILITIES AT A GLANCE

Key
a Toilets and showers
b Launderette
c Chandlery
d Restaurant and bar
e Brokerage
f Dockmaster, marina manager's office
g Waste disposal
h Recycling area

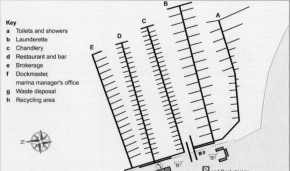

SWANWICK MARINA

Swanwick Marina
Swanwick, Southampton, Hampshire, SO31 1ZL
Tel: 01489 884081 Fax: 01489 579073
Email: swanwick@premiermarinas.com
www.premiermarinas.com

VHF	Ch 80
ACCESS	H24

Situated on the east bank of the River Hamble next to Bursledon Bridge, Swanwick Marina is accessible at all states of the tide and can accommodate yachts up to 20m LOA.

The marina's fully-licensed bar and bistro, the Doghouse, overlooking the river, is open for breakfast, lunch and dinner during the summer. Alternatively, just a short row or walk away is the celebrated Jolly Sailor pub in Bursledon on the west bank, made famous for being the local watering hole in the British television series *Howard's Way*.

FACILITIES AT A GLANCE

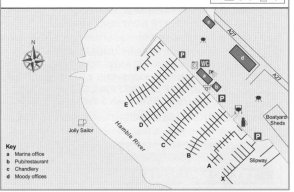

Key
a Marina office
b Pub/restaurant
c Chandlery
d Moody offices

RYDE LEISURE HARBOUR

Ryde Harbour
The Esplanade, Ryde, Isle of Wight, PO33 1JA
Tel: 01983 613879 Fax: 01983 613879
www.rydeharbour.com Email: ryde.harbour@iow.gov.uk

VHF	Ch 80
ACCESS	HW±2

Known as the 'gateway to the Island', Ryde, with its elegant houses and abundant shops, is among the Isle of Wight's most popular resorts. Its well-protected harbour is conveniently close to the exceptional beaches as well

as to the town's restaurants and amusements.

Drying to 2.5m and therefore only accessible to yachts that can take the ground, the harbour accommodates 90 resident boats as well as up to 75 visiting yachts. Fin keel yachts may dry out on the harbour wall.

Ideal for family cruising, Ryde offers a wealth of activities, ranging from ten pin bowling and ice skating to crazy golf and tennis.

FACILITIES AT A GLANCE

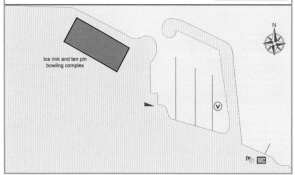

Ice rink and ten pin bowling complex

BEMBRIDGE MARINA

Bembridge Marina
Harbour Office, The Duver, St Helens, Ryde
Isle of Wight, PO33 1YB
Tel: 01983 872828 Fax: 01983 872922
Email: chris@bembridgeharbour.co.uk
www.bembridgeharbour.co.uk

VHF	Ch 80
ACCESS	HW±2.5

Bembridge is a compact, pretty harbour whose entrance, although restricted by the tides (recommended entry for a 1.5m draught is 2½hrs before HW), is well sheltered in all but north north easterly gales. Offering excellent sailing clubs, beautiful beaches and fine restaurants, this Isle of Wight port is a first class haven with plenty of charm. With approximately 100 new visitors' berths on the Duver Marina pontoons, the marina at St Helen's Quay, at the western end of the harbour, is now allocated to annual berth holders only.

FACILITIES AT A GLANCE

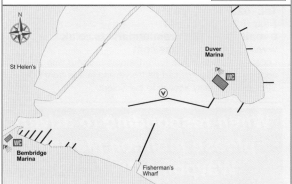

St Helen's
Duver Marina
Bembridge Marina
Fisherman's Wharf

M&WC29/2007/e

Bembridge Harbour

Bembridge Harbour welcomes visiting yachts which are now accommodated at the new Duver Marina providing access to the shore on the north side of the harbour. Rafting will be necessary at busy times. Showers and toilets, formerly in the Marina Office, are now located on the old Duver Boatyard site.

Water Taxi
The Water Taxi operates a service to ferry visitors to other parts of the harbour where there are various pick-up points.

Reservations
Reservations are not accepted for visitors' berths which are allocated strictly on a first-come, first-served basis. Visitors should call VHF Channel 80 for berthing instructions before entering the harbour.

ASSURING YOU OF A WARM AND FRIENDLY WELCOME
Harbour Master: Chris Turvey
Bembridge Harbour Improvements Company Limited.
Harbour Office, The Duver, St Helens, Ryde, Isle of Wight, PO33 1YB
Tel: 01983 872828 · Fax: 01983 872922
email: chris@bembridgeharbour.co.uk
web: www.bembridgeharbour.co.uk

When responding to adverts please mention Marina & Waypoint Guide 2007

HASLAR MARINA

Haslar Marina
Haslar Road, Gosport, Hampshire, PO12 1NU
Tel: 023 9260 1201 Fax: 023 9260 2201
www.haslarmarina.co.uk Email: sales@deanreddyhoff.co.uk

VHF | Ch 80
ACCESS | H24

This modern, purpose-built marina lies to port on the western side of Portsmouth Harbour entrance and is easily recognised by its prominent lightship incorporating a bar and restaurant. Accessible at all states of the tide, Haslar's extensive facilities do not however include fuel, the nearest being at the Camper and Nicholsons jetty only a fuel cables north.

Within close proximity is the town of Gosport where the Royal Navy Submarine Museum and the Museum of Naval Firepower 'Explosion' are well worth a visit.

FACILITIES AT A GLANCE

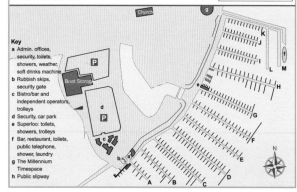

Key
a Admin. offices, security, toilets, showers, weather, soft drinks machine
b Rubbish skips, security gate
c Bistro/bar and independent operators, trolleys
d Security, car park
e Superloo: toilets, showers, trolleys
f Bar, restaurant, toilets, public telephone, shower, laundry
g The Millennium Timespace
h Public slipway

GOSPORT MARINA

Premier Gosport Marina
Mumby Road, Gosport, Hampshire, PO12 1AH
Tel: 023 9252 4811 Fax: 023 9258 9541
Email: gosport@premiermarinas.com
www.premiermarinas.com

VHF | Ch M, 80
ACCESS | H24

A few cables north of Haslar Marina, again on the port hand side, lies Gosport Marina. Boasting 519 fully-serviced visitors' berths, its extensive range of facilities incorporates a fuel barge on its southern breakwater as well as shower and laundry amenities. Numerous boatyard and engineering specialists are also located in and around the premises.

Within easy reach of the marina is Gosport town centre, offering a cosmopolitan selection of restaurants along with several supermarkets and shops.

FACILITIES AT A GLANCE

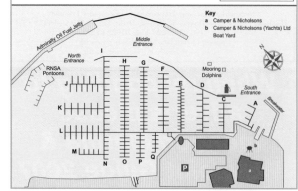

Key
a Camper & Nicholsons
b Camper & Nicholsons (Yachts) Ltd Boat Yard

DEAN & REDDYHOFF LTD - HASLAR MARINA
Haslar Road, Gosport, Hampshire PO12 1NU
Tel: (023) 9260 1201 Fax: (023) 9260 2201
e-mail: sales@haslarmarina.co.uk
www.deanreddyhoff.co.uk
Ideally situated only minutes from open water, Haslar caters for 600 annual berths together with up to 150 visiting berths. Facilities include: Light Ship bar/restaurant, Riggers, Chandlery, Brokers, Engineers, Maintenance, Electronics, Divers, Valeting, Charters, Wine Bar/Bistro, 24hr security and much more. See our full page advert at the end of Area 1 in Nautical Almanac.
2007/M&WEXT12/eb

Gosport Boat Yard Ltd.
THE COMPLETE BOATYARD SERVICE
BOAT REPAIRS, RENOVATIONS & FITTING OUT FOR ALL TYPES OF BOATS
INSURANCE REPAIRS UNDERTAKEN
PRE-SEASON PREPARATIONS, ANTI - FOULING, SCUB OFF, PAINTING, VANISHING ETC
FULL MARINE ENGINEERING SERVICE
Agents for BETA Bukh & Yanmar
CRANAGE WITH SPECIALIST WEIGHT LOAD UP TO 20 TONNES
Moorings - Deep Water & Tidal, Storage - Short & Long Term
Gosport Boat Yard Ltd Sharbour Road, Gosport, Hampshire, PO12 1BJ
TEL: 02392 586216 / 526534 Fax: 586216
2007/M&WC109/fz

Ocean Youth Trust South
❖ Voyages for young people aged 12- 25
❖ 72' Ocean going sail training vessel.
❖ Coastal or cross channel passages
❖ Voyages 3- 6 nights.
❖ Individual or group bookings
❖ Tall Ship Race events for over 15 year olds
❖ Fully qualified sea staff, all CRB cleared.
❖ Originally founded in 1960 as Ocean Youth Club
PO BOX 203, Gosport, PO12 9AZ. Tel:- 0870 241 2252
Web:-oytsouth.org .   email:- office@oytsouth.org
2007/M&WC90/b

GOSPORT MARINA
Mumby Road, Gosport, Hampshire PO12 1AH
Tel: (023) 9252 4811
Fax: (023) 9258 9541
e-mail: gosport@premiermarinas.co.uk
www.permiermarinas.com
Located at the entrance to Portsmouth Harbour with 24 hour access. 519 fully serviced berths varying in size from 5m to 20m. Ideal for easy access to the Solent.
2007/M&WL1/e

When responding to adverts please mention Marina & Waypoint Guide 2007

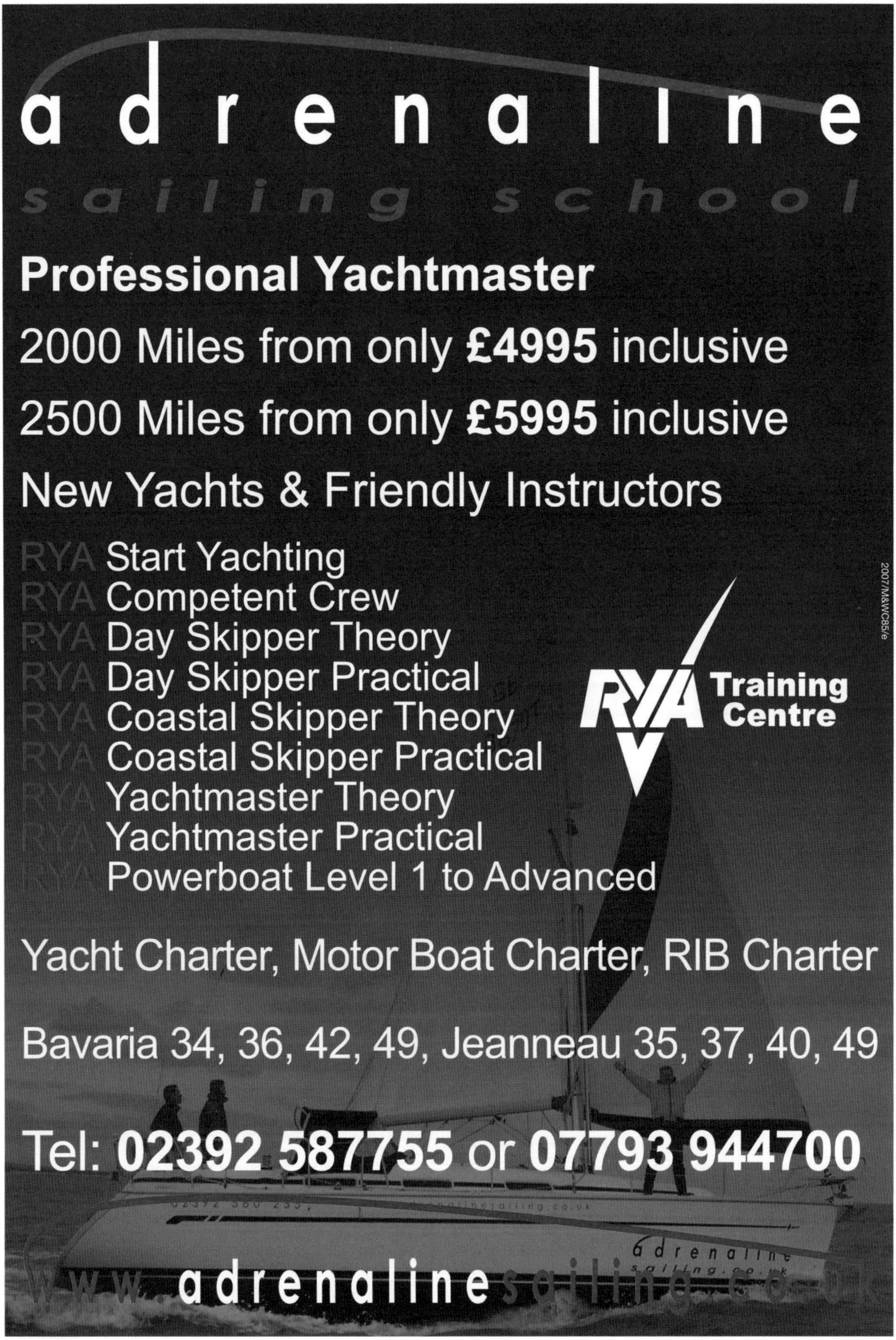

adrenaline
sailing school

Professional Yachtmaster

2000 Miles from only **£4995** inclusive

2500 Miles from only **£5995** inclusive

New Yachts & Friendly Instructors

RYA Start Yachting
RYA Competent Crew
RYA Day Skipper Theory
RYA Day Skipper Practical
RYA Coastal Skipper Theory
RYA Coastal Skipper Practical
RYA Yachtmaster Theory
RYA Yachtmaster Practical
RYA Powerboat Level 1 to Advanced

RYA Training Centre

2007/M&WC85/e

Yacht Charter, Motor Boat Charter, RIB Charter

Bavaria 34, 36, 42, 49, Jeanneau 35, 37, 40, 49

Tel: **02392 587755** or **07793 944700**

www.adrenaline sailing.co.uk

ROYAL CLARENCE MARINA

Royal Clarence Marina, Royal Clarence Yard
Weevil Lane, Gosport, Hampshire PO12 1AX
Tel: 023 9252 3810 Fax: 023 9252 3980
Email: enquiries@royalclarencemarina.co.uk
www.royalclarencemarina.co.uk

VHF	Ch 80
ACCESS	H24

Royal Clarence Marina benefits from a unique setting within a deep-water basin in front of the Royal Navy's former victualling yard. Only 10 minutes from the entrance to Portsmouth Harbour, it forms part of a £100 million redevelopment scheme which, anticipated to be completed in 2005, will incorporate residential homes, waterfront bars and restaurants as well as shopping outlets. Among its facilities are fully serviced finger pontoon berths up to 18m in length, while over 200m of alongside berthing will accommodate Yacht Club rallies and other maritime events.

FACILITIES AT A GLANCE

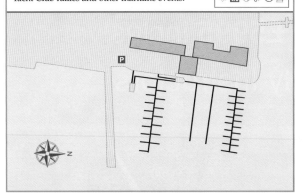

AN HISTORIC MARITIME LOCATION

Telephone: 023 9252 3810
E-mail: enquiries@royalclarencemarina.co.uk

royal clarence marina

- **1 Nautical north of the entrance to Portsmouth Harbour.**
- **Sheltered and accessible at all states of the tide**
- **Ideal location for annual berthing, visitors, rallies and events**
- **Modern pontoons and facilities**
- **Berthing for boats up to 40 metres**
- **Comprehensive boatyard services available at nearby "Endeavour Quay"**

Royal Clarence Marina enjoys a spectacular setting within a deep-water basin fronting the Royal Navy's former victualling yard in Portsmouth Harbour. This modern and professionally managed marina is less than 10 minutes by sea from the harbour entrance and close to Gosport town centre, there are also links to Gunwharf Quays. Our comprehensive boat facility is located half a mile away at the former Camper & Nicholson Shipyard, now renamed Endeavaour Quay

A unique location amongst historic naval buildings

M&WC28/2007/e

PORT SOLENT MARINA

Port Solent Marina
South Lockside, Portsmouth, PO6 4TJ
Tel: 023 9221 0765 Fax: 023 9232 4241
www.premiermarinas.com
Email: portsolent@premiermarinas.com

VHF	Ch 80
ACCESS	H24

Port Solent Marina is located to the north east of Portsmouth Harbour, not far from the historic Portchester Castle. Accessible via a 24-hour lock, this purpose built marina offers a full range of facilities. The Boardwalk comprises an array of shops and restaurants, while close by is a David Lloyd Health and Fitness Club and a large UCI cinema.

No visit to Portsmouth Harbour is complete without a trip to the Historic Dockyard, home to Henry VIII's *Mary Rose*, Nelson's HMS *Victory* and the first iron battleship, HMS *Warrior*, built in 1860.

FACILITIES AT A GLANCE

Key	a	Laundry, berth holders showers, toilets and baby change	c	Chandlery, marine engineers	f	David Lloyd Health and Fitness Club
	b	Portsmouth Harbour YC	d	Under cover boat shed	g	The Boardwalk - bars/restaurants
			e	Berth holders showers, toilets and public toilets, baby change	h	UCI cinema
					i	Marina control and Port Solent reception
					j	Residential building

Bridgeheads ① ② ③

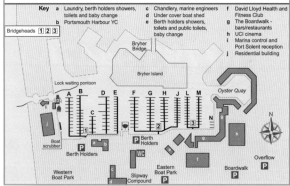

PORT SOLENT MARINA
South Lockside, Port Solent, Portsmouth,
Hampshire PO6 4TJ
Tel: (023) 9221 0765
Fax: (023) 9232 4241
e-mail: portsolent@premiermarinas.co.uk
www.permiermarinas.com
Situated in Portsmouth Harbour, Port Solent offers every facility a boatowner could wish for.

2007/M&WL1/e

When responding to adverts please mention Marina & Waypoint Guide 2007

SOUTH COAST MARINE

SERVICES
All woodwork undertaken

CABIN SOLES	Teak & Holly patterned fitted and/or supplied
DECKS	Teak repaired or replace
HARDWOOD	Sold and machined if required
HEAD LININGS	Replaced
PERSPEX	Supplied cut to pattern
PLYWOOD	Marine ply stocked & cut to pattern
STANCHIONS	Replaced
TOE RAILS	Supplied and fitted alloy or wood

Winter Refits - free estimates

Tel: 0239246 1011
Mob: 07958 540904

2007/M&WC118/e

SOUTHSEA MARINA

Southsea Marina
Fort Cumberland Road, PO4 9RJ
Tel: 02392 822719 Fax: 02392 822220
Email: southsea@premiermarinas.com
www.premiermarinas.com

VHF Ch 80
ACCESS HW±3

Southsea Marina is a small and friendly marina located on the western shore of Langstone Harbour, an expansive tidal bay situated between Hayling Island and Portsmouth. The channel is clearly marked by seven starboard and nine port hand markers. A tidal gate allows unrestricted movement in and out of the marina up to 3 hours either side of HW operates the entrance. The minimum depth in the marina entrance during this period is 1.6m and a waiting pontoon is available. There are excellent on site facilities including a bar, restaurant and chandlery. The nearest town is Southsea with its numerous local attractions.

FACILITIES AT A GLANCE

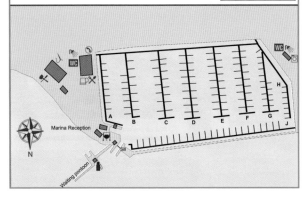

SOUTHSEA MARINA
Fort Cumberland Marina, Portsmouth,
Hampshire PO4 9RJ
Tel: (023) 9282 2719
Fax: (023) 9282 2220
e-mail: southsea@premiermarinas.co.uk
www.permiermarinas.com
A small and friendly Marina on the doorstep of the Solent.
2007/M&WL1/e

When responding to adverts please mention Marina & Waypoint Guide 2007

AG MARINE
Specialist Outboard Engineers
FOUR-STROKE & EFI SPECIALISTS

Factory trained:
SUZUKI
HONDA
YAMAHA
MERCURY
MARINER
EVINRUDE
JOHNSON

Tel: 02392 460777
SPARKES BOATYARD & MARINA
38 Wittering Road, Hayling Island, Hants. PO11 9SR
2007/M&WC120/z

SPARKES MARINA

Sparkes Yacht Harbour
Wittering Road, Hayling Island, Hampshire, PO11 9SR
Tel: 023 9246 3572 Fax: 023 9246 5741
Email: info@sparkes.co.uk www.sparkes.co.uk

VHF Ch 80
ACCESS H24

Just inside the entrance to Chichester Harbour, on the eastern shores of Hayling Island, lies Sparkes Marina and Boatyard. Its approach channel has been dredged to 2m MLW and can be identified by an unlit ECM. One of two marinas in Chichester to have full tidal access, its facilities include a wide range of marine services as well as a well-stocked chandlery and first class restaurant. Within close proximity are a newsagent, farm shop and various takeaways, while a taxi ride away are Capers and Jaspers, two restaurants on Hayling Island renowned for their top quality cuisine.

FACILITIES AT A GLANCE

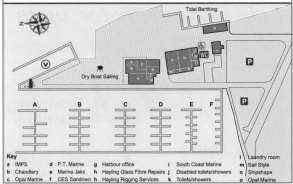

Key
a IMPS	d P.T. Marine	g Harbour office	i South Coast Marine
b Chandlery	e Marina Jaks	h Hayling Glass Fibre Repairs	j Disabled toilets/showers
c Opal Marine	f CES Sandown	h Hayling Rigging Services	k Toilets/showers

l Laundry room
m Sail Style
n Shipshape
o Opal Marine

SEA 'N' SKI

Steve Brown

RYA
BWSF

Powerboat Training
RYA Level 1
RYA Level 2
Intermediate
Advanced
Safety Boat
Water Ski & Driving
I.C.C. Issued

SCHOOL (U.K.)
Tel 02392 466041
Mob 07831 899959
2007/M&WM21/e

RJ WELLS *marine*

Heating and Refrigeration
Installations, Servicing
& Repairs
ROB WELLS
Tel: 07909 950979
robertjwells@ntlworld.com

MIKUNI
MARINE & VEHICLE HEATING

frigoboat
MARINE REFRIGERATION

2007/M&WC117/f

NORTHNEY MARINA

Northney Marina
Northney Road, Hayling Island, Hampshire, PO11 0NH
Tel: 023 9246 6321 Fax: 023 9246 1467
www.marinas.co.uk Email: northney@mdlmarinas.co.uk

VHF Ch 80
ACCESS H24

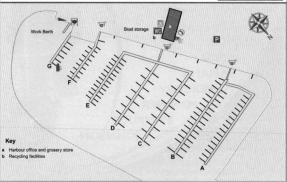

One of two marinas in Chichester Harbour to be accessible at all states of the tide, Northney Marina is on the northern shore of Hayling Island in the well marked Sweare Deep Channel, which branches off to port almost at the end of the Emsworth Channel. With a new facilities block having recently been completed, the marina now incorporates a very basic grocery store as well as improved ablution facilities. There is an events area for rallies.

FACILITIES AT A GLANCE

Key
a Harbour office and grocery store
b Recycling facilities

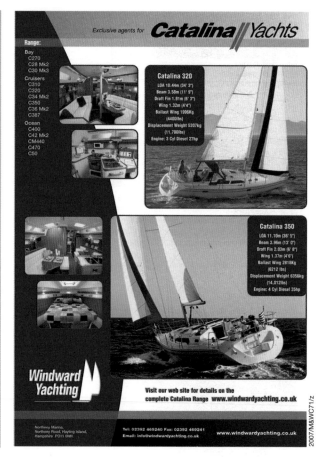

Exclusive agents for **Catalina Yachts**

Range:
Bay
C270
C28 Mk2
C30 Mk3
Cruisers
C310
C320
C34 Mk2
C350
C36 Mk2
C387
Ocean
C400
C42 Mk2
CM440
C470
C50

Catalina 320
LOA 10.44m (34' 3")
Beam 3.58m (11' 9")
Draft Fin 1.91m (6' 3")
Wing 1.32m (4'4")
Ballast Wing 1996Kg
(4400lbs)
Displacement Weight 5307kg
(11,700lbs)
Engine: 3 Cyl Diesel 27hp

Catalina 350
LOA 11.10m (36' 5")
Beam 3.96m (13' 0")
Draft Fin 2.03m (6' 8")
Wing 1.37m (4'6")
Ballast Wing 2818Kg
(6212 lbs)
Displacement Weight 6356kg
(14,012lbs)
Engine: 4 Cyl Diesel 35hp

Windward Yachting

Visit our web site for details on the complete Catalina Range www.windwardyachting.co.uk

Northney Marina,
Northney Road, Hayling Island,
Hampshire PO11 0NH

Tel: 02392 469240 Fax: 02392 469241
Email: info@windwardyachting.co.uk
www.windwardyachting.co.uk

2007/M&WC71/z

Individual Memberships from £76 per year

BOATABILITY.

Fancy a Free RYA Powerboat Course?

Join Boatability today, and not only could you get a free RYA Powerboat course, you could also qualify for up to 20% discount on our other RYA courses

Ground Floor Offices
Lock Control Building
South Lock Side
Port Solent
PO6 4TJ

0845 2608 777
www.boatability.co.uk

RYA Training Centre

2007/M&WC131/e

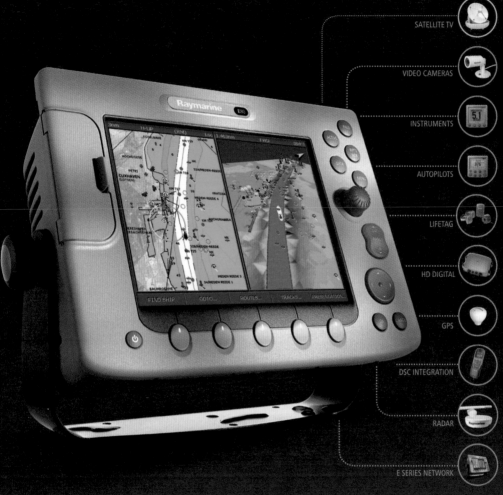

Displays this good
deserve to be shared.

SATELLITE TV

VIDEO CAMERAS

INSTRUMENTS

AUTOPILOTS

LIFETAG

HD DIGITAL

GPS

DSC INTEGRATION

RADAR

E SERIES NETWORK

☑ **E Series** now with Navtex and AIS Support

Raymarine®

Raymarine's E Series gives you everything you need from networkable multi function marine displays. Chartplotter, Fishfinder, Radar, Instrument data, Engine data – even live video feeds and LifeTag 'man overboard' tracking. All at your fingertips instantly, thanks to Raymarine's super-fast SeaTalk® networking software. Add in powerful 3D graphics, unbeatable functionality and a high-bright screen you can view even in bright sunlight, and you really have got the whole picture.

E SERIES NETWORK DISPLAYS

To see what Raymarine can do for you call:
+44 (0) 8080 729627 for your FREE copy of
our 2006 main product brochure or visit our
website **www.raymarine.com**

| RADAR | NAVIGATION AIDS | INSTRUMENTS | FISHFINDERS | AUTOPILOTS | COMMUNICATIONS | SOFTWARE | SYSTEMS |

2007/M&WC107/e

EMSWORTH YACHT HARBOUR

Emsworth Yacht Harbour
Thorney Road, Emsworth, Hants, PO10 8BP
Tel: 01243 377727 Fax: 01243 373432
Email: info@emsworth-marina.co.uk
www.emsworth-marina.co.uk

VHF Ch 80
ACCESS HW±2

Accessible about one and a half to two hours either side of high water, Emsworth Yacht Harbour is a sheltered site, offering good facilities to yachtsmen.

Created in 1964 from a log pond, the marina is within easy walking distance of the pretty little town of Emsworth, which boasts at least 10 pubs, several high quality restaurants and two well-stocked convenience stores.

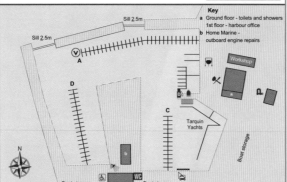

Key
a Ground floor - toilets and showers
   1st floor - harbour office
b Home Marine -
   outboard engine repairs

CHICHESTER MARINA

Chichester Marina
Birdham, Chichester, West Sussex, PO20 7EJ
Tel: 01243 512731 Fax: 01243 513472
Email: chichester@premiermarinas.com
www.premiermarinas.com

VHF Ch 80
ACCESS HW±5

Chichester Marina, nestling in an enormous natural harbour, has more than 1,000 berths, making it one of the largest marinas in the UK. Its approach channel can be easily identified by the CM SHM pile. The channel was dredged to 0.5m below CD in 2004, giving

access of around five hours either side of HW at springs. Besides the wide ranging marine facilities, there are also a restaurant and small convenience store on site. Chichester, which is only about a five minute bus or taxi ride away, has several places of interest, the most notable being the cathedral.

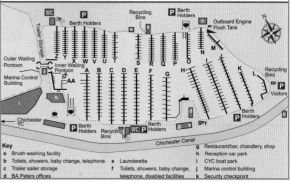

Key
a Brush washing facility
b Toilets, showers, baby change, telephone
c Trailer sailer storage
d BA Peters offices
e Launderette
f Toilets, showers, baby change, telephone, disabled facilities
g Restaurant/bar, chandlery, shop
h Reception car park
i CYC boat park
j Marina control building
k Security checkpoint

EMSWORTH YACHT HARBOUR LTD
Emsworth
Friendly marina in Chichester Harbour. Full facilities available – water, electricity, diesel, Calor gas, 40-tonne mobile crane, showers, toilets. Boat repairs, engineers, hard standing/storage, slipways, chandlery and car parking.
Thorney Road, Emsworth, Hants PO10 8BP.
Tel: (01243) 377727 Fax: (01243) 373432
Website: www.emsworth-marina.co.uk   2007/M&WMD10/e

HOLMAN RIGGING
Tel/Fax: 01243 514000
Chichester Marina, Chichester, West Sussex PO20 7EJ
Insurance Rig Checks
Expert inspection, report and recommendation. Mast, Rigging and reefing systems. Agents for major suppliers in this field. Also for Hyde Sails. Purpose designed mast trailer for quick and safe transportation.   2007/M&WMD20/e
E-mail: enquiries@holmanrigging.co.uk   www.holmanrigging.co.uk

CHICHESTER MARINA
Birdham, Chichester, West Sussex PO20 7EJ
Tel: (01243) 512731
Fax: (01243) 513472
e-mail: chichester@premiermarinas.co.uk
www.permiermarinas.com
A peaceful and relaxing Marina situated in a stunning natural harbour.
2007/M&WL1/e

BIRDHAM POOL MARINA

Birdham Pool Marina
Birdham Pool, Chichester, Sussex
Tel: 01243 512310 Fax: 01243 513163
Email: bpool@petersplc.com

VHF Ch 80
ACCESS HW±3

Birdham Pool must be among Britain's most charming and rustic marinas. Only accessible three hours either side of HW via a lock, any visiting yachtsman will not be disappointed by its unique and picturesque setting. To get to Birdham Pool, enter the channel at the Birdham SHM beacon. The channel is marked by green piles that should be left no more than 3m to starboard. There is a wide range of marine facilities on hand, including a small chandlery that opens six days a week.

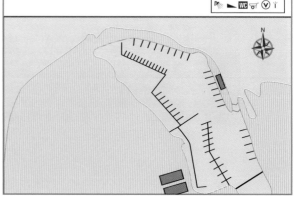

When responding to adverts please mention Marina & Waypoint Guide 2007

Yarmouth Harbour
ISLE OF WIGHT

www.yarmouth-harbour.co.uk

Yarmouth (IOW) Harbour Commissioners

Yarmouth Harbour extends a warm welcome to visiting yachtsmen.

∧ John Cleave (Yarmouth Gallery)

∧ Martin Williams www.island-photography.co.uk

Yarmouth Harbour is accessible at all states of the tide and offers a wide range of moorings and excellent facilities.

The harbour provides so much more than just a place to moor a boat. It is situated in the scenic Western Yar valley and is just a short stroll away from the historical town offering a range of shops, pubs, cafes and restaurants.

Whether cruising or relaxing for the day, Yarmouth Harbour is well worth a visit.

tel. 01983 760321 fax. 01983 761192
email. info@yar-iow-harbour.demon.co.uk

- Pontoon, pile & walk ashore moorings
- Buoy moorings outside of the breakwater during summer
- Rally booking arrangements
- Individual bookings welcomed on walk ashore pontoons
- Shower/toilet facilities for bona fide yachtsmen only, includes facilities for disabled visitors
- Berthing Masters available on the water to assist
- Laundry
- Cranage
- Waste disposal
- Shops close by - including bank & cashpoint
- Pubs, restaurants and cafés
- Local attractions
- Public transport
- Tourist Information Office
- Walkers paradise
- Chandlery
- Harbour Taxi
- Marine Engineers /Boatyards
- Yacht Clubs /Sailing Clubs

2007/M&WC57/e

THE YACHT CANOPY COMPANY

COCKPIT CANOPIES	COCKPIT COVERS
SPRAYHOODS	SUN AWNINGS
BIMINIS	WINTER COVERS
TONNEAU COVERS	LETTERED DODGERS

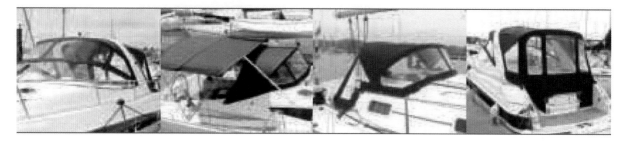

`Tailored to Perfection`

Skilled craftsmanship from generations of experience combine with the very latest in manufacturing technology to bring you the finest tailored marine products.

Original equipment suppliers to: ANCASTA

SEA VENTURES

HUNTER BOATS

PORTWAY SOUTH and EAST

... and many prominent yacht importers.

2007/M&WC146/e

TECSEW LIMITED
Units 3 & 4 Camden Street,
Gosport, Hampshire, PO12 3LU

Tel: 0845 402 4310
Fax: 0845 402 4311
Email: sales@tecsew.com

PAY US A VISIT...

www.tecsew.com

ADLARD COLES NAUTICAL
WEATHER FORECASTS
BY FAX & TELEPHONE

Coastal/Inshore	2-day by Fax	5-day by Phone
Mid Channel	09065 222 347	09068 969 647
Channel East	09065 222 346	09068 969 646
Anglia	09065 222 345	09068 969 645
East	09065 222 344	09068 969 644
National (3-5 day)	09065 222 340	09068 969 640

Offshore	2-5 day by Fax	2-5 day by Phone
English Channel	09065 222 357	09068 969 657
Southern North Sea	09065 222 358	09068 969 658
Northern North Sea	09065 222 362	09068 969 662
Biscay	09065 222 360	09068 969 660

09068 CALLS COST 60P PER MIN. 09065 CALLS COST £1.50 PER MIN.

Key to Marina Plans symbols

Calor Gas		P	Parking
Chandler			Pub/Restaurant
Disabled facilities			Pump out
Electrical supply			Rigging service
Electrical repairs			Sail repairs
Engine repairs			Shipwright
First Aid			Shop/Supermarket
Fresh Water			Showers
Fuel - Diesel			Slipway
Fuel - Petrol		WC	Toilets
Hardstanding/boatyard			Telephone
Internet Café	@		Trolleys
Laundry facilities		V	Visitors berths
Lift-out facilities			Wi-Fi

3

Area 3 - South East England

MARINAS
Telephone Numbers
VHF Channel
Access Times

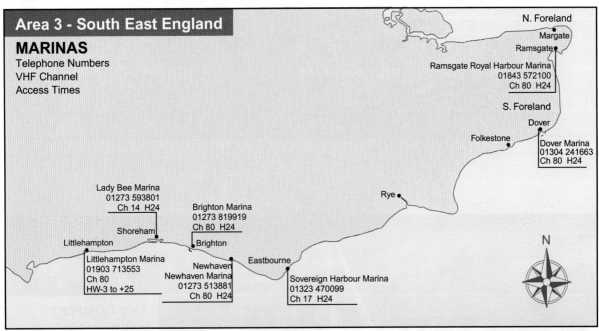

N. Foreland
Margate
Ramsgate
Ramsgate Royal Harbour Marina
01843 572100
Ch 80 H24

S. Foreland

Dover
Folkestone
Dover Marina
01304 241663
Ch 80 H24

Lady Bee Marina
01273 593801
Ch 14 H24

Brighton Marina
01273 819919
Ch 80 H24

Rye

Shoreham
Littlehampton
Brighton

Littlehampton Marina
01903 713553
Ch 80
HW-3 to +25

Newhaven
Newhaven Marina
01273 513881
Ch 80 H24

Eastbourne

Sovereign Harbour Marina
01323 470099
Ch 17 H24

N

Adlard Coles Nautical
THE BEST SAILING BOOKS

Reeds Astro Navigation Tables 2007
Lt Cdr Harry Baker   **£16.99**   0 7136 7824 0

TO ORDER

Tel: **01256 302692** email: **direct@macmillan.co.uk** or **www.adlardcoles.com**

Adlard Coles Nautical
THE BEST SAILING BOOKS

The Power Boater's Guide
Basil Mosenthal & Richard Mortimer   **£12.99**   0 7136 7569 1

TO ORDER

Tel: **01256 302692** email: **direct@macmillan.co.uk** or **www.adlardcoles.com**

LITTLEHAMPTON MARINA

Littlehampton Marina
Ferry Road, Littlehampton, W Sussex
Tel: 01903 713553 Fax: 01903 732264
Email: sales@littlehamptonmarina.co.uk

VHF	Ch 80
ACCESS	HW-3 to +2.5

A typical English seaside town with funfair, promenade and fine sandy beaches, Littlehampton lies roughly midway between Brighton and Chichester at the mouth of the River Arun. It affords a convenient stopover for yachts either east or west bound, providing you have the right tidal conditions to cross the entrance bar with its charted depth of 0.7m. The marina lies about three cables above Town Quay and Fisherman's Quay, both of which are on the starboard side of the River Arun, and is accessed via a retractable footbridge that opens on request to the HM (note that you should contact him by 1630 the day before you require entry).

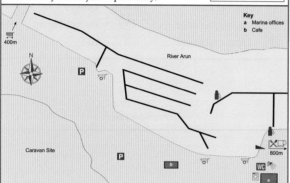

Key
a Marina offices
b Cafe

HILLYARDS

Hillyards
Rope Walk, Littlehampton, West Sussex, BN17 5DG
Tel: 01903 713327 Fax: 01903 722787
www.hillyards.co.uk Email: info@hillyards.co.uk

VHF	
ACCESS	HW-3 to +2.5

Established for more than 100 years Hillyards is a full service boatyard with moorings and storage for up to 50 boats. Based on the south coast within easy reach of London and the main yachting centres of the UK and Europe, Hillyards provides a comprehensive range of marine services.

The buildings of the boatyard are on the River Arun, a short distance from the English Channel. They provide the ideal conditions to accommodate and service craft up to 36m in length and with a maximum draft 3.5m. There is also craning services for craft up to 40 tons and the facilities to slip vessels up to 27m. In addition there are secure facilities to accommodate vessels up to 54m in dry dock.

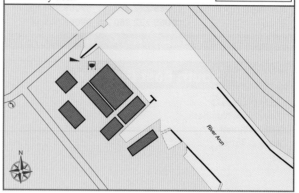

HILLYARDS
EXPERIENCE • EXPERTISE • EXCELLENCE

THE COMPLETE MARINE SERVICE

* Yacht & boat building
* Mainentance, servicing & engineering
* Repair & refits
* Painting & finishing
* Osmosis treatment
* Blast cleaning services
* Stainless & aluminium fabrication
* Shipwrighting
* Rigging
* Electrical & electronic services
* Mooring, lifting & storage
* Brokerage
* Insurance & surveyor work
* Collection & delivery service

With over 100 years of boatbuilding, repair and servicing experience we have the expertise to be of service to you - whether you're sailing a classic wooden yacht or the latest powerboat.
For more details, a quote or a copy of our Information Pack call 01903 713327 or email info@hillyards.co.uk

2007/M&WC112/e

LADY BEE MARINA

Lady Bee Marina
138-140 Albion Street, Southwick
West Sussex, BN42 4EG
Tel: 01273 593801 Fax: 01273 870349

VHF	Ch 14
ACCESS	H24

Shoreham, only five miles west of Brighton, is one of the South Coast's major commercial ports handling, among other products, steel, grain, tarmac and timber. On first impressions it may seem that Shoreham has little to offer the visiting yachtsman, but once through the lock and into the eastern arm of the River Adur, the quiet Lady Bee Marina, with its Spanish waterside restaurant, can make this harbour an interesting alternative to the lively atmosphere of Brighton Marina. Run by the Harbour Office, the marina meets all the usual requirements, although fuel is available in cans from Southwick garage or from Corral's diesel pump situated in the western arm.

FACILITIES AT A GLANCE

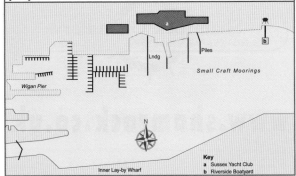

Key
a Sussex Yacht Club
b Riverside Boatyard

ADUR BOAT SALES

YACHT
INSURANCE
VALUATIONS

SALES
YACHT
PURCHASES
BOAT REPAIRS

YACHT BROKERS

Telephone 01273 596680 / 01273 591705
Fax 01273 870349
www.adurboatsales.co.uk

G.P. Barnes Ltd.

MARINA MANAGEMENT & SERVICES CHANDLERY & CALOR CENTRE
138-140 Ladybee Marina ● Albion Street ● Southwick ● West Sussex BN42 4EG

2007/M&WC63/e

boatronics

Marine Electrical and Electronic Sales, Installation and Repairs
The electronics specialist dedicated to Sovereign Harbour

Navigation instruments	Fish Finders	Engine instrumentation
Autopilots	Radios	Battery charging
Radars	Security systems	Rewiring

Tel 01424 892595
Visit our new web shop at boatronicsonline.com

SIMRAD   **Raymarine**   **B&G**   **tacktick**

2007/M&WC122B/z   Sovereign Harbour Registered on-site Contractor

BRIGHTON MARINA

Brighton Marina
West Jetty, Brighton, East Sussex, BN2 5UP
Tel: 01273 819919 Fax: 01273 675082
Email: brighton@premiermarinas.com
www.premiermarinas.com

VHF	Ch 37, 80
ACCESS	H24

Brighton Marina is the largest marina in the country and with its extensive range of shops, restaurants and facilities, is a popular and convenient stop-over for east and west-going passagemakers. Note, however, that it is not advisable to attempt entry in strong S to SE winds.

Only half a mile from the marina is the historic city of Brighton itself, renowned for being a cultural centre with a cosmopolitan atmosphere. Among its numerous attractions are the exotic Royal Pavilion, built for King George IV in the 1800s, and the Lanes, with its multitude of antiques shops.

FACILITIES AT A GLANCE

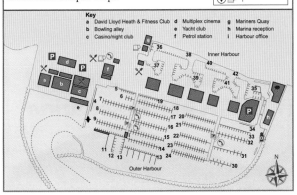

Key
a David Lloyd Heath & Fitness Club
b Bowling alley
c Casino/night club
d Multiplex cinema
e Yacht club
f Petrol station
g Mariners Quay
h Marina reception
i Harbour office

Shop online at...
www.smrmarine.co.uk

Brighton Marina

- Large Chandlery
- Yacht Rigging
- Outboard Centre
- Dinghy's
- Sail Repairs

01273 668900

2007/M&WC55/e
2006/M&WC75/e

BRIGHTON MARINA
West Jetty, Brighton Marina, Brighton,
East Sussex BN2 5UQ
Tel: (01273) 819919
Fax: (01273) 675082
e-mail: brighton@premiermarinas.co.uk
The UK's largest fully serviced Marina, accessible at all states of the tide.

2007/M&WL1/e

When responding to adverts please mention Marina & Waypoint Guide 2007

NEWHAVEN MARINA

Newhaven Marina
The Yacht Harbour, Fort Road, Newhaven
East Sussex, BN9 9BY
Tel: 01273 513881 Fax: 01273 510493
Email: john.stirling@seacontainers.com

VHF Ch 80
ACCESS H24

Some seven miles from Brighton, Newhaven lies at the mouth of the River Ouse. With its large fishing fleet and regular ferry services to Dieppe, the harbour has over the years become progressively commercial, therefore care is needed to keep clear of large vessels under manoeuvre. The marina lies approximately quarter of a mile from the harbour entrance on the west bank and was recently dredged to allow full tidal access except on LWS.

FACILITIES AT A GLANCE

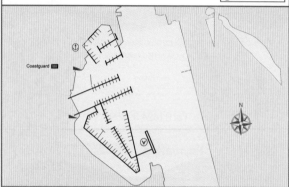

Coastguard

The Yacht Harbour, Fort Road, NEWHAVEN, East Sussex, BN9 9BY
Telephone (01273) 513881
Fax (01273) 510493

newhaven marina

2007/M&WC69/e

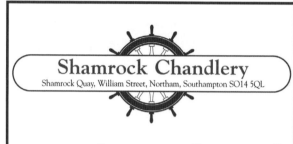

Shamrock Chandlery
Shamrock Quay, William Street, Northam, Southampton SO14 5QL

www.shamrock.co.uk

2007/M&WC160/z

SOVEREIGN HARBOUR MARINA

Sovereign Harbour Marina Ltd
Pevensey Bay Road, Eastbourne, East Sussex, BN23 6JH
Tel: 01323 470099 Fax: 01323 470077
Email: sovereignharbour@carillianplc.com
www.sovereignharbour.co.uk

VHF Ch 15, 17
ACCESS H24

Opened in 1993, Sovereign Harbour is situated a few miles NE of Eastbourne and is accessible at all states of the tide and weather except for in strong NE to SE'ly winds. Entered via a lock at all times of the day or night, the marina is part of one of the largest waterfront complexes in Britain, enjoying close proximity to shops, restaurants and a multiplex cinema. A short bus or taxi ride takes you to Eastbourne, where again you will find an array of shops and eating places to suit all tastes and budgets.

FACILITIES AT A GLANCE

Key
a The Waterfront, shops, restaurants, pubs and offices
b Harbour office - weather information and visitor's information
c Cinema
d Retail park - supermarket and post office
e Restaurant
f Toilets, showers, telephone, launderette and disabled facilities
g 24 hr fuel pontoon (diesel, petrol and holding tank pump out)
h Recycling centre
i Boatyard, boatpark, marine engineers, riggers and electricians

boatronics

Marine Electrical and Electronic Sale, Installation and Repairs

The electronics specialist dedicated to Sovereign Harbour

Navigation instruments
Autopilots
Radars
Fish Finders
Radios

Security systems
Engine instrumentation
Battery charging
Rewiring

Tel: 01424 892595
Vicit our new web shop at boatronicsonline.com

B&G tacktick
SIMRAD Raymarine

2007/M&WC122A/z

Sovereign Harbour Registered on-site Contractor

HARBOUR OF RYE

Harbour of Rye
New Lydd Road, Camber, E Sussex, TN31 7QS
Tel: 01797 225225 Fax: 01797 227429
Email: rye.harbour@environment-agency.gov.uk
www.environment-agency.gov.uk/harbourofrye

| VHF | Ch 14 |
| ACCESS | HW±2 |

The Strand Quay moorings are located in the centre of the historic town of Rye with all of its amenities a short walk away. The town caters for a wide variety of interests with the nearby Rye Harbour Nature Reserve, a museum, numerous antique shops and plentiful pubs, bars and restaurants. Vessels, up to a length of 15 metres, wishing to berth in the soft mud in or near the town of Rye should time their arrival at the entrance for not later than one hour after high water. Larger vessels should make prior arrangements with the Harbour Master. Fresh water, electricity, shower and toilet facilities are available.

FACILITIES AT A GLANCE

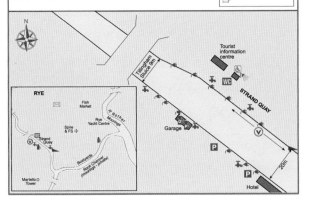

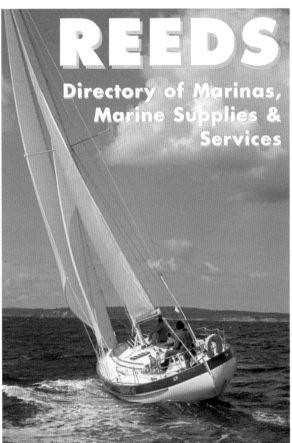

REEDS

Directory of Marinas, Marine Supplies & Services

3

2007/M&WC43/e

next time you visit Rye, why not bring your boat...

Environment Agency

Visitor's berths are available from £10 per night including power, water, shower and toilet facilities. Permanent moorings are also available. The yearly charge for a 9 metre boat is just £794. Contact the Harbour Office for more details.

Rye Harbour Office, New Lydd Road, Camber, Rye, East Sussex TN31 7QS. Tel: 01797 225225.
Email: rye.harbour@environment-agency.gov.uk   Website: www.environment-agency.gov.uk/harbourofrye

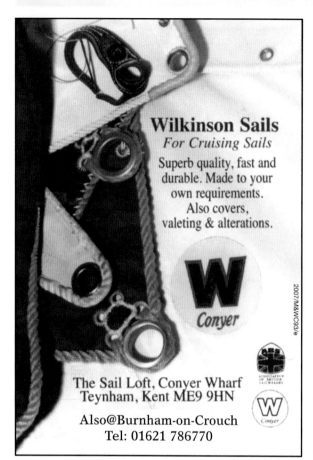

Wilkinson Sails

For Cruising Sails

Superb quality, fast and durable. Made to your own requirements. Also covers, valeting & alterations.

W Conyer

The Sail Loft, Conyer Wharf Teynham, Kent ME9 9HN

Also@Burnham-on-Crouch Tel: 01621 786770

2007/M&WC93/e

NORWOOD MARINE
65 Royal Esplanade, Margate, Kent CT9 5ET
Tel: (01843) 835711
Fax: 01843 832044
e-mail: greenfieldgr@aol.com
Marine consultants and advisers. Specialists in collisions, groundings, pioltage, yachting and RYA examinations - Fellows of Nautical Institute and RIN.

2007/M&Wext6

Shamrock Chandlery
Shamrock Quay, William Street, Northam, Southampton SO14 5QL

www.shamrock.co.uk

MAIL ORDER HOTLINE
Tel: (02380) 632725
Fax (02380) 225611

2007/M&WC160/z

DOVER MARINA

Dover Harbour Board
Harbour House, Dover, Kent, CT17 9TF
Tel: 01304 241663 Fax: 01304 242549
Email: marina@doverport.co.uk

VHF Ch 80
ACCESS H24

Nestling under the famous White Cliffs, Dover sits between South Foreland to the NE and Folkestone to the SW. Boasting a maritime history stretching back as far as the Bronze Age, Dover is today one of Britain's busiest  commercial ports, with a continuous stream of ferries and cruise liners plying to and from their European destinations. However, over the past years the harbour has made itself more attractive to the cruising yachtsman, with the marina, set well away from the busy ferry terminal, offering three sheltered berthing options in the Tidal Harbour, Granville Dock and Wellington Dock.

FACILITIES AT A GLANCE

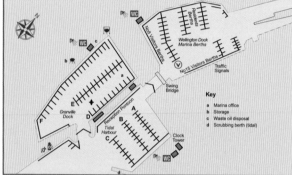

RAMSGATE ROYAL HARBOUR

The Royal Harbour Ramsgate Marina
Harbour Office, Military Road, Ramsgate, Kent, CT11 9LQ
Tel: 01843 572100 Fax: 01843 590941
Email: dominic.evans@thanet.gov.uk
www.ramsgatemarina.co.uk

VHF Ch 14, 80
ACCESS H24

Steeped in maritime history, Ramsgate was awarded 'Royal' status in 1821 by George IV in recognition of the warm welcome he received when sailing from Ramsgate to Hanover with the Royal Squadron. Offering good shelter and modern facilities, the Royal Harbour  can be accessed in all conditions except in strong E'ly winds and comprises an inner marina, entered approximately HW±2, a western marina in 3m of water and an eastern marina with a 2m depth. Permission to enter or leave the Royal Harbour must be obtained from Ramsgate Port Control on Ch 14.

FACILITIES AT A GLANCE

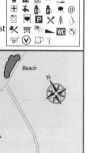

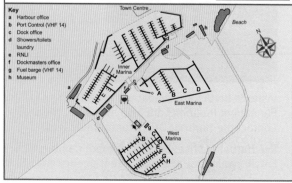

Key
a Harbour office
b Port Control (VHF 14)
c Dock office
d Showers/toilets
   laundry
e RNLI
f Dockmasters office
g Fuel barge (VHF 14)
h Museum

FAMBRIDGE YACHT HAVEN

Formerly 'West-Wick Marina' now the 'Yacht Haven Group's' latest marina on the East coast. Set on the River Crouch in the beautiful Essex countryside.

A natural marina in peaceful & tranquil surroundings with berths & swinging moorings available.

- Deep-Water swinging moorings available at low rates for 2007 to include free ferryservice - contact us for more information.
- Fully serviced deep water pontoon berths.
- Thames and Dutch barges welcome any time of year on fully serviced mud berths.
- Extensive hard standing available for long & short term storage, visitors welcome

- New 25 ton slipway hoist.
- Mobile Crane
- Pressure Washing
- CCTV
- Dedicated Visitor Pontoon
- 'New for 2006/07'- reduced rates for long term boat storage in secure compound.

2007/M&WC150/ez

Fambridge Yacht Haven

Church Road, West Wick, North Fambridge, Essex

Telephone: 01621 740370

www.yachthavens.com   email:fambridge@yachthavens.com

GALLIONS POINT MARINA LTD

Gate 14, Royal Docks, Royal Albert Basin, Woolwich Manor Way, North Woolwich E16 2NJ

"Experience a warm and friendly welcome on the Thames..."

Gallions Point Marina is situated down stream on the North side of Gallions Reach, which makes it particularly convenient, with access via the North Circular Road, the DLR, and numerous bus services. It offers deep water pontoon mooring and hard standing, the peace of mind of 24 hour security, monitored by CCTV, and facilities which include showers and toilets, electricity and water on pontoons, as well as pump out and engineer repairs.

For all enquiries please contact Eric or Leigh who will be happy to assist you.

Tel: 020 7476 7054
Fax: 020 7474 7056
VHF: Channel 37/80
www.gallionspointmarina.co.uk

2007/M&WC15/e

EAST ENGLAND - North Foreland to Great Yarmouth

ADLARD COLES NAUTICAL
WEATHER FORECASTS
BY FAX & TELEPHONE

Coastal/Inshore	2-day by Fax	5-day by Phone
Channel East	09065 222 346	09068 969 646
Anglia	09065 222 345	09068 969 645
East	09065 222 344	09068 969 644
North East	09065 222 343	09068 969 643
National (3-5 day)	09065 222 340	09068 969 640

Offshore	2-5 day by Fax	2-5 day by Phone
English Channel	09065 222 357	09068 969 657
Southern North Sea	09065 222 358	09068 969 658
North West Scotland	09065 222 361	09068 969 661
Northern North Sea	09065 222 362	09068 969 662

09068 CALLS COST 60P PER MIN. 09065 CALLS COST £1.50 PER MIN.

Key to Marina Plans symbols

Calor Gas		Parking	P
Chandler		Pub/Restaurant	
Disabled facilities		Pump out	
Electrical supply		Rigging service	
Electrical repairs		Sail repairs	
Engine repairs		Shipwright	
First Aid		Shop/Supermarket	
Fresh Water		Showers	
Fuel - Diesel		Slipway	
Fuel - Petrol		Toilets	WC
Hardstanding/boatyard		Telephone	
Internet Café	@	Trolleys	
Laundry facilities		Visitors berths	V
Lift-out facilities		Wi-Fi	

4

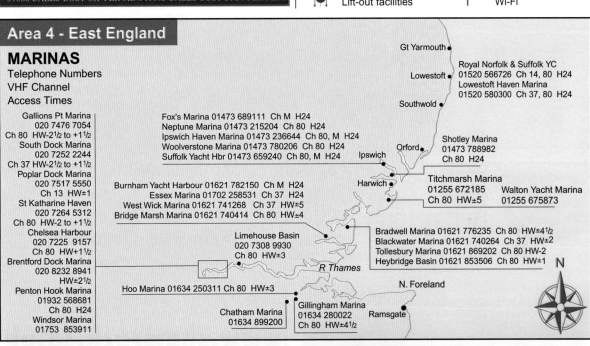

Area 4 - East England

MARINAS
Telephone Numbers
VHF Channel
Access Times

Gallions Pt Marina
020 7476 7054
Ch 80 HW-2½ to +1½
South Dock Marina
020 7252 2244
Ch 37 HW-2½ to +1½
Poplar Dock Marina
020 7517 5550
Ch 13 HW±1
St Katharine Haven
020 7264 5312
Ch 80 HW-2 to +1½
Chelsea Harbour
020 7225 9157
Ch 80 HW+1½
Brentford Dock Marina
020 8232 8941
HW±2½
Penton Hook Marina
01932 568681
Ch 80 H24
Windsor Marina
01753 853911

Fox's Marina 01473 689111 Ch M H24
Neptune Marina 01473 215204 Ch 80 H24
Ipswich Haven Marina 01473 236644 Ch 80, M H24
Woolverstone Marina 01473 780206 Ch 80 H24
Suffolk Yacht Hbr 01473 659240 Ch 80, M H24

Burnham Yacht Harbour 01621 782150 Ch M H24
Essex Marina 01702 258531 Ch 37 H24
West Wick Marina 01621 741268 Ch 37 HW±5
Bridge Marsh Marina 01621 740414 Ch 80 HW±4

Limehouse Basin
020 7308 9930
Ch 80 HW±3

Hoo Marina 01634 250311 Ch 80 HW±3

Chatham Marina
01634 899200

Gt Yarmouth

Lowestoft
Royal Norfolk & Suffolk YC
01520 566726 Ch 14, 80 H24
Lowestoft Haven Marina
01520 580300 Ch 37, 80 H24

Southwold

Orford
Shotley Marina
01473 788982
Ch 80 H24

Ipswich

Harwich
Titchmarsh Marina
01255 672185   Walton Yacht Marina
Ch 80 HW±5   01255 675873

R Thames

Bradwell Marina 01621 776235 Ch 80 HW±4½
Blackwater Marina 01621 740264 Ch 37 HW±2
Tollesbury Marina 01621 869202 Ch 80 HW-2
Heybridge Basin 01621 853506 Ch 80 HW±1

N. Foreland

Gillingham Marina
01634 280022   Ramsgate
Ch 80 HW±4½

N

Adlard Coles Nautical

THE BEST SAILING BOOKS

Pass with
Adlard
Coles
Nautical

Pass Your Yachtmaster
David Fairhall & Mike Peyton
0 7136 7574 8
£12.99

Pass Your Day Skipper – 2nd Edition
David Fairhall
0 7136 7400 8
£12.99

TO ORDER   Tel: **01256 302692** email: **direct@macmillan.co.uk** or **www.adlardcoles.com**

GILLINGHAM MARINA

Gillingham Marina
173 Pier Road, Gillingham, Kent, ME7 1UB
Tel: 01634 280022 Fax: 01634 280164
Email: berthing@gillingham-marina.co.uk
www.gillingham-marina.co.uk

VHF	Ch 80
ACCESS	HW±4.5

Gillingham Marina comprises a locked basin, accessible four and a half hours either side of high water, and a tidal basin upstream which can be entered approximately two hours either side of high water. Deep water moorings in the river cater for yachts arriving at other times.

Visiting yachts are usually accommodated in the locked basin, although it is best to contact the marina ahead of time. Lying on the south bank of the River Medway, the marina is approximately eight miles from Sheerness, at the mouth of the river, and five miles downstream of Rochester Bridge. Facilities include a well-stocked chandlery, brokerage and an extensive workshop.

FACILITIES AT A GLANCE

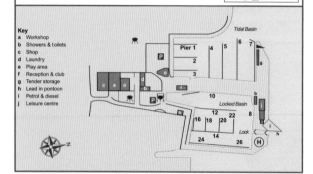

Key
a Workshop
b Showers & toilets
c Shop
d Laundry
e Play area
f Reception & club
g Tender storage
h Lead in pontoon
i Petrol & diesel
j Leisure centre

Enjoy the relaxed and friendly atmosphere and excellent facilities at our 120 floating berth Marina on the Medway. We also offer extensive hard standing, 24 hour security, on-site café and workshop facilities. Our Brokerage offers new sellers coming to the Marina a free lift out and pressure wash plus the first 3 months storage free of charge.
Vicarage Lane   HOO   Rochester   ME3 9LE
Tel: 01634 250311 Fax: 01634 251761

2007/M&WC45/e

marine solutions YACHT CHARTER SERVICE

Charter a comfortable 4 berth performance sailing yacht in some of the most historic and fascinating waters of the British Isles.

Based near the Historical naval dockyard on the Medway River our Marine Coastguard Agency approved vessel will be waiting for you, fully equipped with all the latest knobs and whistles!
For details telephone: Peter or Angela now on 01698 309075 or mobile: 07961 296023.

2007/M&WC123/z

Gillingham Marina

2007/M&WC31a/z

FIVE GOLD ANCHOR BERTHING AND SO MUCH MORE

BROKERAGE
With over 30 years experience
outstanding reliable service from the start to finish
BOAT REPAIRS
• Two boat hoists, of 65t and 20t
• Two modern purpose built spray shops, for boats up to 26m
• Respraying and osmosis specialists
• Leading insurance repair facility
• General hull repairs and maintenance
• Engineering services and overhauls
repairs@gillingham-marina.co.uk
Tel:01634 281333
CHANDLERY
One of the largest in Kent
Extensive stock of Musto & Douglas Gill in addition to all the traditional lines of chandlery
chandlery@gillingham-marina.co.uk
Tel: 01634 283008

British Marine Federation   The Yacht Harbour Association Ltd.

Gillingham Marina 173 Pier Road
Gillingham Kent ME7 1UB
Tel: 01634 280022 Fax: 01634 280164
email: berthing@gillingham-marina.co.uk
www.gillingham-marina.co.uk

Shamrock Chandlery
Shamrock Quay, William Street, Northam, Southampton SO14 5QL

www.shamrock.co.uk

MAIL ORDER
HOTLINE
Tel: (02380) 632725
Fax (02380) 225611

2007/M&WC160/z

EXPANDED BOOK SHOP

HOO MARINA

Hoo Marina
Vicarage Lane, Hoo, Rochester, Kent, ME3 9LE
Tel: 01634 250311 Fax: 01634 251761

VHF Ch 80
ACCESS HW±3

Hoo is a small village on the Isle of Grain, situated on a drying creek on the north bank of the River Medway approximately eight miles inland from Sheerness. Its marina was the first to be constructed on the East Coast and comprises finger berths supplied by all the usual services. It can be approached either straight across the mudflats near HW or, for a 1.5m draught, three hours either side of HW via a creek known locally as Orinoco. The entrance to this creek, which is marked by posts that must be left to port, is located a mile NW of Hoo Ness. Note that the final mark comprises a small, yellow buoy which you should pass close to starboard just before crossing the marina's sill.

Grocery stores can be found either in the adjacent chalet park or else in Hoo Village, while the Hoo Ness Yacht Club welcomes visitors to its bar and restaurant. There are also frequent bus services to the nearby town of Rochester.

FACILITIES AT A GLANCE

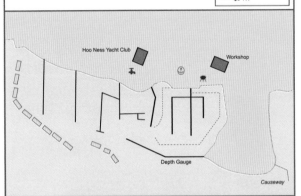

CHATHAM MARITIME MARINA

MDL, The Lock Building, Chatham Maritime Marina
Leviathan Way, Chatham Maritime, Chatham, Medway, ME4 4LP
Tel: 01634 899200 Fax: 01634 899201
Email: chatham@mdlmarinas.co.uk www.marinas.co.uk

VHF Ch 80
ACCESS H24*

Chatham Maritime Marina is situated on the banks of the River Medway in Kent, providing an ideal location from which to explore the surrounding area. There are plenty of secluded anchorages in the lower reaches of the Medway Estuary, while the river is navigable for some 13 miles from its mouth at Sheerness right up to Rochester, and even beyond for those yachts drawing less than 2m. Only 45 minutes from London by road, the marina is part of a multi-million pound leisure and retail development, currently accommodating 300 yachts.

FACILITIES AT A GLANCE

4

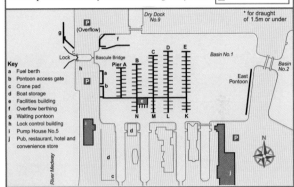

Main Dealers for:
International & Blakes Paint
Plastimo XM Yachting
Raymarine
Seago
Whale & Jabsco Pumps
Crewsaver Products
Silva Compasses
Spinlock
Hummingbird

Pirates Cave Chandlery

Tel: 01634 295233
Fax: 01634 722326

e-mail: piratescaveuk@yahoo.co.uk
Web: www.piratescave.co.uk

Unit 14.
Northpoint Business Estate,
Enterprise Close,
Medway City Estate
Frindsbury,
Rochester,
Kent ME2 4LX

2007/M&WC48/e

GALLIONS POINT MARINA

Gallions Point Marina, Gate 14, Royal Albert Basin
Woolwich Manor Way, North Woolwich
London, E16 2NJ. Tel: 020 7476 7054 Fax: 020 7474 7056
Email: info@gallionspointmarina.co.uk
www.gallionspointmarina.co.uk

VHF Ch M, 80
ACCESS HW≈5

Gallions Point Marina lies about 500 metres downstream of the Woolwich Ferry on the north side of Gallions Reach. Accessed via a lock at the entrance to the Royal Albert Basin, the marina offers deep water pontoon berths as well as hard standing. Future plans to improve facilities include the development of a bar/restaurant, a chandlery and an RYA tuition school.

FACILITIES AT A GLANCE

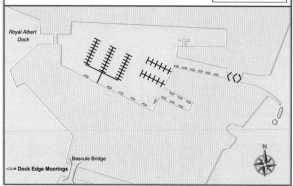

SOUTH DOCK MARINA

Southdown Marina
Southdown Quay, Millbrook, Cornwall, PL10 1HG
Tel: 01752 823084 Fax: 01752 823084
www.southdownmarina.co.uk

VHF
ACCESS HW≈4

South Dock Marina is housed in part of the old Surrey Dock complex on the south bank of the River Thames. Its locked entrance is immediately downstream of Greenland Pier, just a few miles down river of Tower Bridge. For yachts with a 2m draught, the lock can be entered HW-2½ to HW+1½ London Bridge, although if you arrive early there is a holding pontoon on the pier. The marina can be easily identified by the conspicuous arched rooftops of Baltic Quay, a luxury waterside apartment block. Once inside this secure, 200-berth marina, you can take full advantage of all its facilities as well as enjoy a range of restaurants and bars close by or visit historic maritime Greenwich.

FACILITIES AT A GLANCE

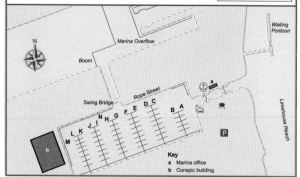

POPLAR DOCK MARINA

Poplar Dock Marina
West India Dock Pierhead
420 Manchester Road
London, E14 9ST
Tel: 020 7517 5550 Fax: 020 7538 5537
Email: sue.king@britishwaterways.co.uk

VHF Ch 13
ACCESS HW≈1 0700-1900

Poplar Dock was originally designed and constructed to maintain the water level in the West India Docks. Nowadays, with Canary Wharf lying to the west and the Millennium Dome to the east, it has been converted into London's newest marina and was officially opened by the Queen in June 1999. Canary Wharf, boasting as many as 90 shops, bars and restaurants, is just a five minute walk away, while slightly further north of this is West India Quay, where Grade I listed warehouses have been converted into waterside eating places, a 12-screen cinema and fitness centre.

FACILITIES AT A GLANCE

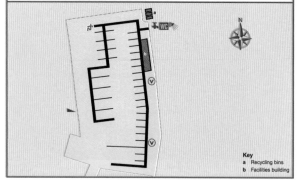

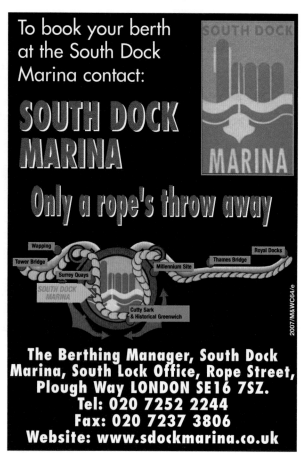

To book your berth at the South Dock Marina contact:

SOUTH DOCK MARINA

Only a rope's throw away

The Berthing Manager, South Dock Marina, South Lock Office, Rope Street, Plough Way LONDON SE16 7SZ.
Tel: 020 7252 2244
Fax: 020 7237 3806
Website: www.sdockmarina.co.uk

2007/M&WC64/e

LIMEHOUSE MARINA

Limehouse Marina
46 Goodhart Place, London, E14 8EG
Tel: 020 7308 9930 Fax: 020 7363 0428
www.bwml.co.uk

VHF Ch 80
ACCESS HW±3

Limehouse Marina, situated where the canal system meets the Thames, is now considered the 'Jewel in the Crown' of the British inland waterways network. With complete access to 2,000 miles of inland waterway systems and with access to the Thames at most stages of the tide except around low water, the marina provides a superb location for river, canal and sea-going pleasure craft alike. Boasting a wide range of facilities and up to 90 berths, Limehouse Marina is housed in the old Regent's Canal Dock.

FACILITIES AT A GLANCE

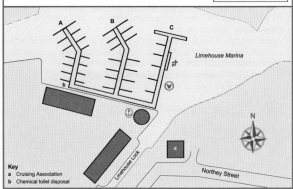

Limehouse Marina

Key
a Cruising Association
b Chemical toilet disposal

CHERTSEY MARINE

FOR ROPES, BOATS, MOST THAT FLOATS & OTHER BITS BESIDE LOOS, SHOES, ELSON BLUE, WITH LOTS MORE INSIDE

INTERNATIONAL FLAGSHIP DEALER

We stock:- BSS parts, Ropes, Fenders, Cleats, Water/Bilge Pumps, Anodes, Elsan Chemicals, Filters, Hoses, Impellors, Oils, Engine-Filters, Taps, Sinks, TVs, Cookers, Calor Gas, Polish Cleaners, Paint, Bic Dinghies, Sealants, Gas Fittings, S/S Screws, Nuts, Bolts, Maps, Mags, Books etc...

The Chandlery on the Thames
TOHATSU MAIN DEALER
VOLVO PENTA PARTS STOCKIST

WATER IN YOUR FUEL D-TX-IT

Chertsey Marine Ltd
Penton Hook Marina
Staines Road, Chertsey,
Surrey KT16 8QR

Opening Times:
Tues - Fri 9.30 - 5.30
Sat-Sun 9.30 - 4.00

TEL: 01932 565195 FAX: 01932 571668
Email: sharron@chertsey-marine.fsnet.co.uk

ST KATHARINE HAVEN

St Katharine's Marina Ltd
50 St Katharine's Way, London, E1W 1LA
Tel: 020 7264 5312 Fax: 020 7702 2252
Email: reception@skdocks.co.uk
www.skdocks.co.uk

VHF Ch 80
ACCESS HW -2 to +1.5

St Katharine Docks has played a significant role in worldwide trade and commerce for over 1,000 years. Formerly a working dock, today it is an attractive waterside development housing a mixture of shops, restaurants, luxury flats and offices as well as a state-of-the-art marina. St Katharine Haven is ideally situated for exploring central London and taking full advantage of the West End's theatres and cinemas. Within easy walking distance are Tower Bridge, the Tower of London and the historic warship HMS *Belfast*. No stay at the docks is complete without a visit to the famous Dickens Inn, an impressive three storey timber building incorporating a pizza bar and stylish restaurant.

FACILITIES AT A GLANCE

Key
a Ivory House
b Dickens Inn
c Haven office
d Tower Hotel

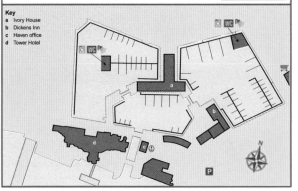

St Katharine's Haven

St Katharine's Investments, L.P.,
50 St Katharine's Way, London E1W 1LA
Tel: 020 7264 5312
Fax: 020 7702 2252
Email: haven.reception@skdocks.co.uk

CHELSEA HARBOUR MARINA

Chelsea Harbour Marina
Estate Managements Office
C2-3 The Chambers, London, SW10 0XF
Tel: 020 7225 9108 Fax: 020 7352 7868
Email: paul.ray@chelsea-harbour.co.uk

VHF Ch 80
ACCESS HW±1.5

Chelsea Harbour is now widely thought of as one of London's most significant maritime sites. It is located in the heart of South West London, therefore enjoying easy access to the amenities of Chelsea and the West End. On site is the Chelsea Harbour Design Centre, where 80 showrooms exhibit the best in British and International interior design, while offering superb waterside views along with excellent cuisine is the Conrad Hotel.

The harbour lies approximately 48 miles up river from Sea Reach No 1 buoy in the Thames Estuary and is accessed via the Thames Flood Barrier in Woolwich Reach. With its basin gate operating one and a half hours either side of HW (+ 20 minutes at London Bridge), the marina welcomes visiting yachtsmen.

FACILITIES AT A GLANCE

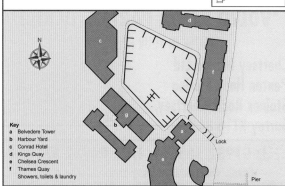

Key
a Belvedere Tower
b Harbour Yard
c Conrad Hotel
d Kings Quay
e Chelsea Crescent
f Thames Quay
   Showers, toilets & laundry

Lock

Pier

Sailing Information

2007/M&WC4/e

Location and Access:
From the sea, Chelsea Harbour is 48 nautical miles upriver from Sea Reach No: 1 Buoy in the Thames Estuary. For vessels entering or leaving the Thames, the recommended overnight mooring, if required, is at Queenbough at the river entrance to the River Medway. Vessels bound for Chelsea Harbour will pass through the Thames Floor Barrier located in Woolwich Reach. Traffic is controlled by Woolwich Radio (VHF Ch 14), and vessels equipped with VHF are required to call up Barrier Control on passing Margaret Ness when proceeding upstream, or on passing Blackwall Point when heading downstream. There is a speed limit of 8 knots on the tideway above Wandsworth Bridge.

Visitors:
Visitor yachtsmen from home and abroad are most welcome to Chelsea Harbour Marina, and are able to make prior arrangements by telephoning the Harbour Master's office on +44 (0) 7770 542783

Basin Gate Operation:
Approximately 1? hours either side of high water +20 minutes at London Bridge. With spring tide it may be necessary to close the outer gates around high water to control marina level.

Marina Lock Dimensions (Maximum for Craft):
Beam 5.5m (18')
Draught 2.5m (8')

Recommended Charts and Publications:
Admiralty: 1183, 2151 2484, 3319
Imray: C1, C2.

Cruising Opportunities:
Chelsea Harbour is ideally located for day, weekend or longer trips either upstream to Kew, Richmond, Hampton Court, or downstream to Rochester.

BRENTFORD DOCK MARINA

Brentford Dock Marina
2 Justine Close, Brentford, Middlesex, TW8 8QE
Tel: 020 8232 8941 Fax: 020 8560 5486
Mobile: 07920 143 987

VHF
ACCESS HW±2.5

Brentford Dock Marina is situated on the River Thames at the junction with the Grand Union Canal. Its hydraulic lock is accessible for up to two and a half hours either side of high water, although boats over 9.5m LOA enter on high water by prior arrangement. There is a Spar grocery store on site. The main attractions within the area are the Royal Botanic Gardens at Kew and the Kew Bridge Steam Museum at Brentford.

FACILITIES AT A GLANCE

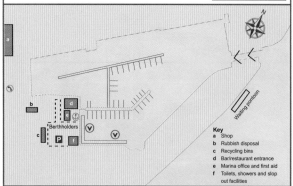

Key
a Shop
b Rubbish disposal
c Recycling bins
d Bar/restaurant entrance
e Marina office and first aid
f Toilets, showers and slop out facilities

PENTON HOOK MARINA

Penton Hook
Staines Road, Chertsey, Surrey, KT16 8PY
Tel: 01932 568681 Fax: 01932 567423
Email: pentonhook@mdlmarinas.co.uk
www.marinas.co.uk

VHF Ch 80
ACCESS H24

Penton Hook Marina is situated on what is considered to be one of the most attractive reaches of the River Thames, close to Chertsey and about a mile downstream of Runnymede. Providing unrestricted access to the River Thames through a deep water channel below Penton Hook Lock, the marina can accommodate ocean-going craft of up to 21m LOA and is ideally placed for a visit to Thorpe Park, reputedly one of Europe's most popular family leisure attractions.

FACILITIES AT A GLANCE

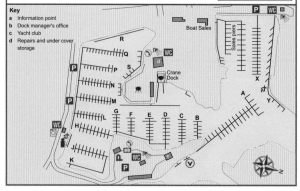

Key
a Information point
b Dock manager's office
c Yacht club
d Repairs and under cover storage

Boat Sales
Crane Dock

WINDSOR MARINA

Windsor Marina
Maidenhead Road, Windsor
Berkshire, SL4 5TZ
Tel: 01753 853911 Fax: 01753 868195
Email: windsor@mdlmarinas.co.uk www.marinas.co.uk

VHF | Ch 80
ACCESS | H24

Situated on the outskirts of Windsor town on the south bank of the River Thames, Windsor Marina enjoys a peaceful garden setting. On site are the Windsor Yacht Club as well as boat lifting and repair facilities, a chandlery and brokerage.

A trip to the town of Windsor, comprising beautiful Georgian and Victorian buildings, would not be complete without a visit to Windsor Castle. With its construction inaugurated over 900 years ago by William the Conqueror, it is the oldest inhabited castle in the world and accommodates a priceless art and furniture collection.

FACILITIES AT A GLANCE

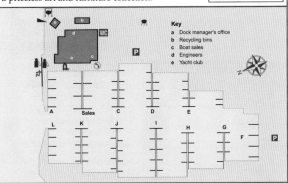

Key
a Dock manager's office
b Recycling bins
c Boat sales
d Engineers
e Yacht club

BRAY MARINA

Bray Marina
Monkey Island Lane, Bray
Berkshire, SL6 2EB
Tel: 01628 623654 Fax: 01628 773485
Email: bray@mdlmarinas.co.uk www.marinas.co.uk

VHF | Ch 80
ACCESS | H24

Bray Marina is situated in a country park setting among shady trees, providing berth holders with a delightfully tranquil mooring. From the marina there is direct access to the Thames and there are extensive well-maintained facilities available for all boat owners. Also on site is the highly acclaimed Riverside Brasserie. Twice winner of the AA rosette award for culinary excellence and short-listed for the Tatler best country restaurant, the Brasserie is especially popular with Club Outlook members who enjoy a 15% discount. The 400-berth marina boasts an active club, which holds social functions as well as boat training lessons and handling competitions, a chandlery and engineering services.

FACILITIES AT A GLANCE

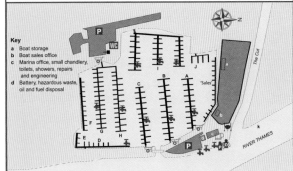

Key
a Boat storage
b Boat sales office
c Marina office, small chandlery, toilets, showers, repairs and engineering
d Battery, hazardous waste, oil and fuel disposal

BURNHAM YACHT HARBOUR MARINA

Burnham Yacht Harbour Marina Ltd
Burnham-on-Crouch, Essex, CM0 8BL
Tel: 01621 782150 Fax: 01621 785848
Email: admin@burnhamyachtharbour.co.uk

VHF | Ch 80
ACCESS | H24

Boasting four major yacht clubs, each with comprehensive racing programmes, Burnham-on-Crouch has come to be regarded by some as 'the Cowes of the East Coast'. At the western end of the town lies Burnham Yacht Harbour, dredged 2.2m below datum. Offering a variety of on site facilities, its entrance can be easily identified by a yellow pillar buoy with an 'X' topmark.

The historic town, with its 'weatherboard' and early brick buildings, elegant quayside and scenic riverside walks, exudes plenty of charm. Among its attractions are a sports centre, a railway museum and a two-screen cinema.

FACILITIES AT A GLANCE

Key
a Workshop
b Yacht sales
c Marina office
d Shower block
e The Swallowtail
f RNLI shore station
g Country park

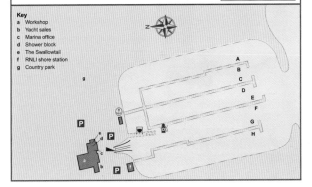

LONTON & GRAY SAILMAKERS

E-mail GryIan@aol.com
or dicklonton@clara.net

Tel 01621 786200
Fax 01621786201

Whatever Your Yacht Speak To Us

The Sail Loft, 61c High Street, Burnham on Crouch, Essex CMO 8AH

2007/M&WC66/e

MarineStore

Burnham-on-Crouch, Essex
www.marinestore.co.uk

Excellent range of day to day chandlery and wide selection of clothing

STOCKIST OF
INTERNATIONAL • BLAKES • S P SYSTEMS • WEST
MUSTO • CREWSAVER

THE EASTCOAST CHANDLERY SPECIALISTS

TEL: 01621 783090 EMAIL: chandlery@marinestore.co.uk

2007/M&WM6b/z

FAMBRIDGE YACHT HAVEN

Fambridge Yacht Haven
Church Road, North Fambridge, Essex, CM3 6LR
Tel: 01621 740370 Fax: 01621 742359
Email: fambridge@yachthavens.com

VHF	Ch 37, 80
ACCESS	H24

Just under a mile upstream of North Fambridge, Stow Creek branches off to the north of the River Crouch. The creek, marked with occasional starboard hand buoys and leading lights, leads to the entrance to Fambridge Yacht Haven, which enjoys an unspoilt, tranquil setting between saltings and farmland. Home to West Wick Yacht Club, the marina has 180 berths and can accommodate vessels up to 17m LOA.

The nearby village of North Fambridge incorporates a small convenience store as well as the Ferryboat Inn, a favourite haunt with the boating fraternity. Only six miles down river lies Burnham-on-Crouch, while the Essex and Kent coasts are within easy sailing distance.

FACILITIES AT A GLANCE

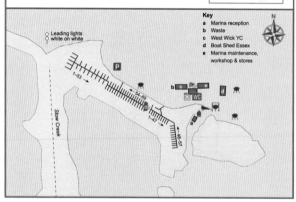

Key
a Marina reception
b Waste
c West Wick YC
d Boat Shed Essex
e Marina maintenance, workshop & stores

ESSEX MARINA

Essex Marina
Wallasea Island, Essex, SS4 2HF
Tel: 01702 258531 Fax: 01702 258227
Email: info@essexmarina.co.uk
www.essexmarina.co.uk

VHF	Ch 37
ACCESS	H24

Surrounded by beautiful countryside in an area of Special Scientific Interest, Essex Marina is situated in Wallasea Bay, about half a mile up river of Burnham on Crouch. Boasting 500 deep water berths, including 50 swinging moorings, the marina can be accessed at all states of the tide. On site are a 70 ton boat hoist, a chandlery and brokerage service as well as the Essex Marina Yacht Club.

Buses run frequently to Southend-on-Sea, just seven miles away, while a ferry service takes passengers across the river on weekends to Burnham, where you will find numerous shops and restaurants. Benefiting from its close proximity to London (just under an hour's drive away) and Rochford Airport (approximately four miles away), the marina provides a suitable location for crew changeovers.

FACILITIES AT A GLANCE

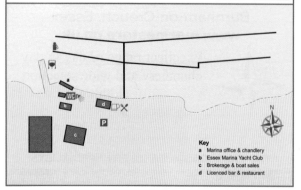

Key
a Marina office & chandlery
b Essex Marina Yacht Club
c Brokerage & boat sales
d Licenced bar & restaurant

ECHOMAX RADAR REFLECTORS
A significant advance in marine safety

2007/M&WC99/z

ECHOMAX 230 MIDI

Halyard/mast mount

Base mount with optional navigation light

Compact and highly efficient

The smallest of the Echomax polyethylene models for halyard/mast mounting (optional s/s deck mount brackets available) or base mounting.

Now used on RNLI RIBs, giving 100% paints at 3.8 miles and 80% at 5+ miles (sea state fair, mounted only 2m above sea level)

Performance
+/-3° 20m² peak. 100%@ 1.25m², 75%@2.5m², 58%@5m², 20%@10m²
The Midi exceeds the RORC and ORC requirement of 10m²

Halyard/mast mount
Height 450mm; diameter 245mm; fixing centres 408mm; fixing holes 8mm; weight 1.7kg

Base mount
Height 432mm (with light 522); diameter 245mm; fixing 4 x 10mm bolts at 80mm pcd; weight 2.3kg

All models available in white, orange or black

ECHOMAX 230

Light & robust for mid-size vessels

Made of 2.6mm polyethylene Meets ISO 8729, Ships Wheel Mark, SOLAS, RORC, ORC, and sec A1/1.33 & A1/4.39 of Marine Directive 98/95/EC

Performance
+/-3° 24m² peak
+/-15° 10m² peak

Halyard/mast/deck mount
Height 610mm; fixing centres 560mm; dia 245mm; fixing holes 8mm; weight 2.4 kg

For details on inflatable and larger ECHOMAX plus full specifications see www.echomax.co.uk
email: echomaxsales@aol.com
Tel: +44 (0)1371 830216 • Fax: +44 (0)1371 831733
The only one to be seen with

4

BRIDGEMARSH MARINA

Bridge Marsh Marine
Fairholme, Bridge Marsh Lane, Althorne, Essex
Tel: 01621 740414 Mobile: 07968 696815 Fax: 01621 740414

VHF Ch 80
ACCESS HW±4

On the north side of Bridgemarsh Island, just beyond Essex Marina on the River Crouch, lies Althorne Creek. Here Bridgemarsh Marine accommodates over 100 boats berthed alongside pontoons supplied with water and electricity. A red beacon marks the entrance to the creek, with red can buoys identifying the approach channel into the marina. Accessible four hours either side of high water, the marina has an on site yard with two docks, a slipway and crane. The village of Althorne is just a short walk away, from where there are direct train services (taking approximately one hour) to London.

FACILITIES AT A GLANCE

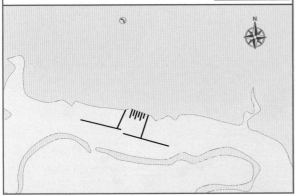

BRADWELL MARINA

Bradwell Marina, Port Flair Ltd, Waterside
Bradwell-on-Sea, Essex, CM0 7RB
Tel: 01621 776235 Fax: 01621 776393
Email: info@bradwellmarina.com
www.bradwellmarina.com

VHF Ch M, 80
ACCESS HW±4.5

Opened in 1984, Bradwell is a privately-owned marina situated in the mouth of the River Blackwater, serving as a convenient base from which to explore the Essex coastline or as a departure point for cruising further afield to Holland and Belgium. The yacht basin can be accessed four and a half hours either side of HW and offers plenty of protection from all wind directions. With a total of 300 fully serviced berths, generous space has been allocated for manoeuvring between pontoons. Overlooking the marina is Bradwell Club House, incorporating a bar, restaurant, launderette and ablution facilities.

FACILITIES AT A GLANCE

Key
a Clubhouse
b Tower office

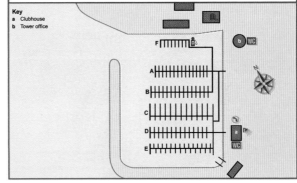

BLACKWATER MARINA

Blackwater Marina
Marine Parade, Maylandsea, Essex
Tel: 01621 740264 Tel: 01621 742122
Email: info@blackwater-marina.co.uk

VHF Ch 37
ACCESS HW±2

Blackwater Marina is a place where families in day boats mix with Smack owners and yacht crews; here seals, avocets and porpoises roam beneath the big, sheltering East Coast skies and here the area's rich heritage of working Thames Barges and Smacks remains part of daily life today. But it isn't just classic sailing boats that thrive on the Blackwater. An eclectic mix of motor cruisers, open boats and modern yachts enjoy the advantages of a marina sheltered by its natural habitat, where the absence of harbour walls allows uninterrupted views of some of Britain's rarest wildlife and where the 21st century shoreside facilities are looked after by experienced professionals, who are often found sailing on their days off.

FACILITIES AT A GLANCE

Key
a Maylandsea Bay YC
b Harlow (Blackwater) Sailing Club
c Main office

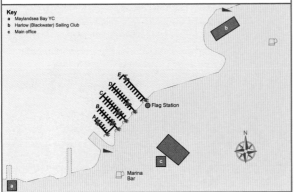

Bradwell Marina

- 300 Pontoon Berths in Rural Setting
- Access 4hrs either side H.W.
- VHF monitoring 9CH.M,P1,37+80)
- Water/Electricity to all Pontoons
- Fuel jetty – Petrol and Diesel
- Chandlery
- Hot Showers
- 1st Class Workshop/Repairs
- Marine Slip to 20 tons
- Boat Hoistage to 16 tons
- Winter Storage
- Licensed Club (Membership Free)
- Yacht Brokerage

Port Flair Ltd., Waterside, Bradwell-on-Sea, Essex CM0 7RB (01621) 776235/776391

Shamrock Chandlery
Shamrock Quay, William Street, Northam, Southampton SO14 5QL

www.shamrock.co.uk

TOLLESBURY MARINA

Tollesbury Marina
The Yacht Harbour, Tollesbury, Essex, CM9 8SE
Tel: 01621 869204 Fax: 01621 868489
email: marina@woodrolfe.com

VHF	Ch M, 80
ACCESS	HW-2

Tollesbury Marina lies at the mouth of the River Blackwater in the heart of the Essex countryside. Within easy access from London and the Home Counties, it has been designed as a leisure centre for the whole family, with on-site activities comprising tennis courts and a covered heated swimming pool as well as a convivial bar and restaurant. Accommodating over 240 boats, the marina can be accessed two hours either side of HW and is ideally situated for those wishing to explore the River Crouch to the south and the Rivers Colne, Orwell and Deben to the north.

FACILITIES AT A GLANCE

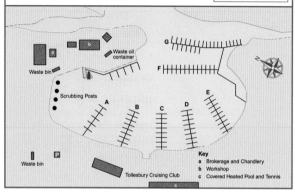

Key
a Brokerage and Chandlery
b Workshop
c Covered Heated Pool and Tennis

HEYBRIDGE BASIN

Heybridge Basin
Lock Hill, Heybridge Basin, Maldon, Essex, CM9 4RX
Tel: 01621 853506 Fax: 01621 859689
Email: colinandmargeret@lockkeepers.fsnet.co.uk
www.cbn.co.uk

VHF	Ch 80
ACCESS	HW±1

Towards the head of the River Blackwater, not far from Maldon, lies Heybridge Basin. Situated at the lower end of the 14–mile long Chelmer and Blackwater Navigation Canal, it can be reached via a lock about one hour either side of HW for a yacht drawing around 2m. If you arrive too early, there is good holding ground in the river just outside the lock. Incorporating as many as 200 berths, the basin has a range of facilities, including shower and laundry amenities. It is strongly recommendedthat you book 24 hours in advance for summer weekends.

FACILITIES AT A GLANCE

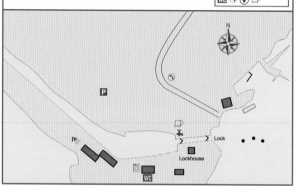

Shamrock Chandlery

Shamrock Quay, William Street, Northam, Southampton SO14 5QL

www.shamrock.co.uk

2007/M&WC160/z

TITCHMARSH MARINA

Titchmarsh Marina Ltd
Coles Lane, Walton on the Naze, Essex, CO14 8SL
Tel: 01255 672185 Fax: 01255 851901
Email: info@titchmarshmarina.co.uk
www.titchmarshmarina.co.uk

VHF	Ch 37, 80
ACCESS	HW±5

Titchmarsh Marina sits on the south side of The Twizzle in the heart of the Walton Backwaters. As the area is designated as a 'wetland of international importance', the marina has been designed and developed to function as a natural harbour. The 420 berths are well sheltered by the high-grassed clay banks, offering good protection in all conditions. Access to Titchmarsh is over a sill, which has a depth of about 1m at LWS, but once inside the basin, the depth increases to around 2m. Among the excellent facilities are an on site chandlery as well as the Harbour Lights Restaurant & Bar serving breakfasts, lunch and dinners.

FACILITIES AT A GLANCE

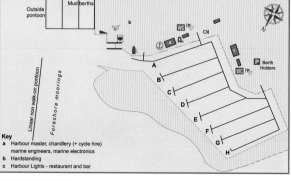

Key
a Harbour master, chandlery (+ cycle hire)
   marine engineers, marine electronics
b Hardstanding
c Harbour Lights - restaurant and bar

TITCHMARSH marina

Friendly service in the peaceful Backwaters.
Visiting yachtsmen welcome.
Sheltered Marina berths with Full Marina facilities:
16 amp electricity supply, diesel,
LPG, Calor Gas, Travel-lift, concrete hard standing, Winter storage - afloat & ashore.
Restaurant and Bar - Harbour Lights Restaurant
Brokerage - Westwater Yacht Sales - www.wwys.co.uk
www.titchmarshmarina.co.uk

Coles Lane, Walton-on-the-Naze, Essex, CO14 8SL
Marina Office Tel: 01255 672 185
Harbour Master Tel/Fax: 01255 851 899 VHF: Channel 80 & 37

2007/M&WC10/e

4

SHOTLEY MARINA

Shotley Marina Ltd
Shotley Gate, Ipswich, Suffolk, IP9 1QJ
Tel: 01473 788982 Fax: 01473 788868
Email: sales@shotley-marina.co.uk
www.shotleymarina.co.uk

| VHF | Ch 80 |
| ACCESS | H24 |

Based in the well protected Harwich Harbour where the River Stour joins the River Orwell, Shotley Marina is only eight miles from the county town of Ipswich. Entered via a lock at all states of the tide, its first class facilities include extensive boat repair and maintenance services as well as a well-stocked chandlery and on site bar and restaurant. The marina is strategically placed for sailing up the Stour to Manningtree, up the Orwell to Pin Mill or exploring the Rivers Deben, Crouch and Blackwater as well as the Walton Backwaters.

FACILITIES AT A GLANCE

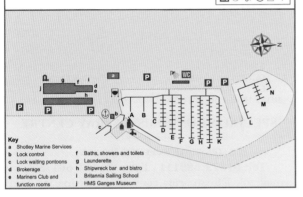

Key
a Shotley Marine Services
b Lock control
c Lock waiting pontoons
d Brokerage
e Mariners Club and function rooms
f Baths, showers and toilets
g Launderette
h Shipwreck bar and bistro
i Britannia Sailing School
j HMS Ganges Museum

SHOTLEY MARINA LTD

SHOTLEY GATE, IPSWICH, SUFFOLK IP9 1QJ.
TEL: (01473) 788982
FAX: (01473) 788868

350-berth, modern state of the art marina offering all the services expected. Open 24 hours with full security - Access all states of tide.

CHANDLERY • GENERAL STORE • RESTAURANT • BAR
LAUNDRY & IRONING CENTRE • SHOWERS BATHS TOILETS • CHILDREN'S ROOM
• TV AND FUNCTION ROOM
FULLY EQUIPPED BOATYARD OFFERING REPAIRS TO FULL REFITS.
DISABLED FACILITIES AVAILABLE.

E-mail: sales@shotley-marina.co.uk
Website: www.shotley-marina.co.uk

2007/M&WM3/e

Adlard Coles Nautical
THE BEST SAILING BOOKS

Sail in Safety with
Adlard Coles Nautical

REEDS VHF DSC HANDBOOK

Reeds VHF/DSC Handbook
2nd edition
Sue Fletcher
0 7136 7573 X
£12.99

TO ORDER Tel: **01256 302692** or visit **www.adlardcoles.com**

WALTON YACHT BASIN

Walton and Frinton Yacht Trust
Mill Lane, Walton on the Naze, CO14 8PF
Managed by Bedwell & Co Tel: 01255 675873
Fax: 01255 677405 After hours Tel: 01255 672655

| VHF | |
| ACCESS | HW-0.75, HW+0.25 |

Walton Yacht Basin lies at the head of Walton Creek, an area made famous in Arthur Ransome's *Swallows & Amazons* and *Secret Waters*. The creek can only be navigated two hours either side of HW, although yachts heading for the Yacht Basin should arrive on a rising tide as the entrance gate is kept shut once the tide turns in order to retain the water inside. Before entering the gate, moor up against the Club Quay to enquire about berthing availability.

A short walk away is the popular seaside town of Walton, full of shops, pubs and restaurants. Its focal point is the pier which, overlooking superb sandy beaches, offers various attractions including a ten-pin bowling alley. Slightly further out of town, the Naze affords pleasant coastal walks with striking panoramic views.

FACILITIES AT A GLANCE

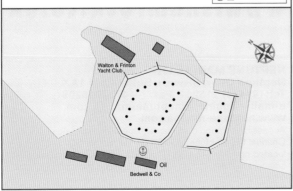

WALTON Yacht Basin

Mill Lane, Walton-on-the-Naze, Essex CO14 8PF

2007/M&WC40/b

The Yacht Basin has a gate-controlled minimum depth of 2 metres, providing up to 60 sheltered berths with access to fresh water and electricity. The Basins owned by the Walton & Frinton Yacht Trust Ltd, which is run by enthusiastic yachtsmen to serve the interests of the Club and visitors alike.

With vehicle access to all berths, the Basin is ideal for winter lay-up as well as for summer-time use. Its facilities are available to all yacht-owners, whilst any who join the Club will also find a warm welcome there. Day to day management is provided by Bedwell & Co, who should be contacted in advance (especially by persons with larger boats) to arrange gate-opening for entrance or exit, berth allocation, and payment of fees.

Telephone Numbers
Clubhouse: 01255 675526   Bedwell & Co: 01255 675873

FOX'S MARINA

Fox's Marina Ipswich Ltd
The Strand, Wherstead, Ipswich, Suffolk, IP2 8SA
Tel: 01473 689111 Fax: 01473 601737
Email: foxs@foxsmarina.com

VHF	Ch 68
ACCESS	H24

One of five marinas on the River Orwell, Fox's provides good shelter in all conditions and, dredged to 2m below chart datum, benefits from full tidal access from Ostrich Creek. Accommodating yachts up to 21m LOA, it has enough storage ashore for over 200 vessels and offers a comprehensive refit, repair and maintenance service. Since becoming part of the Oyster Group of Companies, Fox's facilities have further improved with ongoing investment. Besides several workshops, other services on hand include an osmosis centre, a spray centre, engineering, rigging and electronic specialists as well as one of the largest chandleries on the East Coast. In addition there are regular bus services to Ipswich, which is only about one to two miles away.

FACILITIES AT A GLANCE

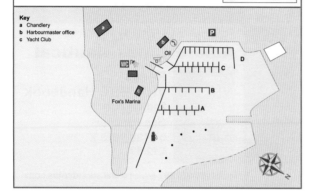

Key
a Chandlery
b Harbourmaster office
c Yacht Club

≈O≈

OYSTER
BROKERAGE

International Specialists in Pre-owned Oyster Yachts

www.oysterbrokerage.com

FOX'S MARINA, IPSWICH, SUFFOLK IP2 8SA
TEL: +44 (0)1473 695100 FAX: (0)1473 695120

FOX'S SINCE 1927

MARINE
SERVICE CENTRE

....

WORKSHOPS	DIESEL
STAINLESS STEEL	ELECTRONICS
MARINA BERTHING	ENGINEERING
YACHT SPRAY CENTRE	MASTS & RIGGING
BOAT HOIST 70/50 TONS	LARGE CHANDLERY

SPECIALIST OSMOSIS & SPRAY CENTRE

....

IPSWICH, SUFFOLK IP2 8SA

Tel: 01473 689111 Fax: 01473 601737

email: foxs@foxsmarina.com www.foxsmarina.com

FOX'S MARINA IPSWICH LTD
The Strand, Ipswich, Suffolk IP2 8SA
Tel: (01473) 689111
Fax: (01473) 601737
e-mail: foxs@foxsmarina.com
www.foxsmarina.com
Comprehensive boatyard. Osmosis, spray painting, rigging, electronics, engineering, stainless, chandlery.

NEPTUNE MARINA

Neptune Marina Ltd
Neptune Quay, Ipswich, IP4 1AX
Tel: 01473 215204 Fax: 01473 215206
Email: enquiries@neptune-marina.com

VHF	Ch 37, 80
ACCESS	H±2.5

The Wet Dock at Ipswich, which was opened in 1850, became the largest in Europe and was in use right up until the 1930s. Now the dock incorporates Neptune Marina, situated at Neptune Quay on the Historic Waterfront, and ever increasing shoreside developments. This 26-acre dock is accessible through a 24-hr lock gate, with a waiting pontoon outside. The town centre is a 10 minute walk away, while Cardinal Park, a relatively new complex housing an 11-screen cinema and several eating places, is nearby. There are also a number of other excellent restaurants along the quayside and adjacent to the Marina. The new Neptune Marina building occupies an imposing position in the NE corner of the dock with an over-the-quay restaurant and associated retail units.

FACILITIES AT A GLANCE

Key
a Old Custom House
b Conference centre
c Floating French
   restaurant
d Bistro
e Bellway apartments
f Neptune Marina
   office & facilities
g Marina storage yard

Shamrock Chandlery
Shamrock Quay, William Street, Northam, Southampton SO14 5QL

www.shamrock.co.uk

NEPTUNE MARINA LTD
Neptune Quay, Ipswich, Suffolk IP4 1AX
Tel: (01473) 215204 Fax: (01473) 215206
e-mail: enquiries@neptune-marina.com
www.neptune-marina.com
Accessible through continuously operating lockgates (VHF Channel 68) Neptune Marina (VHF Channels 80 or 37) is located on the north side of Ipswich wet dock immediately adjacent to the town centre and integrated into the rapidly regenerating northern quays.

M&Wext7

FOR FULL MARINE SERVICES IN THE UNIQUE & UNSPOILT SOUTHWOLD HARBOUR

HARBOUR MARINE SERVICES LTD

2007/M&WC147/e

BOATBUILDING & MARINE ENGINEERING CHANDLERS & NAUTICAL GIFTS

Blackshore,
Southwold Harbour,
Southwold,
Suffolk IP18 6TA

www.southwoldharbour.co.uk
Email: info@southwoldharbour.uk.com

Tel: (01502) 724721 24 HOURS
Fax: (01502) 722060

IPSWICH HAVEN MARINA

Ipswich Haven Marina
Associated British Ports
New Cut East, Ipswich, Suffolk, IP3 0EA
Tel: 01473 236644 Fax: 01473 236645
Email: ipswichhaven@abports.co.uk

| VHF | Ch 37, 68 & 80 |
| ACCESS | H24 |

Lying at the heart of Ipswich, the Haven Marina enjoys close proximity to all the bustling shopping centres, restaurants, cinemas and museums that this County Town of Suffolk has to offer. The main railway station is only a 10-minute walk away, where there are regular connections to London, Cambridge and Norwich, all taking just over an hour to get to.

Within easy reach of Holland, Belgium and Germany, East Anglia is proving an increasingly popular cruising ground. The River Orwell, displaying breathtaking scenery, was voted one of the most beautiful rivers in Britain by the RYA.

FACILITIES AT A GLANCE

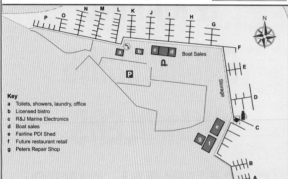

Key
a Toilets, showers, laundry, office
b Licensed bistro
c R&J Marine Electronics
d Boat sales
e Fairline PDI Shed
f Future restaurant retail
g Peters Repair Shop

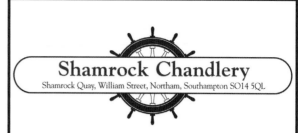

Shamrock Chandlery
Shamrock Quay, William Street, Northam, Southampton SO14 5QL

www.shamrock.co.uk

MAIL ORDER HOTLINE
Tel: (02380) 632725
Fax (02380) 225611

EXPANDED BOOK SHOP

2007/M&WC160/z

IPSWICH & LOWESTOFT HAVEN MARINAS
For more information please contact:

IPSWICH
Telephone:+44 (0) 1473 236644
Facsimile:+44 (0) 1473 236645
e-mail: ipswichhaven@abports.co.uk

LOWESTOFT
Telephone:+44 (0) 1502 580300
Facsimile:+44 (0) 1502 581851
e-mail: lowestofthaven@abports.co.uk

Welcome to our Marinas, both situated in the heart of the towns they serve, the New Lowestoft Haven Marina and the now well established Ipswich Haven Marina

Both offer outstanding facilities with Ipswich Haven already holding the very coveted T.Y.H.A. five gold anchor award

- 70 tonne boat hoist
- Shower and toilet facilities
- Refuse and waste oil disposal facilities
- Diesel fuel and bottle gas supplies
- Boat storage ashore
- Emergency telephone
- Large car park for berth holders and visitors

- Repair and re-fit workshops
- Chandlery shop
- Marine electronic sales installation and service
- A new and used boat sales centre
- Bar/Restaurant
- Superb location

ABP   THE YACHT HARBOUR ASSOCIATION LTD.

2007/NC78/e

LOWESTOFT HAVEN MARINA

Lowestoft Haven Marina
School Road, Lowestoft, Suffolk, NR33 9NB
Tel: 01502 580300 Fax: 01502 581851
Email: lowestofhaven@abports.co.uk

VHF	Ch 37, 80
ACCESS	H24

Lowestoft HavenLowestoft Haven Marina is phase 1 of a new marina complex for Lowestoft and is based on Lake Lothing and offering easy access to both the open sea and the Norfolk Broads. The town centres of both Lowestoft and Oulton Broad are within a short distance of the marina. The marina's 140 berths can accommodate vessels from 7-20m. Offering a full range of modern facilities the marina welcomes all visitors.

FACILITIES AT A GLANCE

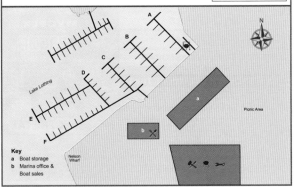

Key
a Boat storage
b Marina office &
   Boat sales

Lake Lothing
Picnic Area
Nelson Wharf

The Marine Safety Centre Limited

NEED A LIFERAFT?
WE ARE SPECIALISTS IN LIFERAFT

SALES • HIRE • SERVICE

Also Fenders, Life Jackets, Pyrotechnics

Unit 4 Colville Road Works, Colville Road
Lowestoft, Suffolk NR33 9QX
Tel: 01502 500940 Fax: 01502 500937
After Hours: 01502 566044

2007/M&WC127/e

4

LOWESTOFT YACHT SERVICES
For friendly Advice and Guaranteed Quality
SPECIALISING IN RIGGING AND YACHT SERVICES
YACHT COMMISSIONING TO OFFSHORE STANDARD

'Complete' rigging service, wire and rope swaging and splicing

Mast & 'Spar' overhauls /replacements, reefing systems, lazyjacks, Jib furling gear

'Boat refits', all deck gear supplied and fitted

'CALL-IN' service berth, slipping, cranage, and moorings

'BOSUN'S STORE' chandlery, yacht equipment supplied and fitted

'Mobile Rigging Services', Yacht and Cruiser sea delivery

2007/M&WC38/e

Also @ Lowestoft Haven Marina - on site services available
The Boatyard, Harbour Road, Oulton Broad, Lowestoft, Suffolk, NR32 3LX.

BOATYARD Tel/Fax: 01502 585535
Website: www.lowestoftyachts@.co.uk

Mobile: 07887 616846
E-mail: info@lowestoftyachts.co.uk

WOOLVERSTONE MARINA

Woolverstone Marina
Woolverstone, Ipswich, Suffolk, IP9 1AS
Tel: 01473 780206 Fax: 01473 780273
www.marinas.co.uk Email: t.barnes@mdlmarinas.co.uk

VHF Ch 80
ACCESS H24

Set in 22 acres of parkland, within close proximity to the Royal Harwich Yacht Club, Woolverstone Marina boasts 210 pontoon berths as well as 120 swinging moorings, all of which are served by a water taxi. Besides boat repair services, an on site chandlery and excellent ablution facilities, the marina also incorporates a sailing school and yacht brokerage.

Woolverstone's location on the scenic River Orwell makes it ideally placed for exploring the various cruising grounds along the East Coast, including the adjacent River Stour, the Colne and Blackwater estuaries to the south and the River Deben to the north.

FACILITIES AT A GLANCE

Key
a Marina office, toilets, showers, launderette and boat sales
b Restaurant/bar
c Royal Harwich Yacht Club

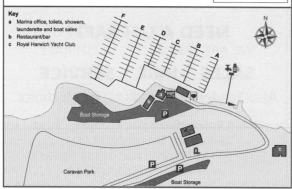

SUFFOLK YACHT HARBOUR

Suffolk Yacht Harbour Ltd
Levington, Ipswich, Suffolk, IP10 0LN
Tel: 01473 659240 Fax: 01473 659632
Email: enquiries@suffolkyachtharbour.ltd.uk
www.suffolkyachtharbour.ltd.uk

VHF Ch M
ACCESS H24

A friendly, independently-run marina on the East Coast of England, Suffolk Yacht Harbour enjoys a beautiful rural setting on the River Orwell, yet is within easy access of Ipswich (a mile away), Woodbridge and Felixstowe. With approximately 500 berths, the marina offers extensive facilities while the Haven Ports Yacht Club provides a bar and restaurant.

FACILITIES AT A GLANCE

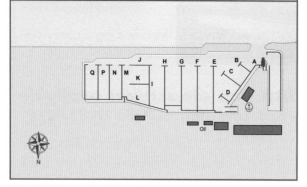

ROYAL HARWICH YACHT CLUB
Visit the Club on the River Orwell
Enjoy some of the best river views on the East Coast.
Hammer heads available for visitors.
Bar and catering service 7 days a week during the sailing season.

For further information, contact the Club on 01473 780319 / 219 or Geoff Prentice, our Berth Master, at weekends on 07742 145 994.

A.S.A.P. SUPPLIES LTD — Equipment & Spares Worldwide
- ENGINE & TRANSMISSION SPARES
- MARINISATION & PUMPS
- FUEL FILTERS & COMPONENTS
- INTAKES & EXHAUSTS
- GENERAL PUMPS & DOMESTICS
- STEERING & CONTROLS
- GAUGES & ELECTRICAL
- STERN GEAR & ACCESSORIES

REQUEST YOUR CATALOGUE TODAY

Email: sales@asap-supplies.com
Website: www.asap-supplies.com
Local Rate UK: 0845 1300 870
International Tel: +44 1502 716993
Free Fax UK: 0800 316 2727
International Fax +44 1502 711680
Beccles, Suffolk, England NR34 7TD

Parker & Kay Sailmakers (South)
Hamble Point Marina, School Lane, Hamble, Southampton, Hampshire SO31 4JD
Tel: 023 8045 8213 Fax: 023 8045 8228
Parker & Kay Sailmakers (East)
Suffolk Yacht Harbour, Levington, Ipswich, Suffolk IP10 0LN
Tel: 01473 659878 Fax: 01473 659197
PARTNERS IN THE QUANTUM SAIL DESIGN GROUP

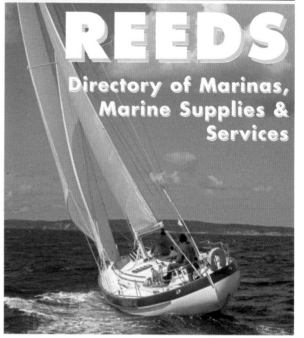
REEDS Directory of Marinas, Marine Supplies & Services

ROYAL NORFOLK & SUFFOLK YACHT CLUB

Royal Norfolk and Suffolk Yacht Club
Royal Plain, Lowestoft, Suffolk, NR33 0AQ
Tel: 01502 566726 Fax: 01502 517981
Email: marinaoffice@rnsyc.co.uk

| VHF | Ch 14, 80 |
| ACCESS | H24 |

With its entrance at the inner end of the South Pier, opposite the Trawl Basin on the north bank, the Royal Norfolk and Suffolk Yacht Club marina occupies a sheltered position in Lowestoft Harbour. Lowestoft has always been an appealing destination to yachtsmen due to the fact that it can be accessed at any state of the tide, 24 hours a day. Note, however, that conditions just outside the entrance can get pretty lively when the wind is against tide. The clubhouse is enclosed in an impressive Grade 2 listed building overlooking the marina and its facilities include a bar and restaurant as well as a formal dining room with a full à la carte menu.

FACILITIES AT A GLANCE

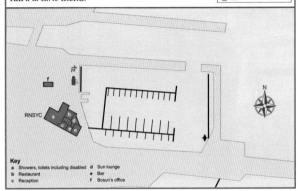

Key
a Showers, toilets including disabled   d Sun lounge
b Restaurant   e Bar
c Reception   f Bosun's office

For full marine services in the unique & unspoilt Southwold Harbour

HARBOUR MARINE SERVICES LTD

BOATBUILDING & MARINE ENGINEERING CHANDLERS & NAUTICAL GIFTS

Blackshore, Southwold Harbour, Southwold, Suffolk IP18 6TA
www.southwoldharbour.co.uk
Email: info@southwoldharbour.uk.com
Tel: (01502) 724721 24 HOURS
Fax: (01502) 722060

Breathtakingly Beautiful Burgh

BURGH CASTLE MARINA & CARAVAN PARK
Cruise centre for Broadland and the Norfolk Coast
Our peaceful location at the confluence of the Waveney and Yare rivers and at the head of Breydon Water is ideal for cruising inland or at sea.
Tel: 01493 780331 Fax: 01493 780163
Email: info@burghcastlemarina.co.uk
Web site: www.burghcastlemarina.co.uk

NORFOLK MARINE
CHURCH ROAD, WROXHAM, NORWICH, NORFOLK. NR12 8 UG
TEL: 01603-783150 • FAX: 01603-782471
E-mail: sales@norfolkmarine.co.uk
www.norfolkmarine.co.uk

Large well stocked Chandlery, open 7 days a week for all your requirements for all types of boating at sea and inland.

Electronics: Raymarine, Simrad, Nasa, Echopilot, Navman, Icom, Silva, Lowrance, Humminbird, Eagle & Magellan.
Paints: International, Blakes & Epifanes.
Safety Equipment: Plastimo, XM, Seago, Crewsaver, Paines Wessex.
Inflatables & Engines: Quicksilver, Valiant, Seago, Mercury Minkota.
Hardware: Harken, Barton, Ronstan, Holt, RWO, Lewmar.
General Chandlery: Huge stock from manufacturers from all over the world.
Clothing: Musto, Gill, Crewsaver, Splashdown, Quayside, Chatham, Henry Lloyd, Yak,
Canoes & Kayaks: Perception, Pyranha, Dagger, Islander, Mobile Adventure, Old Town

"DISCOVER THE WASH"

WISBECH YACHT HARBOUR

The finest moorings between the Humber & Lowestoft
128 Berths, fully serviced pontoon moorings in the heart of historic Wisbech.

Visitors welcome.

Fuel bunkering facilities   Commercial berths 24m LOA
80 Ton boat hoist   Secure hardstanding.
CCTV   Unbeatable rates   Special Winter Rates

**Prime East Coast Location, Inland Waterway Access
Midlands - Under 2 hours by road.**

For a Pilot Guide and Brochure:-
Harbour Masters Office, Dock Cottage
Crab Marsh, Wisbech, Cambs PE13 3JJ

Tel:- 01945-588059   www.fenland.gov.uk

2007/M&WC148/z

NORTH EAST ENGLAND - Great Yarmouth to Berwick-upon-Tweed

ADLARD COLES NAUTICAL
WEATHER FORECASTS
BY FAX & TELEPHONE

Coastal/Inshore	2-day by Fax	5-day by Phone
Anglia	09065 222 345	09068 969 645
East	09065 222 344	09068 969 644
North East	09065 222 343	09068 969 643
Scotland East	09065 222 342	09068 969 642
National (3-5 day)	09065 222 340	09068 969 640

Offshore	2-5 day by Fax	2-5 day by Phone
English Channel	09065 222 357	09068 969 657
Southern North Sea	09065 222 358	09068 969 658
Northern North Sea	09065 222 362	09068 969 662
North West Scotland	09065 222 361	09068 969 661

09068 CALLS COST 60P PER MIN. 09065 CALLS COST £1.50 PER MIN.

Key to Marina Plans symbols

Calor Gas		P	Parking
Chandler		✗	Pub/Restaurant
Disabled facilities			Pump out
Electrical supply			Rigging service
Electrical repairs			Sail repairs
Engine repairs			Shipwright
First Aid			Shop/Supermarket
Fresh Water			Showers
Fuel - Diesel			Slipway
Fuel - Petrol		WC	Toilets
Hardstanding/boatyard			Telephone
@ Internet Café			Trolleys
Laundry facilities		V	Visitors berths
Lift-out facilities			Wi-Fi

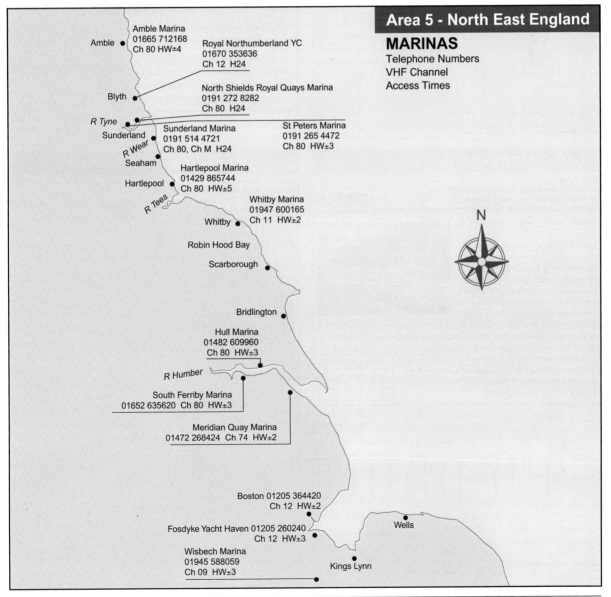

Area 5 - North East England

MARINAS
Telephone Numbers
VHF Channel
Access Times

Amble
Amble Marina
01665 712168
Ch 80 HW±4

Royal Northumberland YC
01670 353636
Ch 12 H24

North Shields Royal Quays Marina
0191 272 8282
Ch 80 H24

Blyth

R Tyne

Sunderland
Sunderland Marina
0191 514 4721
Ch 80, Ch M H24

St Peters Marina
0191 265 4472
Ch 80 HW±3

R Wear

Seaham

Hartlepool
Hartlepool Marina
01429 865744
Ch 80 HW±5

R Tees

Whitby Marina
01947 600165
Ch 11 HW±2

Whitby

Robin Hood Bay

Scarborough

Bridlington

Hull Marina
01482 609960
Ch 80 HW±3

R Humber

South Ferriby Marina
01652 635620 Ch 80 HW±3

Meridian Quay Marina
01472 268424 Ch 74 HW±2

Boston 01205 364420
Ch 12 HW±2

Wells

Fosdyke Yacht Haven 01205 260240
Ch 12 HW±3

Wisbech Marina
01945 588059
Ch 09 HW±3

Kings Lynn

N

WISBECH YACHT HARBOUR

Wisbech Yacht Harbour
Harbour Master, Harbour Office, Dock Cottage
Wisbech, Cambridgeshire PE13 3JJ
Tel: 01945 588059 Fax: 01945 580589
Email: torbeau@btinternet.com www.fenland.gov.uk

VHF | Ch 9
ACCESS | HW±3

Regarded as the capital of the English Fens, Wisbech is situated about 25 miles north east of Peterborough and is a market town of considerable character and historical significance. Rows of elegant houses line the banks of the River Nene, with the North and South Brink still deemed two of the finest Georgian streets in England.

Wisbech Yacht Harbour, linking Cambridgeshire with the sea, is proving increasingly popular as a haven for small craft, despite the busy commercial shipping. In recent years the facilities have been developed and improved upon and the HM is always on hand to help with passage planning both up or downstream.

FACILITIES AT A GLANCE

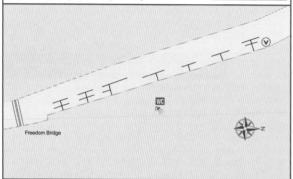

"DISCOVER THE WASH"

WISBECH YACHT HARBOUR

The finest moorings between the Humber & Lowestoft 128 Berths, fully serviced pontoon moorings in the heart of historic Wisbech.

Visitors welcome.

Fuel bunkering facilities
80 Ton boat hoist
CCTV

Commercial berths 24m LOA
Secure hardstanding.
Unbeatable rates

Prime East Coast Location, Inland Waterway Access
Midlands - Under 2 hours by road.

For a Pilot Guide and Brochure:-
Harbour Masters Office, Dock Cottage
Crab Marsh, Wisbech, Cambs PE13 3JJ

Tel:- 01945-588059   www.fenland.gov.uk

2007/M&WC1/j

BOSTON MARINA

Boston Marina
5/7 Witham Bank East, Boston, Lincs, PE21 9JU
Tel: 01205 364420 Fax: 01205 364420
www.bostonmarina.co.uk Email: bostonmarina@5witham.fsnet

VHF | Ch 12
ACCESS | H±2

Boston Marina, located near Boston Grand Sluice in Lincolnshire, is an ideal location for both seagoing vessels and for river boats wanting to explore the heart of the Fens. However, berths are only available from 1 April to 31 October when all vessels must leave the marina to find winter storage. The on site facilities include a fully-stocked chandlery and brokerage service, while nearby is the well-established Witham Tavern, decorated in a rustic theme to reflect the pub's close proximity to The Wash.

The old maritime port of Boston has numerous modern-day and historical attractions, one of the most notable being St Botolph's Church, better known as the 'Boston Stump'.

FACILITIES AT A GLANCE

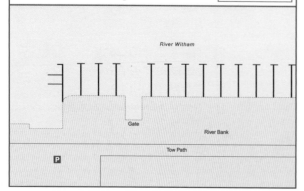

MERIDIAN QUAY MARINA

Humber Cruising Assn
Meridian Quay Marina, Meridian Quay
Auckland Road, Fish Dock, Grimsby
Tel: 01472 268424 Fax: 01472 269832
www.hca-grimsby.freeserve.co.uk

VHF | Ch 74
ACCESS | HW±2

Situated in the locked fish dock of Grimsby, at the mouth of the River Humber, Meridian Quay Marina is run by the Humber Cruising Association and comprises approximately 160 alongside berths plus 30 more for visitors. Accessed two hours either side of high water via lock gates, the marina should be contacted on VHF Ch 74 (call sign 'Fish Dock Island') as you make your final approach. The pontoon berths are equipped with water and electricity, while the fully licensed clubhouse serves light meals and incorporates a pool table, television and laundry facilities.

FACILITIES AT A GLANCE

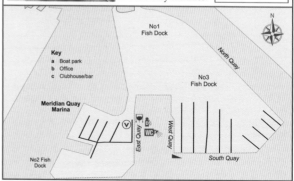

SOUTH FERRIBY MARINA

South Ferriby Marina
Barton on Humber, Lincolnshire, DN18 6JH
Tel: 01652 635620 (Lock 635219) Fax: 01652 660517
www.clapsons.co.uk Email: marina@clapsons.co.uk

VHF	Ch 80
ACCESS	HW±3

South Ferriby Marina is run by Clapson & Sons, an established company founded in 1912. The marina site was developed in 1967 and today offers a comprehensive range of services, including heated workshops for osmosis repairs, general boat repairs and ample storage space. Its well stocked on site chandlery is open until 1700 seven days a week.

Situated at Barton upon Humber, the marina lies on the south bank of the River Humber at the southern crossing of the Humber Bridge, approximately eight miles south west of Kingston upon Hull. Good public transport links to nearby towns and villages include train services to Cleethorpes and Grimsby, and bus connections to Scunthorpe and Hull.

FACILITIES AT A GLANCE

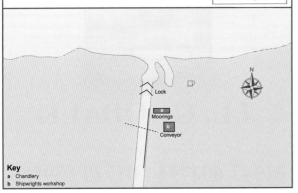

Key
a Chandlery
b Shipwrights workshop

HULL MARINA

Hull Marina
Railway Street, Hull, HU1 2DQ
Tel: 01482 330505 Fax: 01482 224148
www.britishwaterways.co.uk
Email: hullmarina@bwml.co.uk

VHF	Ch 80
ACCESS	HW±3

Situated on the River Humber, Hull Marina is literally a stone's throw from the bustling city centre with its array of arts and entertainments. Besides the numerous historic bars and cafés surrounding the marina itself, there are plenty of traditional taverns to be sampled in the Old Town, while also found here is the Street Life Museum, vividly depicting the history of the city.

Yachtsmen enter the marina via a tidal lock, operating HW±3, and should try to give 15 minutes' notice of arrival via VHF Ch 80. Hull is perfectly positioned for exploring the Trent, Ouse and the Yorkshire coast as well as across the North Sea to Holland or Belgium.

FACILITIES AT A GLANCE

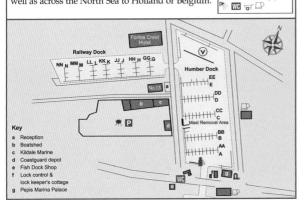

Key
a Reception
b Boatshed
c Kildale Marine
d Coastguard depot
e Fish Dock Shop
f Lock control &
   lock keeper's cottage
g Pepis Marina Palace

RYA Training Centre

BOB WRIDE SCHOOL OF SAILING

HULL MARINA • EAST YORKSHIRE

ALL RYA COURSES

THEORY & PRACTICAL

5 DAY & WEEKENDS

Contact:
Bob or Jan on 01482 635623
Bob on: 07803 011842
Email:
jan@sailingschool.karoo.co.uk
www.bobwridesailing.com

2007/M&WC126/zz

GILL   CREWSAVER

KILDALE MARINE

HULL MARINA, HULL HU1 3DQ
Tel: (01482) 227464 Fax: (01482) 329217

Kildale Marine stocks the largest range of Chandlery, Ropes, Marine Paints and Deck Fittings for all sizes of yacht and motorcruiser in the North East

EXTENSIVE RANGE OF BOOKS, CHARTS AND NAVIGATION AIDS

SERVICES INCLUDE:
LIFERAFT HIRE
• GAS REFILLS
• STANDARD & RUNNING RIGGING & ROPE SPLICING

We are open 6 days a week 9.30 to 5.30
Sunday 10.00 - 4.00 • Closed all day Tuesday

BLAKES PAINTS   INTERNATIONAL PAINTS   BARTON   HARKEN   WHALE   JABSCO   WALLAS HEATERS

2007/M&WC21/e

WEST SYSTEMS   MUSTO   HENRI LLOYD

WHITBY MARINA

Whitby Marina
Whitby Harbour Office, Endeavour Wharf
Whitby, North Yorkshire YO21 1DN
Harbour Office: 01947 602354 Marina: 01947 600165
Email: lesley.dale@scarborough.gov.uk

VHF	Ch 11, 16
ACCESS	HW±2

The only natural harbour between the Tees and the Humber, Whitby lies some 20 miles north of Scarborough on the River Esk. The historic town is said to date back as far as the Roman times, although it is better known for its abbey, which was founded over 1,300 years ago by King Oswy of Northumberland. Another place of interest is the Captain Cook Memorial Museum, a tribute to Whitby's greatest seaman.

A swing bridge divides the harbour into upper and lower sections, with the marina being in the Upper Harbour. The bridge opens on request (VHF Ch 11) each half hour for two hours either side of high water.

FACILITIES AT A GLANCE

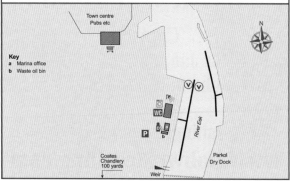

Key
a Marina office
b Waste oil bin

Town centre
Pubs etc

River Esk

Coates
Chandlery
100 yards

Parkol
Dry Dock

Weir

SURVEYS
AND CONDITION REPORTS

PURCHASE AND INSURANCE

TRADITIONAL & MODERN POWER AND SAIL
BENEFIT FROM OVER 40YEARS EXPERIENCE

J.L. GOODALL
SMALL CRAFT SURVEYOR
TELEPHONE:
01947 604791 / 07720 539586

2007/M&WC2/j

HARTLEPOOL MARINA
Lock Office, Slake Terrace,
Hartlepool, Cleveland

A prestigious 500 berth marina alive with busy shops, cafes bars and a wealth of international restaurants. Adjoining the marina site is a retail park; multi screen cinema, health club and a selection of the usual fast food outlets. Visit the Historic Quay and step back through history and enjoy the experience of life at the time of Lord Nelson and step on board HMS Trincomalee 1817 the oldest fighting ship afloat in the UK

In addition to fully serviced pontoon berthing [including broadband internet connection] there are quay wall facilities, a fully equipped boat yard and 40 tonne travel hoist. Our in house Chandlery, sail repairs, Yamaha outboard and diesel inboard dealerships make the marina complete. We are proud to fly our 4 anchor award as assessed by the British Marina Federation.

2007/M&WC1/4/e

Tel: 01429 865744 Fax: 01429 865947

HARTLEPOOL MARINA

Hartlepool Marina
Lock Office, Slake Terrace, Hartlepool, TS24 0UR
Tel: 01429 865744 Fax: 01429 865947
Email: lockoffice@hartlepool-marina.com

VHF	Ch 37, 80
ACCESS	HW±5

Hartlepool Marina is a major boating facility on the North East coast with over 500 fully serviced berths surrounded by a cosmopolitan mix of bars restaurants and hotels. The Historic Quay is nearby with the 17th Century warship, Trincomelee. A tourist town with shopping centre is an easy walk away. Beautiful crusing water north and south access channel dredged to chart datum.

The marina can be accessed five hours either side of high water via a lock: note that yachtsmen wishing to enter should contact the marina on VHF Ch 80 about 15 minutes before arrival.

FACILITIES AT A GLANCE

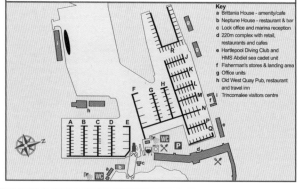

Key
a Brittania House - amenity/cafe
b Neptune House - restaurant & bar
c Lock office and marina reception
d 220m complex with retail, restaurants and cafes
e Hartlepool Diving Club and HMS Abdiel sea cadet unit
f Fisherman's stores & landing area
g Office units
h Old West Quay Pub, restaurant and travel inn
i Trincomalee visitors centre

SUNDERLAND MARINA

The Marine Activities Centre
Sunderland Marina, Sunderland, SR6 0PW
Tel: 0191 514 4721 Fax: 0191 514 1847
Email: mervyn.templeton@marineactivitiescentre.co.uk

VHF Ch 80, 37
ACCESS H24

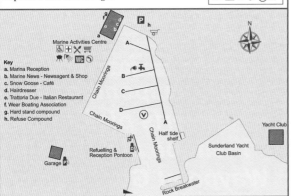

Sunderland Marina sits on the north bank of the River Wear and is easily accessible through the outer breakwater at all states of the tide. Among the extensive range of facilities on site are a newsagent, café, hairdresser and top quality Italian restaurant. Other pubs, restaurants, hotels and cafés are located nearby on the waterfront. Both the Wear Boating Association and the Sunderland Yacht Club are also located in the vicinity and welcome yachtsmen to their respective bars and lounges.

FACILITIES AT A GLANCE

Key
a. Marina Reception
b. Marine News - Newsagent & Shop
c. Snow Goose - Café
d. Hairdresser
e. Trattoria Due - Italian Restaurant
f. Wear Boating Association
g. Hard stand compound
h. Refuse Compound

NORTH SHIELDS ROYAL QUAYS MARINA

North Shields Royal Quays Marina
Coble Dene Road, North Shields, NE29 6DU
Tel: 0191 272 8282 Fax: 0191 272 8288
www.quaymarinas.com
Email: royalquaysmarina@quaymarinas.com

VHF Ch 80
ACCESS H24

North Shields Royal Quays Marina enjoys close proximity to the entrance to the River Tyne, allowing easy access to and from the open sea as well as being ideally placed for cruising further up the Tyne. Just over an hour's motoring upstream brings you to the heart of the city of Newcastle, where you can tie up on a security controlled visitors' pontoon right outside the Pitcher and Piano Bar.

With a reputation for a high standard of service, the marina accommodates 281 pontoon berths, all of which are fully serviced. It is accessed via double sector lock gates which operate at all states of the tide and 24 hours a day.

FACILITIES AT A GLANCE

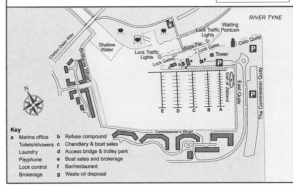

Key
a. Marina office
Toilets/showers
Laundry
Payphone
Lock control
Brokerage
b. Refuse compound
c. Chandlery & boat sales
d. Access bridge & trolley park
e. Boat sales and brokerage
f. Bar/restaurant
g. Waste oil disposal

5

STORRAR MARINE STORE
The Complete Specialists
Covering all areas including Whitby & Berwick

Sailmaking and Canvas Work
New sails made, old sails repaired. Sprayhoods, stackpacks, dodgers, winter covers. Laundry service.

Mercury Outboards
We are a Mercury Dealer for the North East. New & 2nd hand

Safety Equipment
Lifejackets, flares, harnesses, fire extinguishers

Chandlery
(Mail order service available)
Harken, Lewmar (spares center), Plastimo, Jabsco, Spinlock, Wetline, Quicksilver, Valiant inflatables

Spars & Rigging
Selden, Z-Spar etc. rig building & repair. Wire splicing and rope splicing, Furling systems supplied, fitted & refurbished

Electronics
Simrad, Icom, Garmin, Raymarine, Navman, Eagle, NASA etc.

Clothing
Henri Lloyd, Douglas Gill, Musto, Crewsaver
Visit our website @ www.storrarmarine.co.uk
181-183 Coast Road, Cochrane Park,
Newcastle upon Tyne, NE7 7RR
Telephone - 0191 266 1037 · Fax - 0191 240 0436
E-Mail - robbie@storrarmarine.co.uk

2007/M&WC106/e

QUAY MARINAS LTD
Avon House, Newbrick Road, Stokegifford,
Bristol BS34 8RA
Tel: (01179) 236466
Fax: (01179) 236508
e-mail: sriggs@quaymarinas.com
A wholly owned subsidiary of Quay Marinas, operate comprehensive yachting facilities at 5 locations in the UK and are marketing agents for Malahide Marina in Dublin Bay.

2007/M&WEXT9/e

Shamrock Chandlery
Shamrock Quay, William Street, Northam, Southampton SO14 5QL

www.shamrock.co.uk

MAIL ORDER HOTLINE
Tel: (02380) 632725
Fax (02380) 225611

2007/M&WC160/z

ST PETERS MARINA

St Peters Marina, St Peters Basin
Newcastle upon Tyne, NE6 1HX
Tel: 0191 2654472 Fax: 0191 2762618
Email: info@stpetersmarina.co.uk
www.stpetersmarina.co.uk

VHF	Ch 80, M
ACCESS	HW±3

Nestling on the north bank of the River Tyne, some eight miles upstream of the river entrance, St Peters Marina is a fully serviced, 150-berth marina with the capacity to accommodate large vessels of up to 37m LOA. Situated on site is the Bascule Bar and Bistro, while a few minutes away is the centre of Newcastle. This city, along with its surrounding area, offers an array of interesting sites, among which are Hadrian's Wall, the award winning Gateshead Millennium Bridge and the Baltic Art Centre.

FACILITIES AT A GLANCE

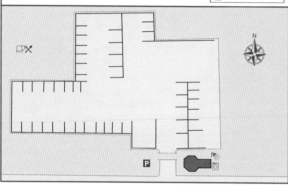

ST. PETERS MARINA

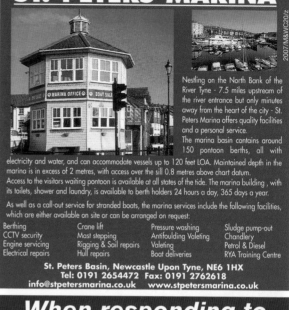

Nestling on the North Bank of the River Tyne - 7.5 miles upstream of the river entrance but only minutes away from the heart of the city - St. Peters Marina offers quality facilities and a personal service.
The marina basin contains around 150 pontoon berths, all with electricity and water, and can accommodate vessels up to 120 feet LOA. Maintained depth in the marina is in excess of 2 metres, with access over the sill 0.8 metres above chart datum.
Access to the visitors waiting pontoon is available at all states of the tide. The marina building, with its toilets, shower and laundry, is available to berth holders 24 hours a day, 365 days a year.

As well as a call-out service for stranded boats, the marina services include the following facilities, which are either available on site or can be arranged on request:

Berthing	Crane lift	Pressure washing	Sludge pump-out
CCTV security	Mast stepping	Antifoulding Valeting	Chandlery
Engine servicing	Rigging & Sail repairs	Valeting	Petrol & Diesel
Electrical repairs	Hull repairs	Boat deliveries	RYA Training Centre

St. Peters Basin, Newcastle Upon Tyne, NE6 1HX
Tel: 0191 2654472 Fax: 0191 2762618
info@stpetersmarina.co.uk www.stpetersmarina.co.uk

When responding to adverts please mention Marina & Waypoint Guide 2007

ROYAL NORTHUMBERLAND YACHT CLUB

Royal Northumberland Yacht Club
South Harbour, Blyth, Northumberland, NE24 3PB
Tel: 01670 353636

VHF	Ch 12
ACCESS	H24

The Royal Northumberland Yacht Club is based at Blyth, a well-sheltered port that is accessible at all states of the tide and in all weathers except for when there is a combination of low water and strong south-easterly winds. The yacht club is a private club with approximately 75 pontoon berths and a further 20 fore and aft moorings.

Visitors usually berth on the north side of the most northerly pontoon and are welcome to use the clubship, HY *Tyne* – a wooden lightship built in 1880 which incorporates a bar, showers and toilet facilities. The club also controls its own boatyard, providing under cover and outside storage space.

FACILITIES AT A GLANCE

Key
a H.Y. Tyne

AMBLE MARINA

Amble Marina Ltd
Amble, Northumberland, NE65 0YP
Tel: 01665 712168 Fax:01665 713363
www.amble.co.uk Email: marina@amble.co.uk

VHF	Ch 80
ACCESS	HW±4

Amble Marina is a small family run business offering peace, security and a countryside setting at the heart of the small town of Amble. It is located on the banks of the beautiful River Coquet and at the start of the Northumberland coast's area of outstanding natural beauty. Amble Marina has 250 fully serviced berths for residential and visiting yachts. Cafes, bars, restaurants and shops are all within a short walk.
From your berth watch the sun rise at the entrance to the harbour and set behind Warkworth Castle or walk on wide empty beaches. There is so much to do or if you prefer simply enjoy the peace, tranquillity and friendliness at Amble Marina.

FACILITIES AT A GLANCE

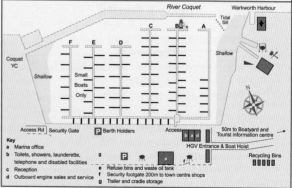

Key
a Marina office
b Toilets, showers, launderette, telephone and disabled facilities
c Reception
d Outboard engine sales and service
e Refuse bins and waste oil tank
f Security footage 200m to town centre shops
g Trailer and cradle storage

ADLARD COLES NAUTICAL
WEATHER FORECASTS
BY FAX & TELEPHONE

Coastal/Inshore	2-day by Fax	5-day by Phone
East	09065 222 344	09068 969 644
North East	09065 222 343	09068 969 643
Scotland East	09065 222 342	09068 969 642
Scotland North	09065 222 341	09068 969 641
National (3-5 day)	09065 222 340	09068 969 640

Offshore	2-5 day by Fax	2-5 day by Phone
English Channel	09065 222 357	09068 969 657
Southern North Sea	09065 222 358	09068 969 658
Northern North Sea	09065 222 362	09068 969 662
North West Scotland	09065 222 361	09068 969 661

09068 CALLS COST 60P PER MIN. 09065 CALLS COST £1.50 PER MIN.

Key to Marina Plans symbols

Calor Gas		P	Parking
Chandler			Pub/Restaurant
Disabled facilities			Pump out
Electrical supply			Rigging service
Electrical repairs			Sail repairs
Engine repairs			Shipwright
First Aid			Shop/Supermarket
Fresh Water			Showers
Fuel - Diesel			Slipway
Fuel - Petrol		WC	Toilets
Hardstanding/boatyard			Telephone
Internet Café			Trolleys
Laundry facilities		V	Visitors berths
Lift-out facilities			Wi-Fi

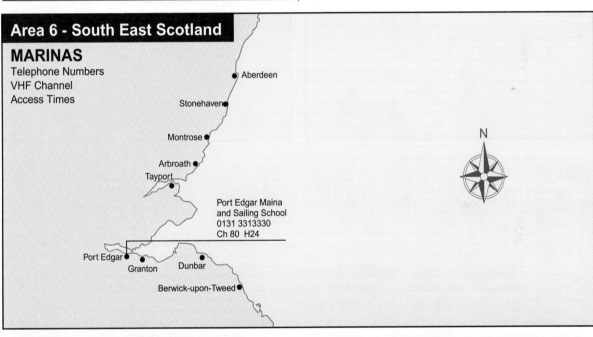

Area 6 - South East Scotland

MARINAS
Telephone Numbers
VHF Channel
Access Times

Aberdeen

Stonehaven

Montrose

Arbroath

Tayport

Port Edgar Maina
and Sailing School
0131 3313330
Ch 80 H24

Port Edgar

Granton   Dunbar

Berwick-upon-Tweed

N

6

Adlard Coles Nautical THE BEST SAILING BOOKS

Tie Yourself in Knots with **Adlard Coles Nautical**

RYA Book of Knots
Peter Owen
£7.99
0 7136 7054 1

Knots in Use
Colin Jarman
£8.99
0 7136 6710 9

Creative Ropecraft
Stuart Grainger
£10.99
0 7136 7401 6

TO ORDER Tel: **01256 302692** email: **direct@macmillan.co.uk** or **www.adlardcoles.com**

PORT EDGAR MARINA

Port Edgar Marina
Shore Road, South Queensferry
West Lothian, EH3 9SX
Tel: 0131 331 3330 Fax: 0131 331 4878
Email: admin.pe@edinburghleisure.co.uk

VHF	Ch 80
ACCESS	H24

Port Edgar is a large watersports centre and marina found on the south bank of the sheltered Firth of Forth. Situated in the village of South Queensferry, just west of the Forth Road Bridge, it is managed by Edinburgh Leisure on behalf of the City of Edinburgh Council and is reached via a deep water channel just west of the suspension bridge.

The nearby village offers a sufficient range of shops and restaurants, while Port Edgar is only a 20-minute walk from Dalmeny Station from where trains run regularly to Edinburgh.

FACILITIES AT A GLANCE

Key
a Changing rooms and toilets
b Landing and trolleys
c Port Edgar Yacht Club
d Sail loft
e Cafe
f Marina office
g Ferry Marine
h Blue V
i Bosuns Locker

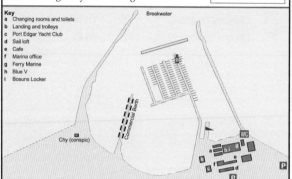

ARBROATH HARBOUR

Arbroath Harbour
Harbour Office, Arbroath, DD11 1PD
Tel: 01241 872166 Fax: 01241 878472
Email: harbourmaster@arbroathharbour.sol.co.uk

VHF	Ch 11, 16
ACCESS	HW±3

Arbroath harbour has 36 floating pontoon berths with security entrance which are serviced with electricity and fresh water to accommodate all types of leisure craft. Half height dock gates with walkway are located between the inner and outer harbours maintaining a minimum of 2.5m of water in the inner harbour.

The town of Arbroath offers a variety of social and sporting amenities to visiting crews and a number of quality pubs, restaurants, the famous twelfth century Abbey and Signal Tower Museum are located close to the harbour. The railway and bus stations are only 1km from the harbour with direct north and south connections.

FACILITIES AT A GLANCE

Key
a Signal Tower Museum
b Tourist Information
c RNLI
d Harbourmaster
e Harbour gates & walkway

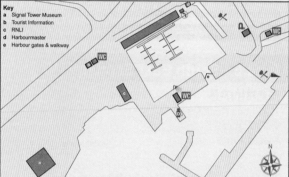

PORT EDGAR MARINA & SAILING SCHOOL

Welcome to **PORT EDGAR MARINA & SAILING SCHOOL**

Our programme has something to offer all types of sailor whatever their experience. To find out more please telephone **0131 331 3330**

What's on offer?

Something for everyone who is interested in Watersports at every level from beginner to instructor. Courses are available throughout the summer, and in the winter months we run a wide range of shore based classes.

Activities include: -

- **Dinghy Sailing At All Levels.**
- **Children's Holiday Sailing Courses**
- **SPLASH! Multi Activity Courses for Youngsters**
- **Catamaran Courses**
- **Dinghy Crusing**
- **Dinghy Racing**

- **Powerboating**
- **Safety Boat Handling**
- **Advanced Powerboating**
- **Canoeing - BCU 1 & 2 Star Courses**
- **SRC/DSC Radio Operators Course**
- **GPS Operator**
- **Yachtmaster, Coastal Skipper, Day Skipper**

The Marina

The marina is fully serviced with power and water to 300 berths. We have storage facilities for craft in boat sheds or boat parks. Cranage is available throughout the year via our fixed crane for craft up to 4.3/4 tons. Other services on site are Chandlery, Sailmakers, Marine engineers, Electronics, Port Edgar Yacht Club.

2007/M&WC5/e

ADLARD COLES NAUTICAL
WEATHER FORECASTS
BY FAX & TELEPHONE

Coastal/Inshore	2-day by Fax	5-day by Phone
North East	09065 222 343	09068 969 643
Scotland East	09065 222 342	09068 969 642
Scotland North	09065 222 341	09068 969 641
Minch	09065 222 354	09068 969 654
National (3-5 day)	09065 222 340	09068 969 640

Offshore	2-5 day by Fax	2-5 day by Phone
Southern North Sea	09065 222 358	09068 969 658
Northern North Sea	09065 222 362	09068 969 662
North West Scotland	09065 222 361	09068 969 661
Irish Sea	09065 222 359	09068 969 659

09068 CALLS COST 60P PER MIN. 09065 CALLS COST £1.50 PER MIN.

Key to Marina Plans symbols

Calor Gas		P	Parking
Chandler			Pub/Restaurant
Disabled facilities			Pump out
Electrical supply			Rigging service
Electrical repairs			Sail repairs
Engine repairs			Shipwright
First Aid			Shop/Supermarket
Fresh Water			Showers
Fuel - Diesel			Slipway
Fuel - Petrol		WC	Toilets
Hardstanding/boatyard			Telephone
Internet Café	@		Trolleys
Laundry facilities		V	Visitors berths
Lift-out facilities			Wi-Fi

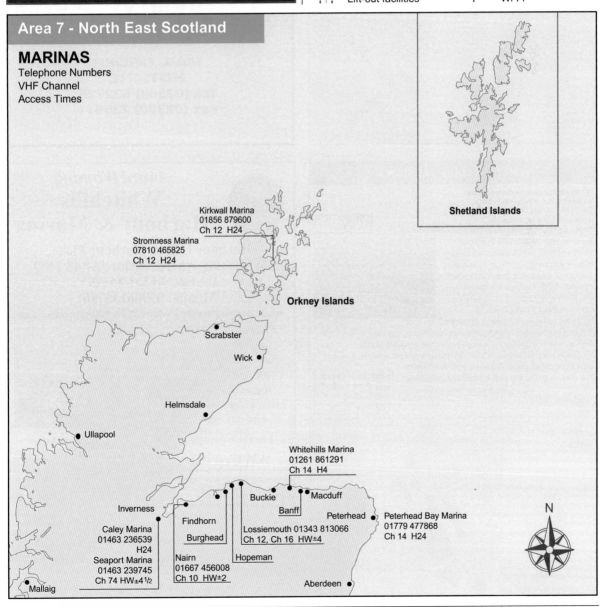

Area 7 - North East Scotland

MARINAS
Telephone Numbers
VHF Channel
Access Times

Kirkwall Marina
01856 879600
Ch 12 H24

Stromness Marina
07810 465825
Ch 12 H24

Shetland Islands

Orkney Islands

Scrabster

Wick

Helmsdale

Ullapool

Whitehills Marina
01261 861291
Ch 14 H4

Inverness

Buckie

Macduff

Banff

Peterhead

Peterhead Bay Marina
01779 477868
Ch 14 H24

Caley Marina
01463 236539
H24

Findhorn

Burghead

Lossiemouth 01343 813066
Ch 12, Ch 16 HW±4

Seaport Marina
01463 239745
Ch 74 HW±4½

Nairn
01667 456008
Ch 10 HW±2

Hopeman

Mallaig

Aberdeen

N

PETERHEAD BAY MARINA

Peterhead Port Authority
Harbour Office, West Pier, Peterhead, AB42 1DW
Tel: 01779 483600 Fax: 01779 475715
Email: info@peterheadport.co.uk
www.peterheadport.co.uk

VHF	Ch 14
ACCESS	H24

Based in the south west corner of Peterhead Bay Harbour, the marina provides one of the finest marine leisure facilities in the east of Scotland. In addition to the services on site, there are plenty of nautical businesses in the vicinity, ranging from ship chandlers and electrical servicing to boat repairs and surveying.

Due to its easterly location, Peterhead affords an ideal stopover for those yachts heading to or from Scandinavia as well as for vessels making for the Caledonian Canal.

FACILITIES AT A GLANCE

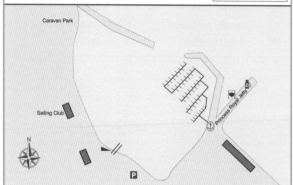

Peterhead PORT AUTHORITY
PETERHEAD BAY MARINA
North East Scotland's Finest

Fully serviced marina offering a warm welcome and access to an excellent range of local services

Tel: **(01779) 474020** Fax: **(01779) 475712**
Website: www.peterheadport.co.uk

2007/M&WMD3/e

Shamrock Chandlery
Shamrock Quay, William Street, Northam, Southampton SO14 5QL

www.shamrock.co.uk

MAIL ORDER HOTLINE
Tel: (02380) 632725
Fax (02380) 225611

2007/M&WC160z

WHITEHILLS MARINA

Whitehills Harbour Commissioners
Whitehills, Banffshire AB45 2NQ
Tel: 01261 861291 Fax: 01261 861291
www.whitehillsharbour.co.uk
Email: harbourmaster@whitehillsharbour.wanadoo.co.uk

VHF	Ch 14, 16
ACCESS	H24

Built in 1900, Whitehills is a Trust Harbour fully maintained and run by nine commissioners elected from the village. It was a thriving fishing port up until 1999, but due to changes in the fishing industry, was converted into a marina during 2000.

Three miles west of Banff Harbour the marina benefits from full tidal access and comprises 38 serviced berths, with electricity, as well as eight non-serviced berths.

The nearby village of Whitehills boasts a selection of local stores and a couple of pubs. A coastal path leads from the marina to the top of the headland, affording striking views across the Moray Firth to the Caithness Hills.

FACILITIES AT A GLANCE

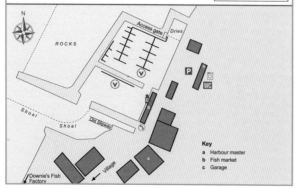

Key
a Harbour master
b Fish market
c Garage

Award Winning
Whitehills Harbour & Marina

Harbour Office, Harbour Place, Whitehills, Aberdeenshire AB45 2NQ
Tel/Fax: 01261 861291
Mobile: 07906135786

email: harbourmaster@whitehillsharbour.wanadoo.co.uk

Friendly welcome give to visitors Power & water on all berths, with diesel available Also toilets, laundry and day room

Further details can be found on our website:
www.whitehillsharbour.co.uk

2007/M&WC56/e

When responding to adverts please mention Marina & Waypoint Guide 2007

NAIRN MARINA

Nairn Marina
Nairn Harbour, Nairnshire, Scotland
Tel: 01667 456008
Email: alex.taylor@highland.gov.uk

| VHF | Ch 10 |
| ACCESS | HW±2 |

Nairn is a small town on the coast of the Moray Firth. Formerly renowned both as a fishing port and as a holiday resort dating back to Victorian times, it boasts miles of award-winning, sandy beaches, famous castles such as Cawdor, Brodie and Castle Stuart, and two championship golf courses. Other recreational activities include horse riding or walking through spectacular countryside.

The marina lies at the mouth of the River Nairn, entry to which should be avoided in strong N to NE winds. The approach is made from the NW at or around high water as the entrance is badly silted and dries out.

FACILITIES AT A GLANCE

Key
a Restaurant
b Yacht Club
c Harbour office

LOSSIEMOUTH MARINA

The Harbour Office
Lossiemouth, Moray, IV31 6NT
Tel: 01343 813066 Fax: 01343 813066
Email: harbourmaster@lossiemarina.fsnet.co.uk

| VHF | Ch 12 |
| ACCESS | HW±4 |

Situated on the beautiful Moray Firth coastline, Lossiemouth Marina provides 47 berths in its East Basin and 25 berths for larger vessels in its West Basin. Although the berths are primarily taken up by residential yachts, during the summer months a certain number are allocated to visitors who can benefit from the friendly, efficient service. The marina lies within easy walking distance of the town, which has a good range of shops and restaurants and boasts an array of leisure facilities, two championship standard golf courses and acres of sandy beaches.

FACILITIES AT A GLANCE

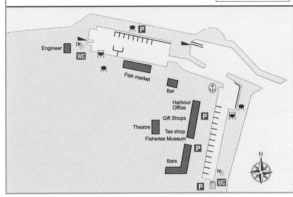

Shamrock Chandlery
Shamrock Quay, William Street, Northam, Southampton SO14 5QL

www.shamrock.co.uk

**MAIL ORDER HOTLINE
Tel: (02380) 632725
Fax (02380) 225611**

EXPANDED BOOK SHOP

Elgin & Lossiemouth Harbour Company

Lossiemouth Harbour Marina is in a perfect location in the Moray Firth, ideally situated for vessels heading to/from Inverness or further afield to Norway and the Continent.
Berths are fully serviced. Additional facilities including showers, toilets and laundry, diesel/gas sales, telephones and engine repair services, bars, hotels and excellent restaurants.
Lossiemouth is an ideal location for visits to the Grampian Mountains and Whisky Trails, and has its own beautiful sandy

*Elgin and Lossiemouth Harbour Marina
6 Pitgaveney Quay Lossiemouth IV31 6NT
Telephone: 01343 813066 (Fax & Ans)
E-mail: harbourmaster@lossiemarina.fsnet.co.uk*

CALEY MARINA

Caley Marina
Canal Road, Inverness, IV3 8NF
Tel: 01463 236539 Fax: 01463 238323
Email: info@caleymarina.com
www.caleycruisers.com

VHF	Ch 74
ACCESS	H24

Caley Marina is a family run business based near Inverness. With the four flight Muirtown locks and the Kessock Bridge providing a dramatic backdrop, the marina runs alongside the Caledonian Canal which, opened in 1822, is regarded as one of the most spectacular waterways in Europe. Built as a short cut between the North Sea and the Atlantic Ocean, thus avoiding the potentially dangerous Pentland Firth on the north coast of Scotland, the canal is around 60 miles long and takes about three days to cruise from east to west. With the prevailing winds behind you, it takes slightly less time to cruise in the other direction.

FACILITIES AT A GLANCE

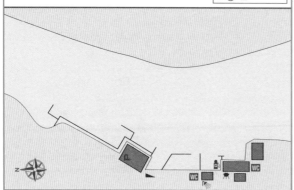

SEAPORT MARINA

Seaport Marina
Muirtown Wharf, Inverness, IV3 5LE
Tel: 01463 725500 Fax: 01463 710942
Email: enquiries.caledonian@britishwaterways.co.uk
www.scottishcanals.co.uk

VHF	Ch 74
ACCESS	HW±4

Seaport Marina is situated at Inverness at the head of the Caledonian Canal. Although it only incorporates 55 berths, it proves a popular location for long term berthing and is accessible four hours either side of HW. The centre of Inverness is just a 15-minute walk away, where you will find a full range of shops, pubs and restaurants, while entertainment venues include a theatre, bowling alley and multiplex cinema.

As the capital of the Highlands, Inverness attracts thousands of visitors each year, providing the ideal base from which to explore the surrounding area by road, coach or train. In addition, Inverness airport is only 20 minutes by taxi from the marina.

FACILITIES AT A GLANCE

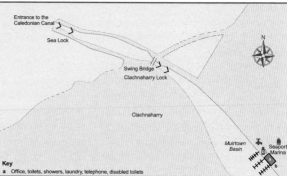

Entrance to the Caledonian Canal

Sea Lock

Swing Bridge
Clachnaharry Lock

Clachnaharry

Muirtown Basin

Seaport Marina

Key
a Office, toilets, showers, laundry, telephone, disabled toilets

Shamrock Chandlery

Shamrock Quay, William Street, Northam, Southampton SO14 5QL

Clothing - Musto MUSTO   Gill **Gill**   Splashdown **splashdown**

Shoes - Dubarry **dubarry** Quayside QUAYSIDE   Gill + Aquashoe AQUASHOE

TYPICALLY 10% OFF RRP

**MAIL ORDER
HOTLINE**
Tel: (02380) 632725
Fax (02380) 225611

www.shamrock.co.uk

2007/M&WC160/z

KIRKWALL MARINA

Kirkwall Marina
Harbour Street, Kirkwall, Orkney, KW15
Tel: 01856 872292 Fax: 01856 852888
www.orkneymarinas.co.uk

VHF	Ch 12
ACCESS	H24

The Orkney Isles, comprising 70 islands in total, provides some of the finest cruising grounds in Northern Europe. The Main Island, incorporating the ancient port of Kirkwall, is the largest, although 16 others have lively communities and are rich in archaeological sites as well as spectacular scenery and wildlife.

Kirkwall Marina is due to open around October 2003 and will offer excellent facilities along with 24hr access and good shelter. The site is very close to the historic Kirkwall, whose original town is one of the best preserved examples of an ancient Norse dwelling.

FACILITIES AT A GLANCE

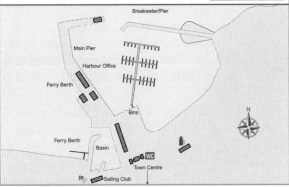

STROMNESS MARINA

Stromness Marina
Stromness
Orkney, KW16
Tel: 01856 850744 Fax: 01856 852888
www.orkneymarinas.co.uk

VHF	Ch 12
ACCESS	H24

Just 16 miles to the west of Kirkwall, Stromness lies on the south-western tip of the Orkney Isles' Mainland. Sitting beneath the rocky ridge known as Brinkie's Brae, it is considered one of Orkney's major seaports, with sailors first attracted to the fine anchorage provided by the bay of Hamnavoe.

Stromness, like Kirkwall, is a brand new marina (due to be completed in Autumn 2003), offering comprehensive facilities including a chandlery and repair services. Also on hand are an internet café, a fitness suite and swimming pool as well as car and bike hire.

FACILITIES AT A GLANCE

Key
a Terminal building, Harbour Master's office
b Cafe
c Rope centre

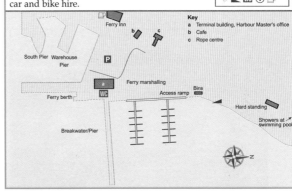

Sail Orkney

Orkney Marinas
126 Victoria Street
Stromness
Orkney KW16 3BU
Tel/Fax 018856 852888   www.orkneymarinas.co.uk   info@orkneymarinas.co.uk

Tel:
01631 566555
Fax:
01631 571044

DUNSTAFFNAGE
MARINA

Dunstaffnage
Marina Ltd,
Dunbeg,
Oban Argyll,
PA37 1PX

Email: info@dunstaffnagemarina.com • Website: www.dunstaffnagemarina.com

Whether you are a first time visitor or regular customer, we hope you enjoy our recently expanded facilities and the magnificent environment in which we are located.

Dunstaffnage Marina is located on the shores of Dunstaffnage Bay overlooking Dunstaffnage Castle at the entrance to Loch Etive.

Just 3 miles from Oban, the gateway to the Western Isles, Dunstaffnage is easily accessible by road, rail and ferry, or by air from Oban Airport at Connel just 2 miles away.

The Marina has excellent facilities with 150 fully serviced berths able to accommodate yachts or motor vessels up to 25 metres loa.

Operating in tandem with the renowned Wide Mouthed Frog, the Marina provides a unique range of services. The Frog is the social hub of the Marina and includes the acclaimed seafood restaurant, a family bistro, a friendly bar and 9 en-suite rooms.

To enter Dunstaffnage Bay from the Firth of Lorne leave Dunstaffnage Castle to starboard and the island Eilean Mor to port. Navigation Lights are fixed on both the Castle and island foreshores.

Entrance to the marina is by following the fairway in a direction of 150 degrees leaving green marker buoys to the starboard.

After the second buoy, the Marina Fairway should become apparent on a course of 270 degrees.

Strong currents exist in the bay due to the effect of tidal flow in Loch Etive. The prevailing current follows the shores of the Bay in an anti-clockwise direction.

Please do not attempt to cut through the Moorings on your approach to the Marina.

Please show consideration to other users by not exceeding 4 knots within the anchorage and bay.

2007/M&WC41a/e

NORTH WEST SCOTLAND - Cape Wrath to Crinan Canal

ADLARD COLES NAUTICAL
WEATHER FORECASTS
BY FAX & TELEPHONE

Coastal/Inshore	2-day by Fax	5-day by Phone
Scotland North	09065 222 341	09068 969 641
Minch	09065 222 354	09068 969 654
Caledonia	09065 222 353	09068 969 653
Clyde	09065 222 352	09068 969 652
National (3-5 day)	09065 222 340	09068 969 640

Offshore	2-5 day by Fax	2-5 day by Phone
Southern North Sea	09065 222 358	09068 969 658
Northern North Sea	09065 222 362	09068 969 662
North West Scotland	09065 222 361	09068 969 661
Irish Sea	09065 222 359	09068 969 659

09068 CALLS COST 60P PER MIN. 09065 CALLS COST £1.50 PER MIN.

Key to Marina Plans symbols

Calor Gas		P	Parking
Chandler			Pub/Restaurant
Disabled facilities			Pump out
Electrical supply			Rigging service
Electrical repairs			Sail repairs
Engine repairs			Shipwright
First Aid			Shop/Supermarket
Fresh Water			Showers
Fuel - Diesel			Slipway
Fuel - Petrol		WC	Toilets
Hardstanding/boatyard			Telephone
Internet Café	@		Trolleys
Laundry facilities		V	Visitors berths
Lift-out facilities			Wi-Fi

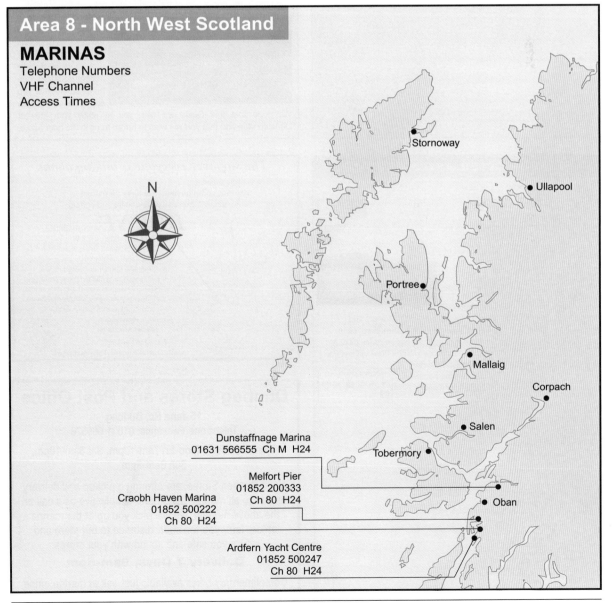

Area 8 - North West Scotland

MARINAS
Telephone Numbers
VHF Channel
Access Times

N

Stornoway

Ullapool

Portree

Mallaig

Corpach

Salen

Tobermory

Oban

Dunstaffnage Marina
01631 566555 Ch M H24

Melfort Pier
01852 200333
Ch 80 H24

Craobh Haven Marina
01852 500222
Ch 80 H24

Ardfern Yacht Centre
01852 500247
Ch 80 H24

DUNSTAFFNAGE MARINA

Dunstaffnage Marina Ltd
Dunbeg, by Oban, Argyll, PA37 1PX
Tel: 01631 566555 Fax: 01631 571044
Email: lizzy@dunstaffnage.sol.co.uk

VHF	Ch M
ACCESS	H24

Located just two to three miles north of Oban, Dunstaffnage Marina has recently been renovated to include an additional 36 fully serviced

berths, a new breakwater providing shelter from NE'ly to E'ly winds and an increased amount of hard standing. Also on site is the Wide Mouthed Frog, offering a convivial bar, restaurant and accomodation with spectacular views of the 13th century Dunstaffnage Castle.

The marina is perfectly placed to explore Scotland's stunning west coast and Hebridean Islands. Only 10 miles NE up Loch Linnhe is Port Appin, while sailing 15 miles S, down the Firth of Lorne, brings you to Puldohran where you can walk to an ancient hostelry situated next to the C18 Bridge Over the Atlantic.

FACILITIES AT A GLANCE

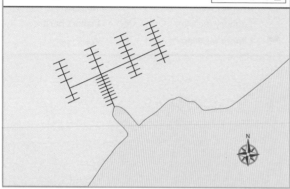

MELFORT PIER AND HARBOUR

Melfort Pier and Harbour
Kilmelford, by Oban, Argyll
Tel: 01852 200333 Fax: 01852 200329
Email: melharbour@aol.com

VHF	
ACCESS	H24

Melfort Pier & Harbour is situated on the shores of Loch Melfort, one of the most peaceful lochs on the south west coast of Scotland. Overlooked by the Pass of Melfort and the Braes of Lorn, it lies approximately 18 miles north of Lochgilphead and 16 miles south of Oban. Its onsite facilities include hot

showers, electricity, water, laundry, telephone, 'WIFI' Hotspot and parking whilst fuel is available at the neighbouring Kilmelford Yacht Haven. Onsite restaurant under construction due late summer 2006. A village shop/post office and pub are available in Kilmelford village. For those who want a few nights on dry land, Melfort Pier & Harbour offers luxury self catering houses, each one equipped with a sauna, spa bath and balcony offering views over the loch.

FACILITIES AT A GLANCE

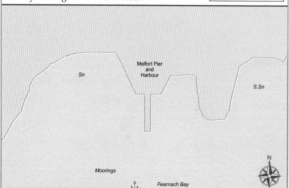

DUNSTAFFNAGE MARINA

Dunbeg, Oban Argyll, PA37 1PX
Tel: 01631 566555
Fax: 01631 571044
email: dunmarina@aol.com

Whether you are a first time visitor or regular customer, we hope you enjoy our facilities and the magnificent environment in which we are located. Dunstaffnage Marina is located on the shores of Dunstaffnage Bay overlooking Dunstaffnage Castle at the entrance to Loch Etive. Just 3 miles from Oban, the gateway to the Western Isles, Dunstaffnage is easily accessible by road, rail and ferry, or by air from Oban Airport at Connel just 2 miles away. The Marina has excellent facilities with 150 fully serviced berths able to accommodate yachts or motor

vessels up to 25 metres loa. Operating in tandem with the renowned Wide Mouthed Frog, the Marina provides a unique range of services. The Frog is the social hub of the Marina and includes the acclaimed

seafood restaurant, a family bistro and a friendly bar. Bookings for meals or our 4 star s t a n d a r d accommodation can be taken whether you are afloat or ashore.

We hope that this Guide will help you to enjoy your stay at Dunstaffnage and that you will wish to return to us in the near future.
2007/M&WC41b/e

The stopover everyone is talking about.

2 free visitors moorings.
Luxurious complimentary showers for patrons.
3 courses + Scottish cheeseboard and coffee.

DOUNE, Knoydart
57° 04.0'N 005° 47.5'W

Freshly prepared single menu with local venison, lamb and shellfish our speciality.
Vegetarian and special diets catered for.
Fresh homemade rolls and delicious puddings.
Fine selection of wines at very reasonable prices.
To book and discuss your menu, call by 5pm latest.
Telephone / weather / water / diesel.

For more information,
contact Martin on
Tel: 01687 462667
email: martin@doune-knoydart.co.uk

www.doune-knoydart.co.uk

Isle of Skye

Ardnamurchan Pt

2006/M&WC70/e

Dunbeg Stores and Post Office

15 Jane Rd, Dunbeg
Telephone/Facsimile: 01631 566576

Opening Hours, Mon-Fri 7am-10pm, Sat 8am-10pm, Sun 8am-9pm

We at Dunbeg Stores, are offering a pickup and delivery service to all marina customers. Simply give us a call on the above number, we will pick you up at the marina office, ferry you the short distance to our store and return you safe and sound with your stores.

Delivery 7 Days, 9am-5pm

Complimentary bikes available just ask at marina office

2007/M&WC114/e

CRAOBH HAVEN MARINA

Craobh Haven Marina
By Lochgilphead, Argyll, Scotland, PA31 8UA
Tel: 01852 500222 Fax: 01852 500252
Email: enquire@kipmarina.co.uk
www.scottishmarinas.co.uk

VHF	Ch M, 80
ACCESS	H24

Pronounced 'Croove', Craobh Marina has been developed from a natural harbour and lies at the heart of Scotland's spectacular west coast cruising grounds. It is strategically placed for entering the Crinan Canal, making a short trip to the Mull of Kintyre and Oban, or visiting Jura and Islay. With 250 berths and the capacity to accommodate

yachts up to 33m LOA, Croabh Marina enjoys deep water at all states of the tide. It sits adjacent to the village of Craobh Haven, where you can find a convenience store, a pub-cum-restaurant and a convivial bistro. Alternative activities to sailing include a well-equipped dive centre as well as a large number of walks through exquisite countryside.

FACILITIES AT A GLANCE

Key
a Holiday cottages
b Village store
c Bar
d Gift shop
e Waste oil
f Boat shed

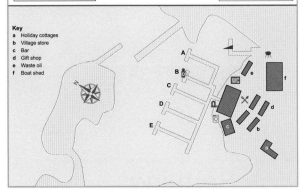

ARDFERN YACHT CENTRE

Ardfern Yacht Centre
Ardfern, by Lochgilphead, Argyll, PA31 8QN
Tel: 01852 500247 Fax: 01852 500624
www.ardfernyacht.co.uk Email: office@ardfernyacht.co.uk

VHF	Ch 80
ACCESS	H24

Developed around an old pier once frequented by steamers, Ardfern Yacht Centre lies at the head of Loch Craignish, one of Scotland's most sheltered and picturesque sea lochs. With several islands and protected anchorages nearby, Ardfern is an ideal place from which to cruise the west coast of Scotland and the Outer Hebrides.

The Yacht Centre comprises pontoon berths and swinging moorings as well as a workshop, boat storage and well-stocked chandlery, while a grocery store and eating places can be found in the village. Among the onshore activities available locally are horse riding, cycling, and walking.

FACILITIES AT A GLANCE

Key
a Workshop
b Showers, toilets and launderette
c Chandlery and office

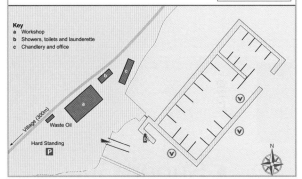

There is always a friendly welcome at Craobh Marina • It is the perfect and most attractive location on the West Coast • boatyard with slipway hoist and crane • service and repair facilities • storage yard • well stocked chandlery • café, pub & gift shop • car hire • call VHF 80 call sign Craobh Marina.

Craobh is the ideal stopping off cruising base. Please contact Jim Berry about your plans.

Craobh Haven
by Lochgilphead
Argyll PA31 8UD

Tel: 01852 500222 Fax: 01852 500252
craobhmarina@talk21.com

website: www.kipmarina.co.uk

2007/M&WMD18B/e

ARDFERN YACHT CENTRE
E-mail: office@ardfernyacht.co.uk Website: www.ardfernyacht.co.uk
The ideal place to visit and keep your boat while cruising the West of Scotland
Tel: (01852) 500247/636 Fax: (01852) 500624
Ardfern By Lochgilphead, Argyll, Scotland PA31 8QN
COMPREHENSIVE FACILITIES. 2007/M&WMD13/e

8

CRINAN BOATYARD LTD
Crinan, Lochgilphead, Argyll PA31 8SW
Tel: (01546) 830232
Fax: (01546) 830281
Chandlery - 01546 830133
Fully stocked chandlery, slipway, engineering and shipwright work and repairs, swinging moorings, water and diesel, shower and laundry facilities, undercover and outside storage.

2007/M&Wext13/e

ARDORAN MARINE
Lerags, Oban, Argyll, Scotland PA34 4SE
Tel: 01631 566123
Fax: 01631 566611
e-mail: colin@ardoran.co.uk
www.ardoran.co.uk
West coast Scotland. All marine facilities.

M&WL3/e

ISLE OF SKYE YACHTS
Ardvasar, Isle of Skye IV45 8RS
Tel: 01471 844216
Fax: 01471 844387
e-mail: enquiries@isleofskyeyachts.co.uk
www.isleofskyeyachts.co.uk
Bareboat and Skippered Yacht Charter, boat repairs, servicing, moorings, supplies.

2007/M&WL5/e

ARISAIG MARINE LTD

Arisaig Harbour, Inverness-shire PH39 4NH
TEL: (01687) 450224
e-mail: info@arisaig.co.uk
Arisaig Harbour for the finest coastal sailing.
60 moorings, 20 ton Roodberg Boat trailed, Linkspan landing, parking, slipway. Services, wintering, repairs, Honda Agents, boat sale etc. Village amenities: Hotel, Bistro, Café, Shop, Post Office & Railway Station.
Website: www.arisaig.co.uk

2007/M&WC1C158/z

When responding to adverts please mention Marina & Waypoint Guide 2007

**British
Waterways
Scotland**

WELCOME
TO SCOTLAND'S CANALS

- Superb Value Marina Berthing

- Winter Lay-up at keen prices

- Canal Information

- Experience the Falkirk wheel

- Download Skipper's Guides

- Everything you need to know Online!

www.britishwaterways.co.uk/scotland

2007/M&WC149/z

SOUTH WEST SCOTLAND - Crinan Canal to Mull of Galloway

ADLARD COLES NAUTICAL
WEATHER FORECASTS
BY FAX & TELEPHONE

Coastal/Inshore	2-day by Fax	5-day by Phone
Minch	09065 222 354	09068 969 654
Caledonia	09065 222 353	09068 969 653
Clyde	09065 222 352	09068 969 652
North West	09065 222 351	09068 969 651
National (3-5 day)	09065 222 340	09068 969 640
Offshore	2-5 day by Fax	2-5 day by Phone
Southern North Sea	09065 222 358	09068 969 658
Northern North Sea	09065 222 362	09068 969 662
North West Scotland	09065 222 361	09068 969 661
Irish Sea	09065 222 359	09068 969 659

09068 CALLS COST 60P PER MIN. 09065 CALLS COST £1.50 PER MIN.

Key to Marina Plans symbols

Calor Gas		P	Parking
Chandler			Pub/Restaurant
Disabled facilities			Pump out
Electrical supply			Rigging service
Electrical repairs			Sail repairs
Engine repairs			Shipwright
First Aid			Shop/Supermarket
Fresh Water			Showers
Fuel - Diesel			Slipway
Fuel - Petrol		WC	Toilets
Hardstanding/boatyard			Telephone
@ Internet Café			Trolleys
Laundry facilities		V	Visitors berths
Lift-out facilities			Wi-Fi

Area 9 - South West Scotland

MARINAS
Telephone Numbers
VHF Channel
Access Times

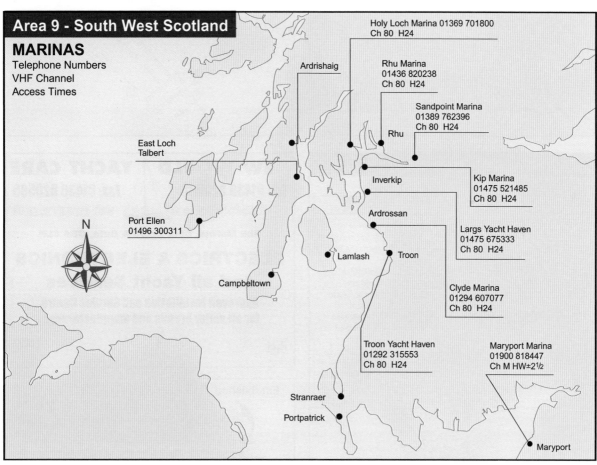

Holy Loch Marina 01369 701800 Ch 80 H24

Ardrishaig

Rhu Marina 01436 820238 Ch 80 H24

Sandpoint Marina 01389 762396 Ch 80 H24

Rhu

East Loch Talbert

Inverkip

Kip Marina 01475 521485 Ch 80 H24

Ardrossan

Largs Yacht Haven 01475 675333 Ch 80 H24

N

Port Ellen 01496 300311

Lamlash   Troon

Clyde Marina 01294 607077 Ch 80 H24

Campbeltown

Troon Yacht Haven 01292 315553 Ch 80 H24

Maryport Marina 01900 818447 Ch M HW±2½

Stranraer

Portpatrick

Maryport

9

Adlard Coles Nautical
THE BEST SAILING BOOKS

Shooting H$_2$O – 2nd Edition
Rick Tomlinson   **£40.00** 0 7136 7480 6

TO ORDER

Tel: **01256 302692** email: **direct@macmillan.co.uk** or **www.adlardcoles.com**

PORT ELLEN MARINA

Port Ellen Marina
Port Ellen, Islay, Argyll, PA42 7DB

VHF
ACCESS H24

A safe and relaxed marina for visitors to the *Malt Whisky Island*. There are seven classic distilleries and yet another still (private) to start production soon. If you are planning a cruise to the north then superb sailing will take you onward via Craighouse on Jura. Meeting guests or short term storage is trouble free with the excellent air and ferry services connecting to Glasgow. Once on Islay you will be tempted to extend your stay so be warned, check www.portellenmarina.com for the many reasons to visit, from golf to music.

FACILITIES AT A GLANCE

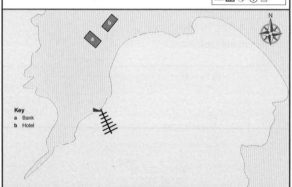

Key
a Bank
b Hotel

HOLY LOCH MARINA

Holy Loch Marina
Rankin's Brae, Sandbank, Dunoon, PA23 8QB
Tel: 01369 701800 Fax: 01369 704749
Email: brochure@holylochmarina.co.uk

VHF Ch 80
ACCESS H24

Holy Loch Marina, reputed for being the Clyde's newest marina, lies on the south shore of the loch, roughly half a mile west of Lazaretto Point. Holy Loch is among the Clyde's most beautiful natural harbours and, besides being a peaceful location, offers an abundance of wildlife, places of local historical interest as well as excellent walking and cycling through the Argyll Forest Park.

The marina can be entered in all weather conditions and is within easy sailing distance of Loch Long and Upper Firth.

FACILITIES AT A GLANCE

Key
a Chandlery
b Office
c Boat Storage
d Fuel Berth
e Holy Loch Sailing Club
f Pier
g Berth Holding Facilities

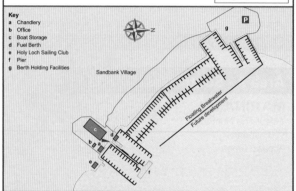

Sandbank Village

RHU MARINA

Rhu Marina Ltd
Rhu, Dunbartonshire, G84 8LH
Tel: 01436 820238 Fax: 01436 821039
Email: dockmaster@rhumarina.co.uk

VHF Ch 37, 80
ACCESS H24

Located on the north shore of the Clyde Estuary, Rhu Marina is accessible at all states of the tide and can accommodate yachts up to 18m in length. It also operates 60 swinging moorings in the bay adjacent to the marina, with a ferry service provided.

Within easy walking distance of the marina is Rhu village, a conservation village incorporating a few shops, a pub and the beautiful Glenarn Gardens as well as the Royal Northern & Clyde Yacht Club. A mile or two to the east lies the holiday town of Helensburgh, renowned for its attractive architecture and elegant parks and gardens, while Glasgow city is just 40 miles away and can be easily reached by train.

FACILITIES AT A GLANCE

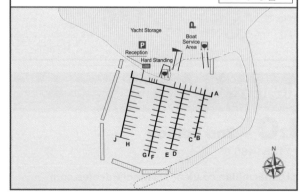

NEW WORLD **YACHT CARE**
Tel: 01436 820586   Fax: 01436 820585
email: sales@nwyc.co.uk   web: www.nwyc.co.uk

Rhu Marina, Rhu, Argyll & Bute, G84 8LH

ELECTRICS & ELECTRONICS and all Yacht Services

Approved Installation and Service Centre for all major brands and manufacturers ..

British Marine Federation

2007/M&WC79/z

Established 1968 **PROFESSIONAL REPAIRS**
Traditional Boat Builders
Glass Fibre Engineers

Family-run Business
Modern Workshop
Temperature Controlled
01389 710070

2007/M&WMD21/f

When responding to adverts please mention Marina & Waypoint Guide 2007

SANDPOINT MARINA

Sandpoint Marina Ltd
Sandpoint, Woodyard Road, Dumbarton, G82 4BG
Tel: 01389 762396 Fax: 01389 732605
Email: sales@sandpoint-marina.co.uk
www.sandpoint-marina.co.uk

VHF	CH M
ACCESS	HW±3

Lying on the north bank of the Clyde estuary on the opposite side of the River Leven from Dumbarton Castle, Sandpoint Marina provides easy access to some of the most stunning cruising grounds in the United Kingdom. It is an independently run marina, offering a professional yet personal service to every boat owner. Among the facilities to hand are an on site chandlery, storage areas, a 40 ton travel hoist and 20 individual workshop units.

Within a 20-minute drive of Glasgow city centre, the marina is situated close to the shores of Loch Lomond, the largest fresh water loch in Britain.

FACILITIES AT A GLANCE

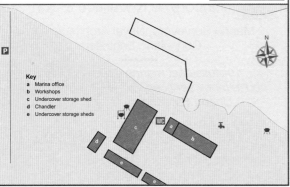

Key
a Marina office
b Workshops
c Undercover storage shed
d Chandler
e Undercover storage sheds

KIP MARINA

Kip Marina, The Yacht Harbour
Inverkip, Renfrewshire, Scotland, PA16 0AS
Tel: 01475 521485 Fax: 01475 521298
www.kipmarina.co.uk Email: enquire@kipmarina.co.uk

VHF	Ch 80
ACCESS	H24

Inverkip is a small village which lies on the south shores of the River Kip as it enters the Firth of Clyde. Once established for fishing, smuggling and, in the 17th century, witch-hunts, it became a seaside resort in the 1860s as a result of the installation of the railway. Today it is a yachting centre, boasting a state-of-the-art marina with over 600 berths and full boatyard facilities. With the capacity to accommodate yachts of up to 23m LOA, Kip Marina offers direct road and rail access to Glasgow and its international airport, therefore making it an ideal location for either a winter lay up or crew changeover.

FACILITIES AT A GLANCE

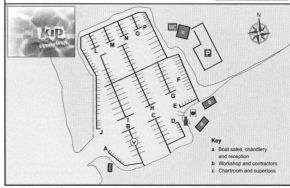

Key
a Boat sales, chandlery and reception
b Workshop and contractors
c Chartroom and superloos

LARGS YACHT HAVEN

Largs Yacht Haven Ltd
Irvine Road, Largs, Ayrshire, KA30 8EZ
Tel: 01475 675333 Fax: 01475 672245
www.yachthavens.com Email: largs@yachthavens.com

VHF	Ch 80, 37
ACCESS	H24

Largs Yacht Haven offers a superb location among lochs and islands, with numerous fishing villages and harbours nearby. Sheltered cruising can be enjoyed in the inner Clyde, while the west coast and Ireland are only a day's sail away. With a stunning backdrop of the Scottish mountains, Largs incorporates 700 fully serviced berths and provides a range of on site facilities including chandlers, sailmakers, divers, engineers, shops, restaurants and club.

A 20-minute coastal walk brings you to the town of Largs, which has all the usual amenities as well as good road and rail connections to Glasgow.

FACILITIES AT A GLANCE

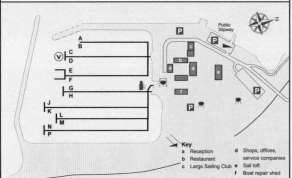

Key
a Reception
b Restaurant
c Largs Sailing Club
d Shops, offices, service companies
e Sail loft
f Boat repair shed

Jeff Rutherford
Yacht Electrical & Electronic Services

Buying a New Boat?

Don't sign up for any boat dealer priced extras until you get a quote from us!

We Offer:
Full Sales, Service, Installation, Design, Setup and Tuition for all instrument Systems by Fully Trained and qualified Engineers
Heating systems from Eberspacher, Webasto and Ardic. We also supply and fit Bow Thrusters, Watermakers and Generators.

Call now for a free no obligation quote

Kip Marina, Inverkip, Renfrewshire, Scotland PA16 0AS
Fairlie Quay Marina, Main road, Fairlie, North Ayrshire KA29 0AS
Phone & Fax 01475 522244 Mobile 07831 445126
Email jeffyees@aol.com www.jeffrutherford.co.uk

2007/M&WC52/e

kip marina

The Yacht Harbour
Inverkip
Renfrewshire PA16 0AS

Renown as Scotland's Premier Marina • Beautifully sheltered marina basin with 700 berths • 50t boat hoist • service and repair facilities • storage yard • well stocked chandlery • bar & restaurant • 24hr security • call VHF 80 call sign Kip Marina.

For full details of all our services please visit our website.

Tel: 01475 521485 Fax: 01475 521298
enquire@kipmarina.co.uk

website: www.kipmarina.co.uk

2007/M&WM18C/z

9

CLYDE MARINA

Clyde Marina Ltd
The Harbour, Ardrossan, Ayrshire, KA22 8DB
Tel: 01294 607077 Fax: 01294 607076
www.clydemarina.com Email: info@clydemarina.com

VHF
ACCESS H24

Situated on the Clyde Coast
between Irvine and Largs,
Clyde Marina is a modern
bustling yacht harbour with
boatyard, 50 Tonne hoist and
active boat sales, set in a landscaped environment. A deep draft
marina accommodating vessels up to 30m LOA, draft up to 5m.
Recent arrivals include tall ships and Whitbread 60s plus a variety of
sail and power craft. Fully serviced pontoons plus all the yard
facilities you would expect from a leading marina
including boatyard and boatshed for repairs or
storage. Good road and rail connections and only
30 minutes from Glasgow and Prestwick airports.
Home of Sunbird International Yacht Sales.

FACILITIES AT A GLANCE

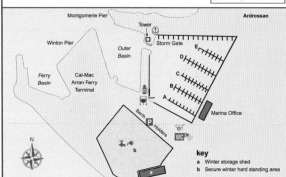

key
a Winter storage shed
b Secure winter hard standing area

The Harbour Ardrossan Ayrshire KA22 8DB
Tel: (01294) 607077 Fax: (01294) 607076
info@clydemarina.com

CLYDE MARINA LTD

2007/M&WMD12/z

250 berth full service marine, large
secure boatyard,
undercover storage,
50 ton hoist, visitors welcome.
Sunbird International Yacht sales

JESSAIL
58 Glasgow Street, Ardrossan KA22 8EH
Tel: (01294) 467311
Fax: (01294) 467311
e-mail: jessail@btinternet.com
Sails, covers, upholstery.

2007/M&WL11/e

A Adamson & Co
Incorp E K Wallace & Son

Marine Surveyors, Naval Architects and
Consulting Engineers

*Professional marine surveying and
consultancy services, carried out across the
United Kingdom and Worldwide*

Offices at Glasgow, Edinburgh, Grangemouth
and Shetland

info@aadamson.co.uk   www.aadamson.co.uk
Call 08450 SURVEY

2007/M&WC128/e

Shamrock Chandlery
Shamrock Quay, William Street, Northam, Southampton SO14 5QL

Clothing - Musto   Gill  Splashdown splashdown

Shoes - Dubarry Quayside  Gill + Aquashoe

TYPICALLY 10% OFF RRP

MAIL ORDER
HOTLINE
Tel: (02380) 632725
Fax (02380) 225611

www.shamrock.co.uk

2007/M&WC160/z

TROON YACHT HAVEN

Troon Yacht Haven Ltd
The Harbour, Troon, Ayrshire, KA10 6DJ
Tel: 01292 315553 Fax: 01292 312836
Email: troon@yachthavens.com
www.yachthavens.com

VHF: Ch 80, M
ACCESS H24

Troon Yacht Haven, situated on the Southern Clyde Estuary, benefits from deep water at all states of the tide. Tucked away in the harbour of Troon, it is well sheltered and within easy access of the town centre. There are plenty of cruising opportunities to be had from here, whether it be hopping across to the Isle of Arran, with its peaceful anchorages and mountain walks, sailing round the Mull or through the Crinan Canal to the Western Isles, or heading for the sheltered waters of the Clyde.

FACILITIES AT A GLANCE

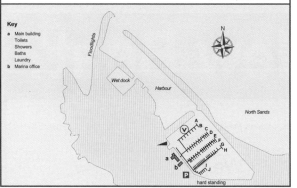

Key
a Main building
   Toilets
   Showers
   Baths
   Laundry
b Marina office

MARYPORT MARINA

Maryport Development Ltd
Marine Road, Maryport, Cumbria, CA15 8AY
Tel: 01900 814431 Fax: 01900 810212
www.maryportmarina.com
Email: enquires@maryportmarina.com

VHF: Ch 12, 16, 80
ACCESS HW±2.5

Maryport Marina lies in the historic Senhouse Dock, which was originally built for sailing clippers. The old stone harbour walls provide good shelter to this 161-berth, Blug Flag marina in all wind directions. Set within a quiet spot, although still within easy walking distance of Maryport town centre, it affords a perfect location from which to explore the west coast of Scotland as well as the Isle of Man and the Galloway Coast. For those who wish to venture inland, then the Lake District is only seven miles away.

FACILITIES AT A GLANCE

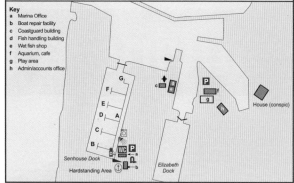

Key
a Marina Office
b Boat repair facility
c Coastguard building
d Fish handling building
e Wet fish shop
f Aquarium, cafe
g Play area
h Admin/accounts office

KYLE CHANDLERS

**Troon Yacht Haven, Harbour Road,
Troon, Ayrshire, KA10 6DJ**

*Tel: (01292) 311880   Fax: (01292) 319910
e-mail: kylechandlers@hotmail.com*

Situated in Troon Yacht Haven.
Established 17 years.
Stockist of main brands - Open 7 Days during season
Calor Gas - Paraffin - Camping Gas

2007/M&WC11/e

Maritime Connection
Sailing and Powerboat
Tuition Yacht Charter & Delivery

Courses also available in VHF Radiotelephony.
Diesel Engine Maintenance, RYA First Aid and Radar

**Troon Yacht Haven,
The Harbour, Troon KA10 6DJ**
Telephone/Fax: 01292 315492
Email: mariconn@dial.pipex.com
Website: www.maritimeconnection.co.uk

2007/M&WC87/e

WEST COAST MARINE SERVICES

The Guild of Master Craftsmen
Certificate of Quality & Service

SHIPWRIGHTS AND MARINE ENGINEERING

GRP & WOOD REPAIRS
★ OSMOSIS TREATMENT
★ FITTING OUT
★ ENGINE SERVICING
and INSTALLATIONS

UNDERCOVER REPAIR FACILITIES

The Boat Shed, Troon Yacht Haven, Troon
Tel: 01292 318121

2007/M&WC133/f

WEST COAST MARINE (Work Boats)
TOWING, MOORINGS,
SURVEY

9

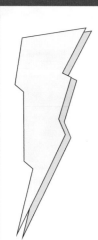 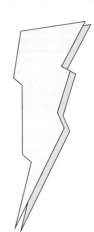

Jeff Rutherford
Yacht Electrical &
Electronic Services

Buying a New Boat?

Don't sign up for any boat dealer priced extras until you get a quote from us!

We Offer:

Full Sales, Service, Installation, Design, Setup and Tuition for all instrument Systems by Fully Trained and qualified Engineers Heating systems from Eberspacher, Webasto and Ardic. We also supply and fit Bow Thrusters, Watermakers and Generators.

Call now for a free no obligation quote

Kip Marina, Inverkip, Renfrewshire, Scotland PA16 0AS
Fairlie Quay Marina, Main road, Fairlie, North Ayrshire KA29 0AS
Phone & Fax 01475 522244   Mobile 07831 445126
Email jeffyees@aol.com   www.jeffrutherford.co.uk

NW ENGLAND, ISLE OF MAN & N WALES - Mull of Galloway to Bardsey Is

ADLARD COLES NAUTICAL
WEATHER FORECASTS
BY FAX & TELEPHONE

Coastal/Inshore	2-day by Fax	5-day by Phone
Northern Ireland	09065 222 355	09068 969 655
Clyde	09065 222 352	09068 969 652
North West	09065 222 351	09068 969 651
Wales	09065 222 350	09068 969 650
National (3-5 day)	09065 222 340	09068 969 640

Offshore	2-5 day by Fax	2-5 day by Phone
Northern North Sea	09065 222 362	09068 969 662
North West Scotland	09065 222 361	09068 969 661
Irish Sea	09065 222 359	09068 969 659
English Channel	09065 222 357	09068 969 657

09068 CALLS COST 60P PER MIN. 09065 CALLS COST £1.50 PER MIN.

Key to Marina Plans symbols

🔋 Calor Gas		P Parking	
Chandler		Pub/Restaurant	
Disabled facilities		Pump out	
Electrical supply		Rigging service	
Electrical repairs		Sail repairs	
Engine repairs		Shipwright	
First Aid		Shop/Supermarket	
Fresh Water		Showers	
Fuel - Diesel		Slipway	
Fuel - Petrol		WC Toilets	
Hardstanding/boatyard		Telephone	
@ Internet Café		Trolleys	
Laundry facilities		V Visitors berths	
Lift-out facilities		Wi-Fi	

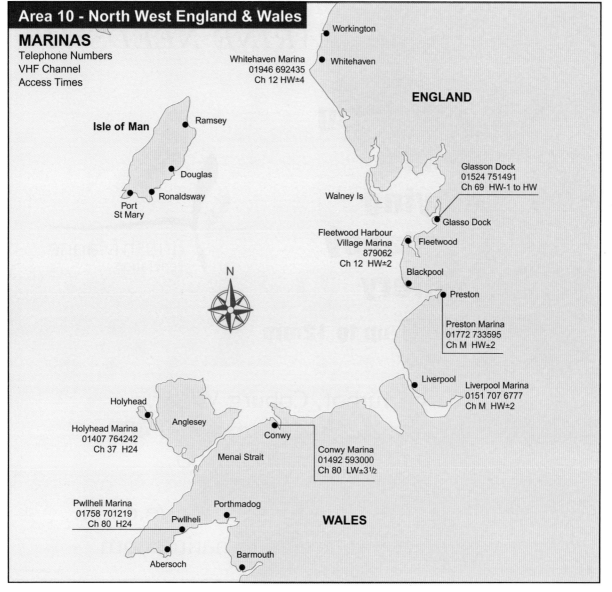

Area 10 - North West England & Wales

MARINAS
Telephone Numbers
VHF Channel
Access Times

Workington

Whitehaven Marina
01946 692435
Ch 12 HW±4

Whitehaven

ENGLAND

Isle of Man

Ramsey

Douglas

Ronaldsway

Port
St Mary

Glasson Dock
01524 751491
Ch 69 HW-1 to HW

Walney Is

Glasso Dock

Fleetwood Harbour
Village Marina
879062
Ch 12 HW±2

Fleetwood

Blackpool

Preston

Preston Marina
01772 733595
Ch M HW±2

N

Liverpool

Liverpool Marina
0151 707 6777
Ch M HW±2

Holyhead

Holyhead Marina
01407 764242
Ch 37 H24

Anglesey

Conwy

Menai Strait

Conwy Marina
01492 593000
Ch 80 LW±3½

Pwllheli Marina
01758 701219
Ch 80 H24

Porthmadog

Pwllheli

WALES

Abersoch

Barmouth

10

S. ROBERTS MARINE LIMITED
at

Liverpool Marina

YOUR ONE STOP SHOP FOR ALL YOUR MARINE NEEDS !!

- ✔ **Boatbuilding**
- ✔ **Repairs**
- ✔ **Surveying**
- ✔ **Consultancy**
- ✔ **Chandlery**
- ✔ **Rigging** up to 12mm

British Marine Federation

Barge Turbot, Coburg Wharf,
South Ferry Quay, Liverpool L3 4BP
Tel/Fax 0151 707 8300

email: stephen@robmar.freeserve.co.uk
website: www.srobertsmarine.com

2007/M&WM10/e

WHITEHAVEN MARINA

Whitehaven Harbour Commissioners, Pears House
1 Duke Street, Whitehaven, Cumbria, CA28 7HW
Tel: 01946 692435 Fax: 01946 61455
Email: office@whitehaven-harbour.co.uk
www.whitehaven-harbour.co.uk

VHF Ch 12
ACCESS HW±4

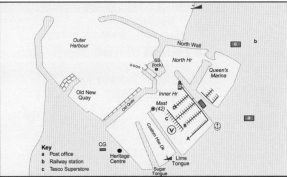

Whitehaven Marina can be found at the south-western entrance to the Solway Firth, providing a strategic departure point for those yachts heading for the Isle of Man, Ireland or Southern Scotland. The harbour is one of the more accessible ports of refuge in NW England, affording a safe entry in most weathers. The approach channel across the outer harbour is dredged to about 1.0m above chart datum, allowing entry into the inner harbour via a sea lock at around HW±4.

Conveniently situated for visiting the Lake District, Whitehaven is an attractive Georgian town, renowned in the C18 for its rum and slave imports.

FACILITIES AT A GLANCE

Key
a Post office
b Railway station
c Tesco Superstore

GLASSON DOCK MARINA

Glasson Basin Yacht Company Ltd
Glasson Dock, Lancaster, LA2 0AW
Tel: 01524 751491 Fax: 01524 752626
Email: info@glassonmarina.com
www.glassonmarina.com

VHF Ch 69
ACCESS HW-1 to HW

Glasson Dock Marina lies on the River Lune, west of Sunderland Point.   Access is via the outer dock which opens 45 minutes before H. W.Liverpool and thence via BWB lock into the inner basin. It is recommended to leave Lune No. 1 Buoy approx 11/2 hrs. before H. W.. Contact the dock on Channel 69.   The Marina can only be contacted by telephone. All the necessary requirements can be found either on site or within easy reach of Glasson Dock, including boat, rigging and sail repair services as well as a launderette, ablution facilities, shops and restaurants.

FACILITIES AT A GLANCE

Key
a Glasson Basin Yacht Co. Ltd
b Glasson Sailing Club
c Harbour House

FLEETWOOD HARBOUR MARINA

Fleetwood Harbour Village Marina
The Dock Office, Wyre Dock, Fleetwood, FY7 6PP
Tel: 01253 872323 Fax: 01253 777549
Email: fleetwood@abports.co.uk

VHF Ch 12
ACCESS HW±1

Fleetwood Harbour Village Marina provides a good location from which to cruise Morecambe Bay and the Irish Sea. To the north west is the Isle of Man, to the north is the Solway Firth and the Clyde Estuary, while to the south west is Conwy, the Menai Straits and Holyhead.

Tucked away in a protected dock which dates back as far as 1835, Fleetwood Harbour Marina has 300 berths and offers extensive facilities. Overlooking the marina is a 15-acre retail and leisure park laid out in a popular American style.

FACILITIES AT A GLANCE

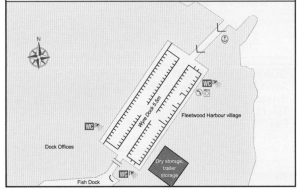

PRESTON MARINA

Preston Marine Services Ltd
The Boathouse, Navigation Way, Preston, PR2 2YP
Tel: 01772 733595 Fax: 01772 731881
Email: info@prestonmarina.co.uk www.prestonmarina.co.uk

VHF Ch 80
ACCESS HW±2

Preston Marina forms part of the comprehensive Riversway Docklands development, meeting all the demands of modern day boat owners. With the docks' history dating back over 100 years, today the marina comprises 40 acres of fully serviced pontoon berths sheltered behind the refurbished original lock gates. Lying 15 miles up the River Ribble, which itself is an interesting cruising ground with an abundance of wildlife,

Preston is well placed for sailing to parts of Scotland, Ireland or Wales. The Docklands development includes a wide choice of restaurants, shops and cinemas as well as being in easy reach of all the cultural and leisure facilities provided by a large town.

FACILITIES AT A GLANCE

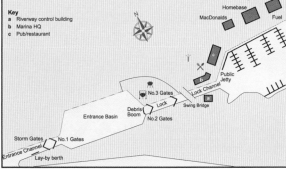

Key
a Riverway control building
b Marina HQ
c Pub/restaurant

10

LIVERPOOL MARINA

Liverpool Marina
Coburg Wharf, Sefton Street, Liverpool, L3 4BP
Tel: 0151 707 6777 Fax: 0151 707 6770
Email: harbourside@liverpoolmarina.co.uk

VHF	Ch M
ACCESS	HW±2

Liverpool Marina is ideally situated for yachtsmen wishing to cruise the Irish Sea. Access is through a computerised lock that opens two and a half hours either side of high water between 0600 and 2200 daily. Once in the marina, you can enjoy the benefits of the facilities on offer, including a first class club bar and restaurant.

Liverpool - recently announced Capital of Culture 2008 - is now a thriving cosmopolitan city, with attractions ranging from numerous bars and restaurants to museums, art galleries and the Beatles Story.

FACILITIES AT A GLANCE

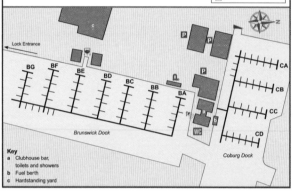

Key
a Clubhouse bar, toilets and showers
b Fuel berth
c Hardstanding yard

Brunswick Dock

Lock Entrance

Coburg Dock

LIVERPOOL MARINA AND HARBOURSIDE CLUB

Coburg Dock, Sefton Street Liverpool L3 4BP

400 berth yacht harbour. All serviced pontoons.
Tidal access HW± 2¹/₂ hrs. approximately depending on draft.
60 ton hoist • Workshops • Bar & Restaurant • Toilets & showers
**CITY CENTRE ONE MILE • OPEN ALL YEAR
• ACTIVE YACHT CLUB**
Tel: 0151 707 6777 & 0151 707 6888 (after 5pm)
Fax 0151 707 6770
email: harbourside@liverpoolmarina.com
www.liverpoolmarina.com

2007/M&WM13/e

HOYLAKE SAILING SCHOOL
MERSEYSIDE

Ships Stores Service
Imray & Admiralty Charts, Books, Hydrographic Publications

5 DAYS or 2 WEEKEND RYA THEORY COURSES
Dayskipper • Coastal Skipper
Yachtmaster Offshore • Yachtmaster Ocean

ONE DAY COURSES
Diesel Engine • VHF • Radar • First Aid • MCA Sea Survival
Practical Power and Sail by Arrangement

RYA Training Centre

Marine House, 86a Market Street, Hoylake, Wirral CH47 3BD
www.sailorsworld.co.uk
0151 632 4664

2007/M&WC139/fz

CONWY MARINA

Conwy Marina
Conwy, LL32 8EP
Tel: 01492 593000 Fax: 01492 572111
Email: jroberts@crestnicholson.com
www.crestnicholsonmarinas.co.uk

VHF	Ch 80
ACCESS	LW±3.5

Situated in an area of outstanding natural beauty, with the Mountains of Snowdonia National Park providing a stunning backdrop, Conwy is the first purpose-built marina to be developed on the north coast of Wales. Enjoying a unique site next to the 13th century Conwy Castle, the third of Edward I's great castles, it provides a convenient base from which to explore the cruising grounds of the North Wales coast. The unspoilt coves of Anglesey and the beautiful Menai Straits prove a popular destination, while further afield are the Llyn Peninsula and the Islands of Bardsey and Tudwells.

The marina incorporates about 500 fully serviced berths which are accessible through a barrier gate between half tide and high water.

FACILITIES AT A GLANCE

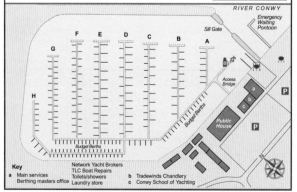

RIVER CONWY

Emergency Waiting Pontoon

Sill Gate

Access Bridge

Budget Berths

Public House

Key
a Main services
Berthing masters office
Network Yacht Brokers
TLC Boat Repairs
Toilets/showers
Laundry store
b Tradewinds Chandlery
c Conwy School of Yachting

YACHT SYSTEMS

M: 07778 516147 T: 01492 584681

AVAILABLE FOR:

■ All types of electrical work caried out
■ Fitting of Electronics
■ GRP Repair specialist
■ Bowthruster installation
■ Deck fittings fitted
■ Seacocks serviced or replaced
■ Vinyl lettering/Striping supplied and fitted
■ Rudder Bearings Replacement
■ General maintenance and Pre-season work

Contact Richard Williams
For a Competitive & Quality Service

2007/M&WC140/fez

QUAY MARINAS LTD
Avon House, Newbrick Road, Stokegifford,
Bristol BS34 8RA
Tel: (01179) 236466
Fax: (01179) 236508
e-mail: sriggs@quaymarinas.com
A wholly owned subsidiary of Quay Marinas, operate comprehensive yachting facilities at 5 locations in the UK and are marketing agents for Malahide Marina in Dublin Bay.

HOLYHEAD MARINA

Holyhead Marina Ltd
Newry Beach, Holyhead, Gwynedd, LL65 1YA
Tel: 01407 764242 Fax: 01407 769152
Email: info@holyheadmarina.co.uk

| VHF | Ch 37 |
| ACCESS | H24 |

One of the few natural deep water harbours on the Welsh coast, Anglesey is conveniently placed as a first port of call if heading to North Wales from the North, South or West. Its marina at Holyhead, accessible at all states of the tide, is sheltered by Holyhead Mountain as well as an enormous harbour breakwater and extensive floating breakwaters, therefore offering good protection from all directions.

Anglesey boasts numerous picturesque anchorages and beaches in addition to striking views over Snowdonia, while only a tide or two away are the Isle of Man and Eire.

FACILITIES AT A GLANCE

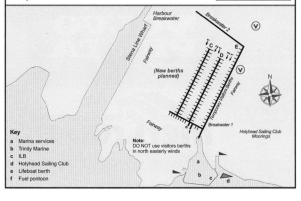

Key
a Marina services
b Trinity Marine
c ILB
d Holyhead Sailing Club
e Lifeboat berth
f Fuel pontoon

Note:
DO NOT use visitors berths in north easterly winds

PWLLHELI MARINA

Pwllheli Marina
Glan Don, Pwllheli, North Wales, LL53 5YT
Tel: 01758 701219 Fax: 01758 701443
Email: wil@hafanpwllheli.co.uk

| VHF | Ch 80 |
| ACCESS | H24 |

Pwllheli is an old Welsh market town providing the gateway to the Llyn Peninsula, which stretches out as far as Bardsey Island to form an 'Area of Outstanding Natural Beauty'. Enjoying the spectacular backdrop of the Snowdonia Mountains, Pwllheli's numerous attractions include an open-air market every Wednesday, 'Neuadd Dwyfor', offering a mix of live theatre and latest films, and beautiful beaches.

Pwllheli Marina is situated on the south side of the Llyn Peninsula. One of Wales' finest marinas and sailing centres, it has over 400 pontoon berths and excellent onshore facilities.

FACILITIES AT A GLANCE

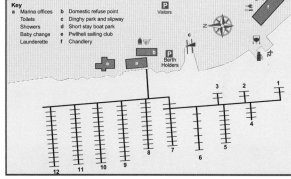

Key
a Marina offices
  Toilets
  Showers
  Baby change
  Launderette
b Domestic refuse point
c Dinghy park and slipway
d Short stay boat park
e Pwllheli sailing club
f Chandlery

LIFERAFT SERVICING
£65 + VAT (Carriage £15)
SALES
ISO9650-1 STANDARD
SOLAS B PACKS SELF RIGHTING
From £570
Liferaft Hire from £30
NORWEST MARINE LTD
6 Cotton Street
Liverpool L3 7DY
Tel/Fax: 0151 207 2860
www.norwestmarine.co.uk

British Marine INDUSTRIES FEDERATION

2007/M&WC138/z

JALSEA MARINE SERVICES LTD

Everything you need from a coastal boatyard in the heart of Cheshire

Indoor & Outdoor Storage & Moorings
BERTHS * REPAIRS * SALES * DIY * WINTER STORE
Inland Marinas with coastal access
• Soft Antifoul Removal • GRP/Metal/Wood/f-cement boat repairs • Gelcoat removal and osmosis treatment • Engine mechanical & electrical repairs • Spray Painting & Varnish •
Ely 01353 664622
Northwich 01606 77870
www.jalsea.co.uk email: info@jalsea.co.uk
WEAVER SHIPYARD, OFF DARWIN STREET, NORTHWICH, CHESHIRE CW8 1LB

2007/M&WM12/e

FIRMHELM Ltd
PWLLHELI BOATYARD

• Boatbuilders
• Maintenance
• Repairs, Refits
• Insurance Work
• Mast and Wire Work
• Rigging and Splicing
• Blakes Osmosis Centre
• Hot Vac Hull Cure Systems
• Spray Centre
• Boat Hoists up to 40 Ton
• Secure Storage
• 25 Ton Mobile Crane Hire
• Chandlery
• Marine Leisure

We pride ourselves in providing the most professional and extensive Boatyard Services in the area together with the areas leading chandlery and leisurewear retail outlet stocking all the major brands e.g. Musto, Henri Lloyd, Gill, Dubarry, Chatham, Quayside, Splashdown, International & Blakes Paints, Harken, Lewmar, Spinlock, Holt, Plastimo, Wichard, Liros Ropes, XM Yachting etc..

Firmhelm Ltd
Pwllheli Marine Centre, Hafan, Pwllheli LL53 5YQ
Tel: 01758 612251 Fax: 01758 613356
Outer Harbour, Pwllheli LL53 5QY
Tel: 01758 612244 Fax: 01758 614790
E-mail: enquiries@firmhelm.com www.firmhelm.com

2007/M&WC36/e

10

Marine Engineering

- Extensive Chandlery

- Rigging wire & swaging

- Mobile repair service

- 25 years experience in the marine industry

Portishead, Bristol

Tel: 01275 815910

www.advancemarine.co.uk

2007/M&WC60/ze

SOUTH WALES & BRISTOL CHANNEL - Bardsey Island to Land's End

ADLARD COLES NAUTICAL
WEATHER FORECASTS
BY FAX & TELEPHONE

Coastal/Inshore	2-day by Fax	5-day by Phone
North West	09065 222 351	09068 969 651
Wales	09065 222 350	09068 969 650
Bristol	09065 222 349	09068 969 649
South West	09065 222 348	09068 969 648
National (3-5 day)	09065 222 340	09068 969 640
Offshore	2-5 day by Fax	2-5 day by Phone
Irish Sea	09065 222 359	09068 969 659
English Channel	09065 222 357	09068 969 657
Biscay	09065 222 360	09068 969 660
North West Scotland	09065 222 361	09068 969 661

09068 CALLS COST 60P PER MIN. 09065 CALLS COST £1.50 PER MIN.

Key to Marina Plans symbols

Calor Gas		P	Parking
Chandler			Pub/Restaurant
Disabled facilities			Pump out
Electrical supply			Rigging service
Electrical repairs			Sail repairs
Engine repairs			Shipwright
First Aid			Shop/Supermarket
Fresh Water			Showers
Fuel - Diesel			Slipway
Fuel - Petrol		WC	Toilets
Hardstanding/boatyard			Telephone
@ Internet Café			Trolleys
Laundry facilities		V	Visitors berths
Lift-out facilities			Wi-Fi

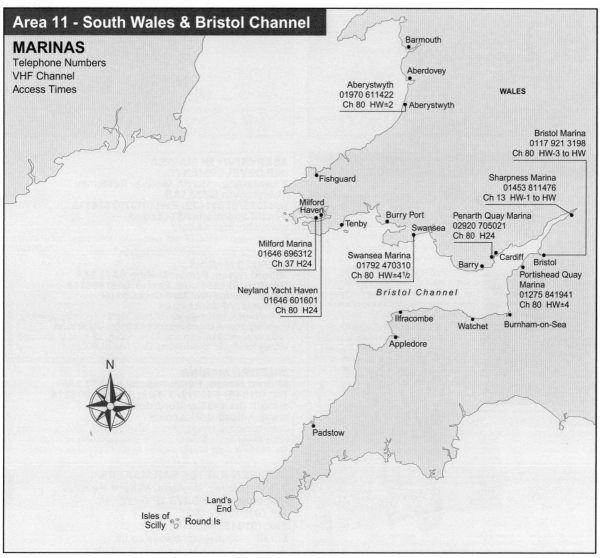

Area 11 - South Wales & Bristol Channel

MARINAS
Telephone Numbers
VHF Channel
Access Times

Barmouth

Aberdovey

WALES

Aberystwyth
01970 611422
Ch 80 HW±2 — Aberystwyth

Bristol Marina
0117 921 3198
Ch 80 HW-3 to HW

Sharpness Marina
01453 811476
Ch 13 HW-1 to HW

Fishguard

Milford Haven

Burry Port

Penarth Quay Marina
02920 705021
Ch 80 H24

Tenby

Swansea

Milford Marina
01646 696312
Ch 37 H24

Swansea Marina
01792 470310
Ch 80 HW±4½

Barry

Cardiff

Bristol

Portishead Quay Marina
01275 841941
Ch 80 HW±4

Neyland Yacht Haven
01646 601601
Ch 80 H24

Bristol Channel

Ilfracombe

Watchet

Burnham-on-Sea

Appledore

N

Padstow

Land's End

Isles of Scilly   Round Is

11

ABERYSTWYTH MARINA

Aberystwyth Marina, IMP Developments
Trefechan, Aberystwyth, Ceredigion, SY23 1AS
Tel: 01970 611422 Fax: 01970 624122
www.abermarina.com Email: abermarina@aol.com

VHF | Ch 80
ACCESS | HW±2

Aberystwyth is a picturesque university seaside town on the west coast of Wales. Its £9 million marina provides over 100 permanent pontoon berths and welcomes on average between 1,500 and 2,000 visiting yachts per year. Accessible two hours either side of high water, its facilities incorporate the usual marine services as well as an on site pub and restaurant.

A short distance away are several pretty Welsh harbours, including Fishguard, Cardigan, Porthmadog and Abersoch, while the east coast of Ireland can be reached within a day's sail.

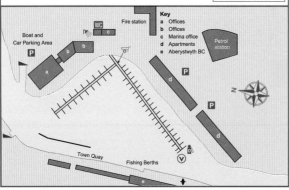

MILFORD MARINA

Milford Marina, Milford Docks
Milford Haven, Pembrokeshire SA73 3AF
Tel: 01646 696312 Fax: 01646 696314
Email: marina@milford-docks.co.uk
www.milford-docks.co.uk

VHF | Ch 18, 37
ACCESS | H24

Set within one of the deepest natural harbours in the world, Milford Marina was opened in 1991 by the Duke of York. Since then its facilities have gradually developed to include hard standing areas, secure boat yards, a diesel pump and chandlery as well as various bars and restaurants.

Accessed via an entrance lock (with waiting pontoons both inside and outside the lock), the marina is ideally situated for exploring the picturesque upper reaches of the River Cleddau or cruising out beyond St Ann's Head to the unspoilt islands of Skomer, Skokholm and Grassholm.

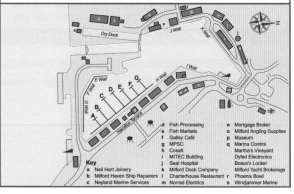

Key
a Neil Hart Joinery
b Milford Haven Ship Repairers
c Neyland Marine Services
d Fish Processing
e Fish Markets
f Galley Café
g MPSC
h Cosalt
i MITEC Building
j Seal Hospital
k Milford Dock Company
l Charterhouse Restaurant
m Norrad Electrics
n Mortgage Broker
o Milford Angling Supplies
p Museum
q Marina Control
Martha's Vineyard
Dyfed Electronics
Bosun's Locker
Milford Yacht Brokerage
r Phoenix Bowl
s Windjammer Marine

NEYLAND YACHT HAVEN

Neyland Yacht Haven Ltd
Brunel Quay, Neyland, Pembrokeshire, SA73 1PY
Tel: 01646 601601 Fax: 01646 600713
Email: neyland@yachthavens.com

VHF | Ch 80, M
ACCESS | H24

Approximately 10 miles from the entrance to Milford Haven lies Neyland Yacht Haven. Tucked away in a well protected inlet just before the Cleddau Bridge, this marina has around 380 berths and

can accommodate yachts up to 25m LOA with draughts of up to 2.5m. The marina is divided into two basins, with the lower one enjoying full tidal access, while entry to the upper one is restricted by a tidal sill.

Offering a comprehensive range of services, Neyland Yacht Haven is within a five minute walk of the town centre where the various shops and takeaways cater for most everyday needs.

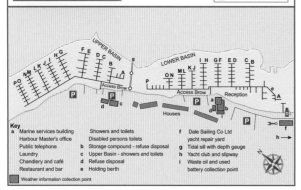

Key
a Marine services building
Harbour Master's office
Public telephone
Laundry
Chandlery and café
Restaurant and bar
■ Weather information collection point
Showers and toilets
Disabled persons toilets
b Storage compound - refuse disposal
c Upper Basin - showers and toilets
d Refuse disposal
e Holding berth
f Dale Sailing Co Ltd
yacht repair yard
g Tidal sill with depth gauge
h Yacht club and slipway
i Waste oil and used
battery collection point

ABERYSTWYTH MARINA -
IMP DEVELOPMENTS
Y Lanfa-Aberystwyth Marina, Trefechan,
Aberystwyth SY23 1AS
Tel: (01970) 611422 Fax: (01970) 624122
e-mail: abermarina@aol.co.uk
www.abermarina.com
Fully serviced marina. Diesel, gas, water, toilets and hot showers.
2007/M&WL19/e

MILFORD MARINA
Milford Haven, Pembrokeshire SA73 3AF
Tel: (01646) 696312/3 Fax: (01646) 696314
e-mail: marina@milford-docks.co.uk
www.milford-docks.co.uk
Marina berths, boat storage, 16t hoist, diesel, electricity, laundery, chandlery, boat & engine repairs, brokerage, engine sales, restaurants, retail park on site, 24 hour staff, 22 miles of sheltered estuary for all year round sailing. Daily rate £1.90.
2007/M&WEXT8/j

MILFORD MARINA
Milford Haven, Pembrokeshire SA73 3AF
Tel: (01646) 696312/3 Fax: (01646) 696314
e-mail: marina@milford-docks.co.uk
www.milford-docks.co.uk
Marina berths, boat storage, 16t hoist, diesel, electricity, laundery, chandlery, boat & engine repairs, brokerage, engine sales, restaurants, retail park on site, 24 hour staff, 22 miles of sheltered estuary for all year round sailing.
2007/M&WL7/e

STEPHEN RATSEY SAILMAKERS
8 Brunel Quay, Neyland, Milford Haven,
Pembrokeshire SA73 1PY
Tel: (01646) 601561
Fax: (01646) 601968
Email: enquiries@ratseys.co.uk
Website: www.stephenratsey.co.uk
New sails, repairs, running, standing rigging, covers, upholstery, seldon & rotostay.
2007/M&WC141/z

SWANSEA MARINA

Swansea Marina
Lockside, Maritime Quarter, Swansea, SA1 1WG
Tel: 01792 470310 Fax: 01792 463948
www.swansea.gov.uk/swanseamarina
Email: swanmar@swansea.gov.uk

VHF	Ch 80
ACCESS	HW±4.5

At the hub of the city's recently redeveloped and award winning Maritime Quarter, Swansea Marina can be accessed HW±4½ hrs via a lock. Surrounded by a plethora of shops, restaurants and marine businesses to cater for most yachtsmen's needs, the marina is in close proximity to the picturesque Gower coast, where there is no shortage of quiet sandy beaches off which to anchor. It also provides the perfect starting point for cruising to Ilfracombe, Lundy Island, the North Cornish coast or West Wales.

Within easy walking distance of the marina is the city centre, boasting a covered shopping centre and market. For those who prefer walking or cycling, take the long promenade to the Mumbles fishing village from where there are plenty of coastal walks.

FACILITIES AT A GLANCE

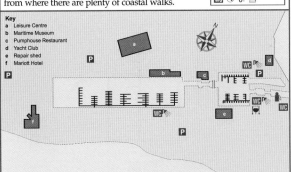

Key
a Leisure Centre
b Maritime Museum
c Pumphouse Restaurant
d Yacht Club
e Repair shed
f Mariott Hotel

PENARTH QUAYS MARINA

Penarth Quay Marina
Penarth, Vale of Glamorgan, CF64 1TQ
Tel: 02920 705021 Fax: 02920 712170
www.quaymarinas.com
Email: sjones@quaymarinas.com

VHF	Ch 80
ACCESS	H24

Constructed around the historic basins of Penarth Dock, which first opened in 1865, Penarth Marina enjoys a prime setting within the sheltered waters of Cardiff Bay. It can be accessed at virtually all states of the tide through the Cardiff Bay Barrage and has become established as one of the major boating facilities in the area.

Although the marina boasts its own high quality restaurants, both of which are housed in the attractively converted Custom House, Penarth town centre is only a 10-minute stroll away and has a selection of shops and eating places as well as a fully-equipped leisure complex.

FACILITIES AT A GLANCE

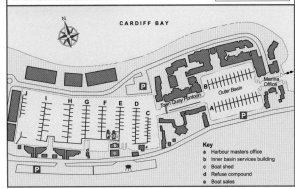

CARDIFF BAY

Key
a Harbour masters office
b Inner basin services building
c Boat shed
d Refuse compound
e Boat sales

---

bay marine insurance

MARINE INSURANCE
YOUR SPECIALIST BROKER
Contact Susanne Newbold
Tel 029 2063 1166

Bay Marine Insurance Consultants Limited

River View
28A Cardiff Road
Taffs Well
CARDIFF
CF15 7RF

Telephone
029 2063 1166

Facsimile
029 2063 1169

Mobile
07774 654 589

- independent advice
- pleasure craft insurance
- specialist assistance
- personal claims service
- competitive premiums from leading insurers
- marina discount

yacht
power
dinghy

admin@baymarineinsurance.co.uk
www.baymarineinsurance.co.uk

Authorised and Regulated by the Financial Services Authority

PENARTH MARINA & CARDIFF BAY ONE STOP MARINE CENTRE

The Area leaders in Marine Engineering, Electrical & Electronic Installations and Repairs. All aspects of boat repairs, GRP a speciality.
Large well stocked Chandlery supplying most well know brands of Marine Leisure Equipment

VOLVO PENTA
YAMAHA
CM
OMREALTY
BLAKES Paint
WIGMORE WRIGHT Marine Services
Authorised Dealers
YANMAR marine
ZF MARINE
vetus
MARINER

2007/M&WC59/f

THE BOATYARD, PENARTH MARINA, PENARTH CF64 1TT
TEL: (029) 2070 9983 / FAX: (029) 2070 7771

QUAY MARINAS LTD
Avon House, Newbrick Road, Stokegifford, Bristol BS34 8RA
Tel: (01179) 236466
Fax: (01179) 236508
e-mail: sriggs@quaymarinas.com
A wholly owned subsidiary of Quay Marinas, operate comprehensive yachting facilities at 5 locations in the UK and are marketing agents for Malahide Marina in Dublin Bay.

2007/M&WEXT9/e

When responding to adverts please mention Marina & Waypoint Guide 2007

11

SHARPNESS MARINA

Sharpness Marina, Sharpness
Berkeley, Gloucestershire GR13 9UN
Tel: 01453 811476
Email: sharpnessmarina@ukonline.co.uk

VHF	Ch 17
ACCESS	HW-2

Sharpness is a small port on the River Severn lying at the entrance to the Gloucester and Sharpness Canal. At the time of its completion in 1827, the canal was the largest and deepest ship canal in the world. However, although once an important commercial waterway, it is now primarily used by pleasure boats. Yachts approaching the marina from seaward can do so via a lock two hours before high water, but note that the final arrival should be timed as late as possible to avoid strong tides in the entrance. From the lock, a passage under two swing bridges and a turn to port brings you to the marina, where pontoon berths are equipped with electricity and water supplies.

FACILITIES AT A GLANCE

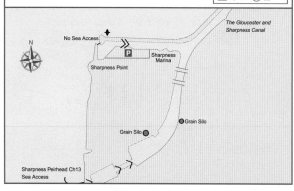

BRISTOL MARINA

Bristol Marina Ltd
Hanover Place, Bristol, BS1 6TZ
Tel: 0117 921 3198 Fax: 0117 929 7672
Email: info@bristolmarina.co.uk

VHF	Ch 80
ACCESS	HW-3 to HW

Situated in the heart of the city, Bristol is a fully serviced marina providing over 100 pontoon berths for vessels up to 20m LOA. Among the facilities are a new fuelling berth and pump out station as well as an on site chandler and sailmaker. It is situated on the south side of the Floating Harbour, about eight miles from the mouth of the River Avon. Accessible from seaward via the Cumberland Basin, passing through both Entrance Lock and Junction Lock, it can be reached approximately three hours before HW.

Shops, restaurants, theatres and cinemas are all within easy reach of the marina, while local attractions include the SS *Great Britain*, designed by Isambard Kingdom Brunel, and the famous Clifton Suspension Bridge, which has an excellent visitors' centre depicting its fascinating story.

FACILITIES AT A GLANCE

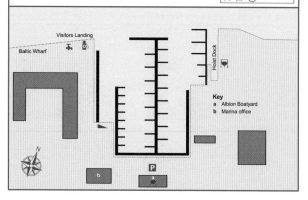

Key
a   Albion Boatyard
b   Marina office

NEW & USED BOATS FOR SALE @ PORTISHEAD MARINA

WALTON MARINE

JEANNEAU

01275 840132
Www.waltonmarine.co.uk

2007/M&WC37/e

PORTISHEAD QUAYS MARINA

Portishead Quays Marina
The Docks, Harbour Road, Portishead, Bristol BS20 7DF
Tel: 01275 841941 Fax: 01275 841942
Email: portisheadmarina@quaymarinas.com
www.quaymarinas.com

VHF	Ch 80
ACCESS	HW±4

Opened in May 2001, Portishead Quays Marina, with its excellent facilities and 24 hour security, is becoming increasingly popular with locals and visitors alike. However, visiting yachtsmen should be aware of the large tidal ranges and strong tidal flows that they are likely to encounter in this part of the Bristol Channel as well as shipping plying to and from the Avonmouth and Portbury Docks. The entrance to the marina is via a lock, with access for a 1.5m yacht being at HW±4½ hrs on neaps and HW±3¾ hrs on springs – contact the marina on VHF Ch 80 ahead of time for the next available lock.

FACILITIES AT A GLANCE

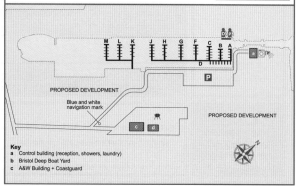

Key
a   Control building (reception, showers, laundry)
b   Bristol Deep Boat Yard
c   A&W Building + Coastguard

QUAY MARINAS LTD
Avon House, Newbrick Road, Stokegifford,
Bristol BS34 8RA
Tel: (01179) 236466
Fax: (01179) 236508
e-mail: sriggs@quaymarinas.com
A wholly owned subsidiary of Quay Marinas, operate comprehensive yachting facilities at 5 locations in the UK and are marketing agents for Malahide Marina in Dublin Bay.

2007/M&WEXT9/e

M.J.BLACKWELL

Marine Surveyor, Designer & Consultant.
Society of Naval Architects & Marine Engineers.
Royal Institute of Naval Architects.
Yacht Designers & Surveyors Association.
Chartered Institute of Arbitrators.

Nominated Surveyor for:
'Code of Practice'. Small Commercial Craft. Power & Sail.
Class V Passenger vessel renewals.
MSA Small workboat certification.

11 Rockwell Avenue,
Rockwell Park
Bristol BS11 0UF

Tel: 0117 938 2160
Fax: 0117 982 9850
Mobile: 08731 888675
E-mail: m.j.blackwell@talk21.com

2007/M&WC111/e

THE BOAT REPAIR CENTRE

**Mobile Repair Service
Fibreglass Specialist**

THE GUILD OF MASTER CRAFTSMEN

Tel: 01275 878136
Mobile: 07947 041916

Email:
jo.line@boatrepaircentre.co.uk

Kenn Road, Kenn, North Somerset, BS21 6TJ

2007/M&WC135/f

www.boatrepaircentre.co.uk

BRISTOL CLASSIC BOAT COMPANY

REDCLIFFE WHARF
BRISTOL BS1 6SR

REPAIRS, REFITS AND NEW BUILDS

2007/M&WC154/z

0117 930 0891

11

docklands

Sail right into the heart of it.

DUBLIN CITY MOORINGS

One of the benefits of berthing at Dublin City Moorings is that you are right in the heart of one of Europe's most exciting capitals – a cosmopolitan young city with a world-renowned cultural scene.

• Berthing available for yachts up to 1000 tonnes
• Draught 4.2 m. LAT
• 3 phase electricity, water, pump-out, wheelchair access

Contact: info@dublindocklands.ie

DUBLIN DOCKLANDS
DEVELOPMENT AUTHORITY

2007/M&WC155/z

52-55 Sir John Rogerson's Quay, Docklands, Dublin 2.
t: +353 1 818 3300   f:+353 1 818 3399   www.dublindocklands.ie

SOUTH IRELAND - Malahide, south to Liscanor Bay

ADLARD COLES NAUTICAL
WEATHER FORECASTS
BY FAX & TELEPHONE

Coastal/Inshore	2-day by Fax	5-day by Phone
Northern Ireland	09065 222 355	09068 969 655
Wales	09065 222 350	09068 969 650
Bristol	09065 222 349	09068 969 649
South West	09065 222 348	09068 969 648
National (3-5 day)	09065 222 340	09068 969 640

Offshore	2-5 day by Fax	2-5 day by Phone
Irish Sea	09065 222 359	09068 969 659
English Channel	09065 222 357	09068 969 657
Biscay	09065 222 360	09068 969 660
North West Scotland	09065 222 361	09068 969 661

09068 CALLS COST 60P PER MIN. 09065 CALLS COST £1.50 PER MIN.

Key to Marina Plans symbols

Calor Gas		Parking	
Chandler		Pub/Restaurant	
Disabled facilities		Pump out	
Electrical supply		Rigging service	
Electrical repairs		Sail repairs	
Engine repairs		Shipwright	
First Aid		Shop/Supermarket	
Fresh Water		Showers	
Fuel - Diesel		Slipway	
Fuel - Petrol		Toilets	
Hardstanding/boatyard		Telephone	
Internet Café		Trolleys	
Laundry facilities		Visitors berths	
Lift-out facilities		Wi-Fi	

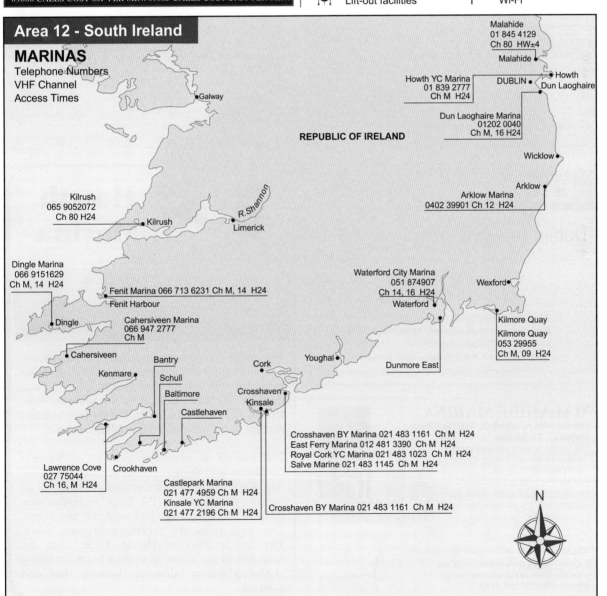

Area 12 - South Ireland

MARINAS
Telephone Numbers
VHF Channel
Access Times

REPUBLIC OF IRELAND

Malahide
01 845 4129
Ch 80 HW±4
Malahide

Howth YC Marina
01 839 2777
Ch M H24

DUBLIN • Howth
Dun Laoghaire

Dun Laoghaire Marina
01202 0040
Ch M, 16 H24

Wicklow

Arklow

Arklow Marina
0402 39901 Ch 12 H24

Galway

Kilrush
065 9052072
Ch 80 H24

Kilrush

R.Shannon
Limerick

Dingle Marina
066 9151629
Ch M, 14 H24

Fenit Marina 066 713 6231 Ch M, 14 H24
Fenit Harbour

Dingle

Cahersiveen Marina
066 947 2777
Ch M

Cahersiveen

Kenmare

Bantry

Schull

Baltimore

Castlehaven

Waterford City Marina
051 874907
Ch 14, 16 H24
Waterford

Youghal

Dunmore East

Cork

Crosshaven
Kinsale

Wexford

Kilmore Quay
Kilmore Quay
053 29955
Ch M, 09 H24

Crosshaven BY Marina 021 483 1161 Ch M H24
East Ferry Marina 012 481 3390 Ch M H24
Royal Cork YC Marina 021 483 1023 Ch M H24
Salve Marine 021 483 1145 Ch M H24

Lawrence Cove
027 75044
Ch 16, M H24

Crookhaven

Castlepark Marina
021 477 4959 Ch M H24
Kinsale YC Marina
021 477 2196 Ch M H24

Crosshaven BY Marina 021 483 1161 Ch M H24

N

12

MALAHIDE MARINA

Malahide Marina
Malahide, Co. Dublin
Tel: +353 1 845 4129 Fax: +353 1 845 4255
Email: info@malahidemarina.net
www.malahidemarina.net

| VHF | Ch 37, 80 |
| ACCESS | HW±4 |

Malahide Marina, situated just 10 minutes from Dublin Airport and 20 minutes north of Dublin's city centre, is a fully serviced marina accommodating up to 350 yachts. Capable of taking vessels of up to 75m in length, its first class facilities include a boatyard with hard standing for approximately 170 boats and a 30-ton mobile hoist. Its on site restaurant, Cruzzo, provides a large seating area in convivial surroundings. The village of Malahide has plenty to offer the visiting yachtsmen, with a wide variety of eating places, nearby golf courses and tennis courts as well as a historic castle and botanical gardens.

FACILITIES AT A GLANCE

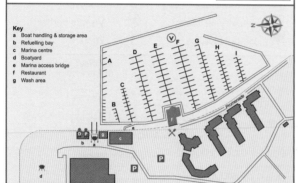

Key
a Boat handling & storage area
b Refuelling bay
c Marina centre
d Boatyard
e Marina access bridge
f Restaurant
g Wash area

HOWTH MARINA

Howth Marina
Howth Marina, Harbour Road, Howth, Co. Dublin
Tel: +353 1 8392777 Fax: +353 1 8392430
Email: marina@hyc.ie
www.hyc.ie

| VHF | Ch 37A, 80 |
| ACCESS | H24 |

Based on the north coast of the rugged peninsula that forms the northern side of Dublin Bay, Howth Marina is ideally situated for north or south-bound traffic in the Irish Sea. Well sheltered in all winds, it can be entered at any state of the tide. Overlooking the marina is Howth Yacht Club, which has in recent years been expanded and is now said to be the largest yacht club in Ireland. With good road and rail links, Howth is in easy reach of Dublin's airport and ferry terminal, making it an obvious choice for crew changeovers.

FACILITIES AT A GLANCE

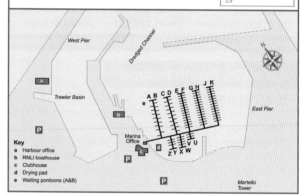

Key
a Harbour office
b RNLI boathouse
c Clubhouse
d Drying pad
e Waiting pontoons (A&B)

---

docklands

Dublin City Moorings

Custom House Quay, Docklands, Dublin 1

the only mooring in the Centre of Dublin City

Beside the Custom House and IFSC.
Electricity/water. Showers/toilets. 24 hour security.
Swipe card access.
Telephone +353 1 8183300 Fax: +353 1 8183399
Email: info@dublindocklands.ie Website: http://www.dublindocklands.ie

2007/M&WC46/e

Howth Marina

The marina is owned and managed by Howth Yacht Club. It is a perfect stopping off point being situated just north of Dublin Bay, mid way through the Irish Sea; it is 30 minutes from Dublin city centre and from Dublin International Airport, both accessible by public transport.

The marina is extremely safe in all weather conditions and there is access at all stages of the tide. Facilities include water and electricity to all berths, diesel pump, 24 hour reception and security, a drying out pad and 15 ton crane. Overnight rates are exceptionally good value. The full facilities of Howth Yacht Club are available to the crews of visiting boats including changing rooms, showers, laundry, bar and catering.

2007/M&WC67/e

MALAHIDE MARINA

Marina Centre, Malahide Marina Village, Malahide, Co. Dublin
350 Berths in fully serviced marina.
On-shore facilities include showers/bath, laundry and Disabled facilities.
Full service boatyard
Covered Repair Facility for re-fits.
10 minutes from Dublin Airport
25 minutes from Dublin City
Idyllic setting with beach, golf, restaurants and many other amenities.
The Ideal Cruise in Company destination.
e-mail: info@malahidemarina.net
website: www.malahidemarina.net
Phone: 003531 845 4129

Irish Marine Federation
Member

British Marine Federation

2007/M&WC88/e

pro rig
SAFETY • MARINE • ARCHITECTURAL
STOCKISTS FOR: GUL · HENRI LLOYD · HARKEN · spinlock · FUSION

2007/M&WC76/e

ProRig caters for all your cruising, racing and dinghy needs offering a complete rigging service, and carrying a wide range of clothing, deck gear, chandlery, electronics and accessories.

16a West Pier, Howth, Co Dublin.
t: +353 1 839 6434 f: +353 1 832 3473
e: info@prorig.ie www.prorig.ie

Specialists in Race Preparation

carrickcraft
2007/M&WC121/e

Chandlery, ropes, nuts and bolts, wetsuits, paint.
Also Bayliner, Orkney, Trophy boats, Funyak dinghies, Mariner outboards.

Carrickcraft
Malahide Marina
Co. Dublin

For more information, visit www.carrickcraft.com or call 01 845 5438

CMC
COLIN COADY MARINE

G.M.D.S.S. G.O.C.

Electrical & Electronic Engineering
For the marine environment:

■ Marine Communications & Navigational Aids
GPS, VHF, /DSC installation / repair

■ Marine Electrical Systems
Distribution Panel, Charging Solutions

■ Refit & Repair

2007/M&WN14312/z

Tel: 087 2656496

Email: colincoadymarine@gmail.com

DUN LAOGHAIRE MARINA

Dun Laoghaire Marina
Harbour Road, Dun Laoghaire, Co Dublin, Eire
Tel: +353 1 202 0040 Fax: +353 1 202 0043
Email: hal@dlmarina.com   www.dlmarina.com

VHF	Ch M, M2, 16
ACCESS	H24

With over 500 berths Dun Laoghaire Marina is Ireland's largest. Plans to add a further 200+ berths are in place. Approval for and installation of the expansion is expected for the summer of 2007. The Marina, located within the Dun Laoghaire Harbour, is adjacent to the STENA High Speed ferry terminal linking Dun Laoghaire with Holyhead – Anglesey – North Wales. Dun Laoghaire town centre is within a stones throw of the Marina and there are many choices of supermarkets, shops, restaurants, and chandlers . Berths are from 8 metres to 40 metres with a minimum draught of 3.6m LWS. With Dublin City centre at 12 km and Dublin Airport 22 km Dun Laoghaire Marina is an ideal location for planned crew change or cruise rest.

FACILITIES AT A GLANCE

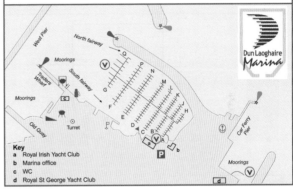

Key
a Royal Irish Yacht Club
b Marina office
c WC
d Royal St George Yacht Club

Dun Laoghaire *Marina*

WESTERN MARINE

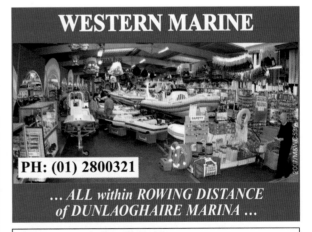

PH: (01) 2800321

... ALL within ROWING DISTANCE of DUNLAOGHAIRE MARINA ...

DUN LAOGHAIRE MARINA
Harbour Road, Dun Laoghaire, Co. Dublin
Tel: ++353 1 2020040
Fax: ++353 1 2020043
e-mail: info@dlmarina.com
www.dlmarina.com
Dun Laoghaire Marina is situated within 12 kms of Dublin City centre. Suburban rail/coach station within 60 metres provides services to City centre and Airport. STENA HSS terminal also within 60 metres. Facilities include: shore power, potable water, showers/toilets incl disabled, laundry, petrol/diesel, gas, pump-out, boatyard and hoist.
2007/M&WEXT4/z

When responding to adverts please mention Marina & Waypoint Guide 2007

12

ARKLOW MARINA

Arklow Marina
North Quay, Arklow, Co. Wicklow, Eire
Tel: +353 402 39901 Fax: +353 402 39902
Mobiles: 087 2375189 or 087 2515699
Email: technical@asl.ie
www.arklowmarina.com

VHF	Ch12
ACCESS	H24

Arklow is a popular fishing port and seaside town situated at the mouth of the River Avoca, just 16 miles south of Wicklow and 11 miles north east of Gorey. Historically noted for building small wooden boats, the town is ideally placed for visiting the many beauty spots of County Wicklow including Glenmalure, Glendalough and Clara Lara.

Lying on the north bank of the river, just upstream of the commercial quays, is Arklow Marina, which provides 42 berths in an inner harbour and 30 berths on pontoons outside the marina entrance. Note that vessels over 14m LOA should moor on the river pontoons. Just a five-minute walk from the town, the marina is within easy reach of as many as 19 pubs and several restaurants.

FACILITIES AT A GLANCE

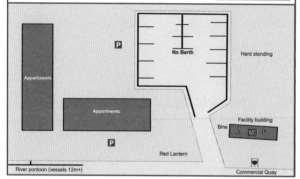

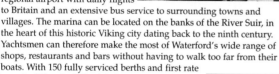

KILMORE QUAY

Kilmore Quay
Wexford, Ireland
Tel: +353 53 29955 Fax: +353 53 29915
Email: hmkilmore@eircom.net

VHF	Ch M
ACCESS	H24

Located in the SE corner of Ireland, Kilmore Quay is a small rural fishing village situated approximately 14 miles from the town of Wexford and 12 miles from Rosslare ferry port.

Its 55-berthed marina, offering shelter from the elements as well as various on shore facilities, has become a regular port of call for many cruising yachtsmen. Kilmore's fishing industry dates back over the last hundred years and among the species of fresh fish available are bass, shark, skate and whiting. With several nearby areas of either historical or natural significance, Kilmore is renowned for its 'green' approach to the environment.

FACILITIES AT A GLANCE

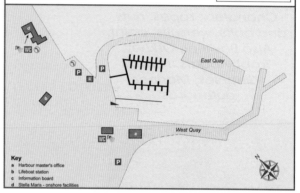

Key
a Harbour master's office
b Lifeboat station
c Information board
d Stella Maris - onshore facilities

WATERFORD MARINA

Waterford City Marina
Waterford, Ireland
Tel: +353 51 309900 Fax: +353 51 870813

VHF	Ch 12
ACCESS	H24

Famous for its connections with Waterford Crystal, now manufactured on the outskirts of the city, Waterford is the capital of the south east region of Ireland. As a major city, it benefits from good rail links with Dublin, Limerick and Rosslare, a regional airport with daily flights to Britain and an extensive bus service to surrounding towns and villages. The marina can be located on the banks of the River Suir, in the heart of this historic Viking city dating back to the ninth century. Yachtsmen can therefore make the most of Waterford's wide range of shops, restaurants and bars without having to walk too far from their boats. With 150 fully serviced berths and first rate security, Waterford City Marina now provides shower, toilet and laundry facilities in its new reception building.

FACILITIES AT A GLANCE

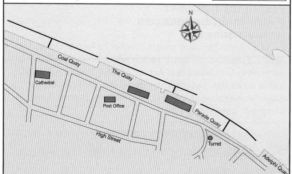

Eugene Curry

Marine Services Ltd.

Eugene F. Curry (Capt.)

Master Mariner

Dip Mar Sur, MNI, IIMM, MIIMS

45 Glenvara Park,

Knocklyon,

Dublin 16, Ireland.

Tel: 00353 1 493 9781

Fax: 00353 1 494 2195

Mobile: 00 353 86 257 0730

E-Mail: currymarineservices@eircom.net

2007/M&WC142/z

CROSSHAVEN BOATYARD MARINA

Crosshaven Boatyard Marina
Crosshaven, Co Cork, Ireland
Tel: +353 214 831161 Fax: +353 214 831603
Email: cby@eircom.net

VHF	Ch M
ACCESS	H24

One of three marinas at Crosshaven, Crosshaven Boatyard was founded in 1950 and originally made its name from the construction of some of the most world-renowned yachts, including *Gypsy Moth* and Denis Doyle's *Moonduster*. Nowadays, however, the yard

has diversified to provide a wide range of services to both the marine leisure and professional industries. Situated on a safe and sheltered river only 12 miles from Cork City Centre, the marina boasts 100 fully-serviced berths along with the capacity to accommodate yachts up to 35m LOA with a 4m draught. In addition, it is ideally situated for cruising the stunning south west coast of Ireland.

FACILITIES AT A GLANCE

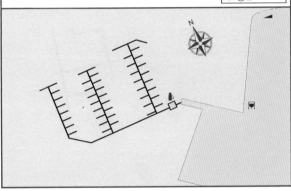

CHMARINE Ltd

Ireland's Largest Chandler - 14,000 Items in Stock
Excellent Spare Parts & Procurement Service

Skibbereen, Co. Cork
Tel: (028) 23190 Fax: (028) 22028

Frankfield Ind. Est. Cork City
Tel: (021) 431 5700 Fax: (021) 431 6160

IRELAND'S PREMIER MARINE SUPPLIER

2007/M&WM15/e

K. P. O'MAHONY & CO. LTD.
Survey House, Upton, County Cork, Ireland
Tel: +353 21 477 6150
Fax: +353 21 477 6152
e-mail: kpom@indigo.ie
We provide comprehensive commercial marine Surveying services, for yachts and all craft, GRP, steel, alloy, timber, machinery, structure, for Underwriters, P&I and Owners, for the South Ireland area.

2007/M&WL10/e

When responding to adverts please mention Marina & Waypoint Guide 2007

SALVE MARINE

Salve Marine
Crosshaven, Co Cork, Ireland
Tel: +353 214 831 145 Fax: +353 214 831 747
Email: salvemarine@eircom.net

VHF	Ch M
ACCESS	H24

Crosshaven is a picturesque seaside resort providing a gateway to Ireland's south and south west coasts. Offering a variety of activities to suit all types, its rocky coves and quiet sandy beaches stretch from Graball to Church Bay and from

Fennell's Bay to nearby Myrtleville. Besides a selection of craft shops selling locally produced arts and crafts, there are plenty of pubs, restaurants and takeaways to suit even the most discerning of tastes. Lying within a few hundred metres of the village centre is Salve Marine, accommodating yachts up to 43m LOA with draughts of up to 4m. Its comprehensive services range from engineering and welding facilities to hull and rigging repairs.

FACILITIES AT A GLANCE

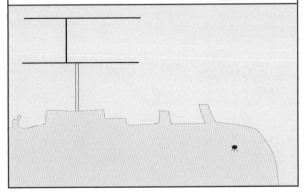

ROYAL CORK YACHT CLUB

Royal Cork Yacht Club Marina
Crosshaven, Co Cork, Ireland
Tel: +353 21 483 1023 Fax: +353 21 483 1586
Email: office@royalcork.com   www.royalcork.com

VHF	Ch M
ACCESS	H24

Founded in 1720, the Royal Cork Yacht Club is one of the oldest and most prominent yacht clubs in the world. Organising, among many other events, the prestigious biennial Ford Cork Week, it boasts a number of World, European and National sailors among its membership.

The Yacht Club's marina is situated at Crosshaven, which nestles on the hillside at the mouth of the Owenabue River just inside the entrance to Cork Harbour. The harbour is popular with yachtsmen as it is accessible and well sheltered in all weather conditions. It also benefits from the Gulf Stream producing a temperate climate practically all year round.

FACILITIES AT A GLANCE

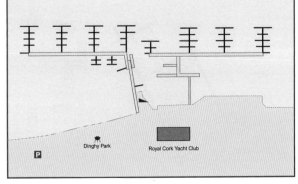

Dinghy Park   Royal Cork Yacht Club

12

EAST FERRY MARINA

East Ferry Marina
Cobh, Co Cork, Ireland
Tel: +353 21 481 1342 Fax: +353 21 481 1342

VHF | Ch 80
ACCESS | H24

East Ferry Marina lies on the east side of Great Island, one of three large islands in Cork Harbour which are now all joined by roads and bridges. Despite its remote, tranquil setting, it offers all the fundamental facilities including showers, water, fuel, electricity and that all important pub. The nearest town is Cobh, which is a good five mile walk away, albeit a pleasant one.

Formerly known as Queenstown, Cobh (pronounced 'cove') reverted back to its original Irish name in 1922 and is renowned for being the place from where thousands of Irish men and women set off to America to build a new life for themselves, particularly during the famine years of 1844–48.

FACILITIES AT A GLANCE

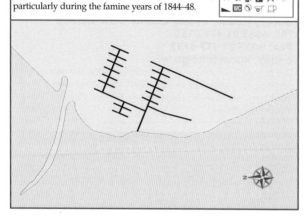

KINSALE YACHT CLUB MARINA

Kinsale Yacht Club Marina
Kinsale, Co Cork, Ireland
Tel: +353 21 4772196 Fax: +353 21 4774455
Email: kyc@iol.ie

VHF | Ch M
ACCESS | H24

Kinsale is a natural, virtually land-locked harbour on the estuary of the Bandon River, approximately 12 miles south west of Cork harbour entrance. Home to a thriving fishing fleet as well as frequented by commercial shipping, it boasts two fully serviced marinas, with the Kinsale Yacht Club & Marina being the closest to the town. Visitors to this marina automatically become temporary members of the club and are therefore entitled to make full use of the facilities, which include a fully licensed bar and restaurant serving evening meals on Wednesdays, Thursdays and Saturdays. Fuel, water and repairs services are also readily available.

FACILITIES AT A GLANCE

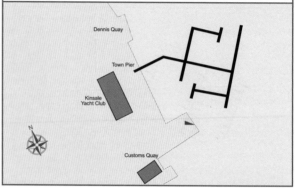

CASTLEPARK MARINA

Castlepark Marina Centre
Kinsale, Co Cork, Ireland
Tel: +353 21 4774959 Fax: +353 21 4774595
Email: maritime@indigo.ie

VHF | Ch M
ACCESS | H24

Situated on the south side of Kinsale Harbour, Castlepark is a small marina with deep water pontoon berths that are accessible at all states of the tide. Surrounded by rolling hills, it boasts its own beach as well as being in close proximity to the parklands of James Fort and a traditional Irish pub. The attractive town of Kinsale, with its narrow streets and slate-clad houses, lies just 1.5 miles away by road or five minutes away by ferry. Known as Ireland's 'fine food centre', it incorporates a number of gourmet food shops and high quality restaurants as well as a wine museum.

FACILITIES AT A GLANCE

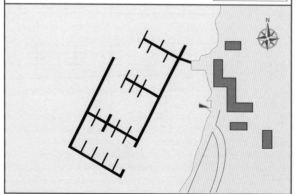

LAWRENCE COVE MARINA

Lawrence Cove Marina
Lawrence Cove, Bere Island, Co Cork, Ireland
Tel: +353 27 75044 Fax: +353 27 75044
Email: lcm@iol.ie
www.lawrencecovemarina.com

VHF | Ch 16
ACCESS | H24

Lawrence Cove enjoys a peaceful location on an island at the entrance to Bantry Bay. Privately owned and run, it offers sheltered and secluded waters as well as excellent facilities and fully serviced pontoon berths. A few hundred yards from the marina you will

find a shop, pub and restaurant, while the mainland, with its various attractions, can be easily reached by ferry. Lawrence Cove lies at the heart of the wonderful cruising grounds of Ireland's south west coast and, just two hours from Cork airport, is an ideal place to leave your boat for long or short periods.

FACILITIES AT A GLANCE

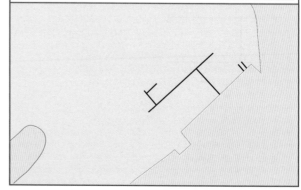

CAHERSIVEEN MARINA

Cahersiveen Marina
The Pier, Cahersiveen, Co. Kerry, Ireland
Tel: +353 66 9472777 Fax: +353 66 9472993
Email: info@cahersiveenmarina.ie
www.cahersiveenmarina.ie

VHF Ch M
ACCESS H24

Situated two miles up Valentia
River from Valentia Harbour,
Cahersiveen Marina is well
protected in all wind directions
and is convenient for sailing to
Valentia Island and Dingle Bay
as well as for visiting some
of the spectacular uninhabited
islands in the surrounding area.

Boasting a host of sheltered sandy beaches, the region is renowned
for salt and fresh water fishing as well as being
good for scuba diving.

Within easy walking distance of the marina lies
the historic town of Cahersiveen, incorporating an
array of convivial pubs and restaurants.

FACILITIES AT A GLANCE

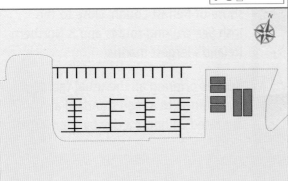

DINGLE MARINA

Dingle Marina
Strand Street, Dingle, Co Kerry, Ireland
Tel: +353 66 9151629 Fax: +353 66 9152629
Email:1dingle@eircom.net   www.dinglemarina.com

VHF Ch M
ACCESS H24

Dingle is Ireland's most
westerly marina, lying at
the heart of the sheltered
Dingle Harbour, and is easily
reached both day and night
via a well buoyed approach
channel. The surrounding
area is an interesting and
unfrequented cruising
ground, with several islands,
bays and beaches for the yachtsman to explore.

The marina lies in the heart of the old market town, renowned for
its hospitality and traditional Irish pub music.
Besides enjoying the excellent seafood restaurants
and 52 pubs, other recreational pastimes include
horse riding, golf, climbing and diving.

FACILITIES AT A GLANCE

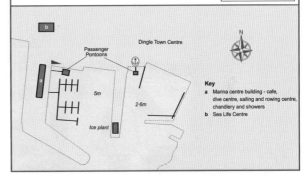

Key
a Marina centre building - cafe,
dive centre, sailing and rowing centre,
chandlery and showers
b Sea Life Centre

FENIT HARBOUR MARINA

Fenit Harbour
Fenit, Tralee, Co. Kerry, Republic of Ireland
Tel: +353 66 7136231 Fax: +353 66 7136473
Email: fenitmarina@eircom.net

VHF Ch M
ACCESS H24

Fenit Harbour Marina is
tucked away in Tralee Bay,
not far south of the
Shannon Estuary. Besides
offering a superb cruising
ground, being within a
day's sail of Dingle and
Kilrush, the marina also

provides a convenient base from which to visit inland attractions such
as the picturesque tourist towns of Tralee and Killarney. This 120-berth
marina accommodates boats up to 15m LOA and benefits from deep
water at all states of the tide.

The small village of Fenit incorporates a grocery
shop as well a several pubs and restaurants, while
among the local activities are horse riding, swimming
from one of the nearby sandy beaches and golfing.

FACILITIES AT A GLANCE

Key
a Fenit Seaworld
b Fish store
c Warehouse
d Marina services, harbour office,
lifeboat station

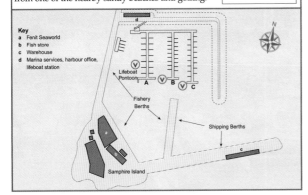

KILRUSH MARINA

Kilrush Creek Marina Ltd
Kilrush, Co. Clare, Ireland
Tel: +353 65 9052072 Fax: +353 65 9051692
Email: hehir@shannon.dev.ie

VHF Ch 80
ACCESS H24

Kilrush Marina and boatyard is
strategically placed for exploring
the unspoilt west coast of
Ireland, including Galway Bay,
Dingle, West Cork and Kerry. It
also provides a gateway to over
150 miles of cruising on Lough
Derg, the River Shannon and the
Irish canal system. Accessed via
lock gates, the marina lies at one

end of the main street in Kilrush, a vibrant market town with a long
maritime history. A 15-minute ferry ride from the marina takes you to
Scattery Island, once a sixth century monastic settlement but now
uninhabited except by wildlife. The Shannon
Estuary is reputed for being the country's first
marine Special Area of Conservation (SAC) and is
home to Ireland's only known resident group of
bottlenose dolphins.

FACILITIES AT A GLANCE

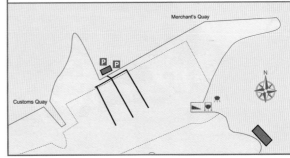

12

CONWY QUAYS

PENARTH QUAYS

PORTISHEAD QUAYS

ROYAL QUAYS

bangor marina

QUAY
M·A·R·I·N·A·S

Bangor Marina is situated on the south shore of Belfast Lough, close to the Irish Sea cruising routes and is Northern Ireland's largest marina.

Besides offering all the usual facilities, maintained to a high standard and operated 24 hours a day by friendly staff, the marina is perfectly situated for visitors to explore the town and the North Down area.

Quay Marinas operate four other large marinas within the UK at Conwy, Penarth, Portishead and Newcastle upon Tyne.

www.quaymarinas.com

2007/M&WC26/e

NORTH IRELAND - Lambay Island, north to Liscanor Bay

ADLARD COLES NAUTICAL
WEATHER FORECASTS
BY FAX & TELEPHONE

Coastal/Inshore	2-day by Fax	5-day by Phone
Caledonia	09065 222 353	09068 969 653
Northern Ireland	09065 222 355	09068 969 655
Clyde	09065 222 352	09068 969 652
North West	09065 222 341	09068 969 641
National (3-5 day)	09065 222 340	09068 969 640

Offshore	2-5 day by Fax	2-5 day by Phone
Irish Sea	09065 222 359	09068 969 659
English Channel	09065 222 357	09068 969 657
Biscay	09065 222 360	09068 969 660
North West Scotland	09065 222 361	09068 969 661

09068 CALLS COST 60P PER MIN. 09065 CALLS COST £1.50 PER MIN.

Key to Marina Plans symbols

Calor Gas		P	Parking
Chandler			Pub/Restaurant
Disabled facilities			Pump out
Electrical supply			Rigging service
Electrical repairs			Sail repairs
Engine repairs			Shipwright
First Aid			Shop/Supermarket
Fresh Water			Showers
Fuel - Diesel			Slipway
Fuel - Petrol		WC	Toilets
Hardstanding/boatyard			Telephone
@ Internet Café			Trolleys
Laundry facilities		V	Visitors berths
Lift-out facilities			Wi-Fi

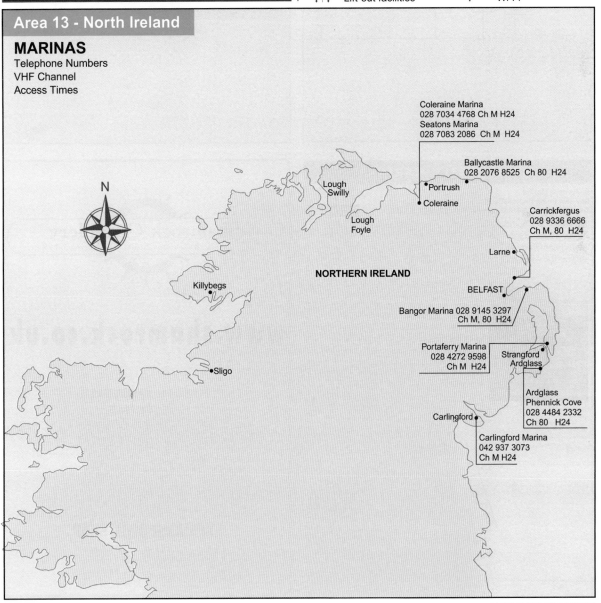

Area 13 - North Ireland

MARINAS
Telephone Numbers
VHF Channel
Access Times

Coleraine Marina
028 7034 4768 Ch M H24
Seatons Marina
028 7083 2086 Ch M H24

Ballycastle Marina
028 2076 8525 Ch 80 H24

Carrickfergus
028 9336 6666
Ch M, 80 H24

Lough Swilly

Lough Foyle

Portrush
Coleraine

Larne

NORTHERN IRELAND

BELFAST

Killybegs

Bangor Marina 028 9145 3297
Ch M, 80 H24

Portaferry Marina
028 4272 9598
Ch M H24

Strangford
Ardglass

Ardglass
Phennick Cove
028 4484 2332
Ch 80 H24

Sligo

Carlingford

Carlingford Marina
042 937 3073
Ch M H24

COLERAINE MARINA

Coleraine Marina
64 Portstewart Road, Coleraine,
Co Londonderry, BT52 1RS
Tel: 028 7034 4768

VHF	Ch M1
ACCESS	H24

Coleraine Marina and Caravan complex enjoys a superb location in sheltered waters just one mile north of the town of Coleraine and four and a half miles south of the River Bann Estuary and the open sea. Besides accommodating vessels up to 18m LOA, this modern marina with 105 berths offers hard standing, fuel, a chandlery and shower facilities.

Among one of the oldest known settlements in Ireland, Coleraine is renowned for its linen, whiskey and salmon. Its thriving commercial centre includes numerous shops, a four-screen cinema and ice rink as well as a state-of-the-art leisure complex.

FACILITIES AT A GLANCE

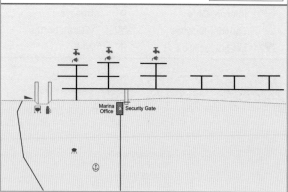

SEATONS MARINA

Seatons Marina
Drumslade Rd, Coleraine, Londonderry, BT52 1SE
Tel: 028 7083 2086
Email: ssp@seatonsmarina.co.uk www.seatonsmarina.co.uk

VHF	Ch M
ACCESS	H24

Seatons Marina is a privately owned business on the north coast of Ireland, which was established by Eric Seaton in 1962. It lies on the east bank of the River Bann, approximately two miles downstream from Coleraine and three miles from the sea. Although facilities are currently rather limited, plans are underway to improve the services available to yachtsmen. The pontoon berths are suitable for yachts up to 13.5m, with a minimum depth of 2.4m on the outer berths, although some of the inner berths do occasionally dry out. Seatons is also able to provide swinging moorings, all of which come with a galvanised chain riser passed over the stem roller.

FACILITIES AT A GLANCE

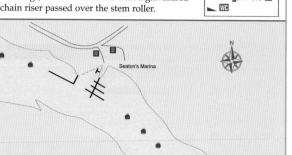

BALLYCASTLE MARINA

Ballycastle Marina
Bayview Road, Ballycastle, Northern Ireland
Tel: 028 2076 8525/07803 505084 Fax: 028 2076 6215

VHF	Ch 80

Ballycastle is a traditional seaside town situated on Northern Ireland's North Antrim coast. The 74-berthed, sheltered marina provides a perfect base from which to explore the well known local attractions such as the Giant's Causeway world heritage site, the spectacular

Nine Glens of Antrim, and Rathlin, the only inhabited island in Northern Ireland. The most northern coastal marina in Ireland, Ballycastle is accessible at all states of the tide, although yachts are required to contact the marina on VHF Ch 80 before entering the harbour. Along the seafront are a selection of restaurants, bars and shops, while the town centre is only about a five-minute walk away.

FACILITIES AT A GLANCE

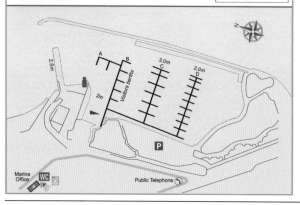

Shamrock Chandlery
Shamrock Quay, William Street, Northam, Southampton SO14 5QL

www.shamrock.co.uk

MAIL ORDER
HOTLINE
Tel: (02380) 632725
Fax (02380) 225611

2007/M&WC160/z

EXPANDED BOOK SHOP

13

CARRICKFERGUS WATERFRONT

Carrickferus Waterfront
3 Quayside, Carrickfergus, Co. Antrim, BT38 8BE
Tel: 028 9336 6666 Fax: 028 9335 0505
Email: gduggan.marina@carrickfergus.org
www.carrickferguswaterfront.co.uk

| VHF | Ch 37, 80 |
| ACCESS | H24 |

Located on the north shore of Belfast Lough, Carrickfergus Waterfront incorporates two sheltered areas suitable for leisure craft. The harbour is dominated by a magnificent 12th century Norman Castle which, recently renovated, includes a film theatre, banqueting room and outdoor models depicting the castle's chequered history.

The marina is located 250 metres west of the harbour and has become increasingly popular since its opening in 1985. A range of shops and restaurants along the Waterfront caters for most yachtsmen's needs.

FACILITIES AT A GLANCE

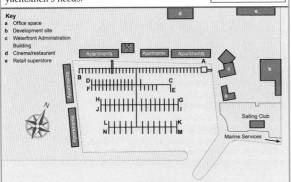

Key
a   Office space
b   Development site
c   Waterfront Administration Building
d   Cinema/restaurant
e   Retail superstore

Carrickfergus Borough

Carrickfergus Marina
3 Quayside, Carrickfergus BT38 8BE
T: +44 (0) 28 9336 6666   F: +44 (0) 28 9335 0505
E: waterfront@carrickfergus.org

SPECIAL OFFER
Upon presentation of this publication, you will receive a second night's accomodation free, subject to the first night being paid in advance.

Adlard Coles Nautical
THE BEST SAILING BOOKS

All Weather Sailing with
Adlard Coles Nautical

Heavy Weather Sailing
Peter Bruce
0 7136 6867 9
£35.00

TO ORDER   Tel: **01256 302692** or visit **www.adlardcoles.com**

On Site Service

MASSEY MARINE

ALL DIESEL & PETROL ENGINES OVERHAULED, SERVICED OR REPAIRED
MARINE ELECTRICAL WIRING INSTALLATIONS CARRIED OUT

WE ARE LOCAL AGENTS FOR   **DockSafe**

▲ Fender system fixed to dock

Enjoy stress-free docking!

▲ Unique energy saving absorption properties

▲ Gives total hull protection

▲ No inflatable fenders needed during docking

▲ For boats up to 25 tonnes

Contact **MASSEY**MARINE to find out more about *stress-free docking!*

4 Sperrin Drive, Belfast BT5 7RY

Tel: 028 9048 7718 (after hours) • Mobile: 07967 688869
Email: masseymarine@googlemail.com

BANGOR MARINA

Quay Marinas Limited
Bangor Marina, Bangor, Co. Down, BT20 5ED
Tel: 028 9145 3297 Fax: 028 9145 3450
Email: ajaggers@quaymarinas.com
www.quaymarinas.com

VHF	Ch 11, 80
ACCESS	H24

Situated on the south shore of Belfast Lough, Bangor is located close to the Irish Sea cruising routes. The Marina is right at the town's centre, within walking distance of shops, restaurants, hotels and bars. The Tourist information centre is across the road from marina reception and there are numerous visitors' attractions in the Borough. The Royal Ulster Yacht Club and the Ballyholme Yacht Club are both nearby and welcome visitors.

FACILITIES AT A GLANCE

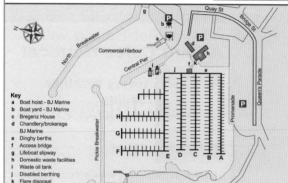

Key
a Boat hoist - BJ Marine
b Boat yard - BJ Marine
c Bregenz House
d Chandlery/brokerage
   BJ Marine
e Dinghy berths
f Access bridge
g Lifeboat slipway
h Domestic waste facilities
i Waste oil tank
j Disabled berthing
k Flare disposal

Bangor Marina is situated on the south shore of Belfast Lough, close to the Irish Sea cruising routes and is Northern Ireland's largest marina.

Besides offering all the usual facilities, maintained to a high standard and operated 24 hours a day by friendly staff, the marina is perfectly situated for visitors to explore the town and the North Down area.

Quay Marinas operate four other large marinas within the UK at Conwy, Penarth, Portishead and Newcastle upon Tyne.

www.quaymarinas.com

QUAY MARINAS LTD
Avon House, Newbrick Road, Stokegifford,
Bristol BS34 8RA
Tel: (01179) 236466
Fax: (01179) 236508
e-mail: sriggs@quaymarinas.com
A wholly owned subsidiary of Quay Marinas, operate comprehensive yachting facilities at 5 locations in the UK and are marketing agents for Malahide Marina in Dublin Bay.

2007/M&WEXT9/e

2007/M&WM14A/e

KTS
SEA SAFETY

The Harbour, Kilkeel, Co. Down, BT34 4AX
Tel: (028) 4176 2655 Fax: (028) 4176 4502

✔ **APPROVED Liferaft**
   Service Station

✔ **Marine Safety Equipment**

✔ **Expert Sales & Service**

NEW OUTLET NOW OPEN!

Jubilee Road
NEWTOWNARDS
Tel: (028) 918 28405
Fax: (028) 918 28410

CHMARINE
(NI) Ltd
Part of CH Marine Ltd. Company

B. J. MARINE LTD

NEW & SECONDHAND BOAT SALES

◆ Large selection of new and secondhand boat sales
◆ Good quality boats always required for brokerage

SAIL
Beneteau
Wauquiez
CNB

POWER
SeaRay　Beneteau Antares
Princess　Bombard Inflatable
Cranchi　& Semi Rigid

SERVICES

B&G
Garmin
Raymarine
Bombard Liferafts
Baltic Lifejackets
Mercruiser

Profurl
Sparcraft

◆ Authorised Brookes & Gatehouse Dealers
◆ Chandlery
◆ Sales & Service
◆ Full boatyard services
◆ Storage
◆ Engine and electrical repair & testing facilities
◆ Approved Mercruiser Service Centre
◆ Emergency call-out service available

2007/M&WM23/z

Bangor Marina, Bangor, Co. Down, BT20 5ED
Telephone: 028 91 271434/271395 Fax: 028 91 271529
Email: bangor@bjmarine.net　　Web: www.bjmarine.net

PORTAFERRY MARINA

Portaferry Marina
11 The Strand, Portaferry, BT22 1PF
Tel: 028 4272 9598 Mobile: 07703 209 780 Fax: 028 4272 9784
Email: barholm.portaferry@virgin.net

VHF	Ch M
ACCESS	H24

Portaferry Marina lies on the east shore of the Narrows, the gateway to Strangford Lough on the north east coast of Ireland. A marine nature reserve of outstanding natural beauty, the Lough offers plenty of recreational activities. The marina, which caters for draughts of up to 2.5m, is fairly small, at present accommodating around 30 yachts. The office is situated about 200m from the marina itself, where you will find ablution facilities along with a launderette.

Portaferry incorporates several pubs and restaurants as well as a few convenience stores, while one of its prime attractions is the Exploris Aquarium. Places of historic interest in the vicinity include Castleward, an 18th century mansion in Strangford, and Mount Stewart House & Garden in Newtownards, both of which are owned by the National Trust.

FACILITIES AT A GLANCE

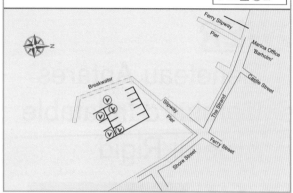

PHENNICK COVE MARINA

Phennick Cove Marina
19 Quay Street, Ardglass, BT30 7SA
Tel: 028 4484 2332 Fax: 028 4484 2332
Email: ardglassmarina@tiscali.co.uk
www.ardglassmarina.co.uk

VHF	Ch 37, 80
ACCESS	H24

Situated just south of Strangford, Ardglass has the capacity to accommodate up to 33 yachts as well as space for small craft. Despite being relatively small in size, the marina boasts an extensive array of facilities, either on site or close at hand. Most of the necessary shops, including grocery stores, a post office, chemist and off-licence, are all within a five-minute walk from the marina. Among the local onshore activities are golf, mountain climbing in Newcastle, which is 18 miles south, as well as scenic walks at Ardglass and Delamont Park.

FACILITIES AT A GLANCE

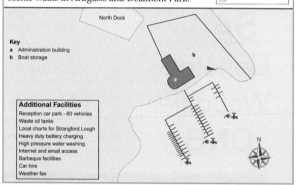

North Dock

Key
a   Administration building
b   Boat storage

Additional Facilities
Reception car park - 60 vehicles
Waste oil tanks
Local charts for Strangford Lough
Heavy duty battery charging
High pressure water washing
Internet and email access
Barbeque facilities
Car hire
Weather fax

PORTAFERRY
MARINA

Portaferry Marina

The gateway to Strangford Lough
An area of outstanding natural beauty

Offers visiting pontoon berthing facilities

Caters for boats with up to 2.5 metres draft
On site water and electric facilities
10 VISITOR BERTHS
Toilets and showers are available at
Barholm which is located nearby

2007M&WM156/a

CONTACT:
John Murray, Berthing Master
Mobile: 0770 320 9780
Office: 028 427 29598

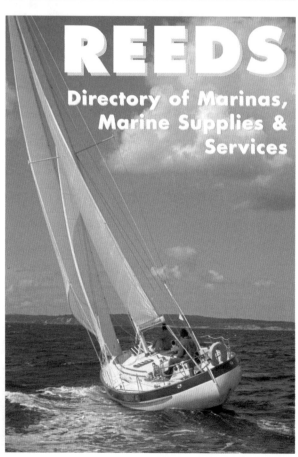

REEDS
Directory of Marinas, Marine Supplies & Services

CARLINGFORD MARINA

Carlingford Marina
Co. Louth, Ireland
Tel: +353 (0)42 937 3073   Fax: +353 (0)42 937 3075
Email: cmarina@iol.ie
www.carlingfordmarina.ie

| VHF | Ch 37 |
| ACCESS | H24 |

Carlingford Lough is an eight-mile sheltered haven between the Cooley Mountains to the south and the Mourne Mountains to the north. The marina is situated on the southern shore, about four miles from Haulbowline Lighthouse, and can be easily reached via a deep water shipping channel. Among the most attractive destinations in the Irish Sea, Carlingford is only 60 miles from the Isle of Man and within a day's sail from Strangford Lough and Ardglass. Full facilities in the marina include a first class bar and restaurant offering superb views across the water.

FACILITIES AT A GLANCE

Key
a Bar and restaurant
b Toilets, showers and laundry
c Refuse
d Office
e Chandlery
f Marina office
g Waiting pontoon

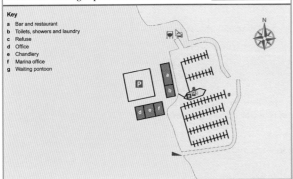

Part of CH Marine Ltd. Company

KTS SEA SAFETY
The Harbour, Kilkeel, Co. Down, BT34 4AX
Tel: (028) 4176 2655   Fax: (028) 4176 4502
- APPROVED Liferaft Service Station
- Marine Safety Equipment
- Expert Sales & Service
NEW OUTLET OPEN in Newtownards!
CHMARINE (NI) Ltd
Jubilee Rd, Newtownards
Tel: (028) 918 28405
Fax: (028) 918 28410
2007/M&WM14B/e

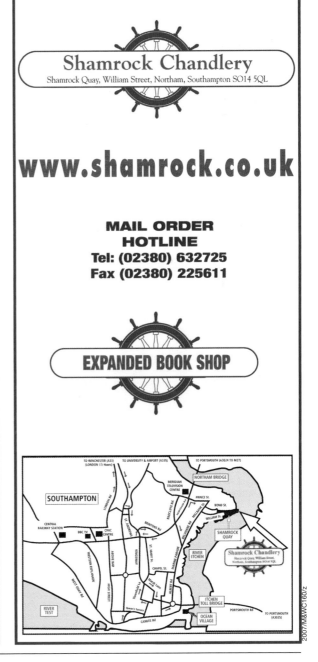

Shamrock Chandlery
Shamrock Quay, William Street, Northam, Southampton SO14 5QL

www.shamrock.co.uk

MAIL ORDER HOTLINE
Tel: (02380) 632725
Fax (02380) 225611

EXPANDED BOOK SHOP

2007/M&WC160/z

Tel: (00353) 42 9373073
Fax: (00353) 42 9373075
Email: cmarine@iol.ie
www.carlingfordmarine.com
VHF Channel 37 or 16

Carlingford Marina situated on the South Western side of Carlingford lough 1Km North of the medieval village of Carlingford, with its hotels, restaurants, pubs, Post Office, supermarket, newsagent, bicycle hire, angling centre, adventure centre, horse riding. Golf course at Greenore.

- **200 Berths most with power (card meter) and water. Max LOA 30 metres.**
- **Diesel available on fuel quay.**
- **Shower, toilets and laundry facilities.**
- **50T travel lift, winter storage and slipway.**
- **Chandlery, Bar and Restaurant with public telephone.**

2007/M&WC50/e

JACKSON YACHT SERVICES

Established for over 20 years, a traditional boatyard owned by Mike and Kay Jackson

Contact Mike about all aspects of yacht management, and Kay to discuss the sale of your vessel and for assistance in your search for the ideal yacht from the largest sailing vessel to the smallest dinghy. Also contact us for boat surveys.

 Zodiac Boat Sales and Service

What we do
Liferaft, Lifejacket, Sales, Hire and Service Jersey's only British Marine and Coastguard Agency (MCA) approved service station qualifying us to service commercial and yachting liferafts to the most stringent specifications. We pride ourselves on meticulous care and attention with your safety equipment and regularly attend manufacturers premises in order to keep abreast of the various liferaft packing methods so that your lifesaving apparatus will operate efficiently when required. We are sales agents and have been awarded servicing certificates for the following manufacturers: - Zodiac, Bombard, RFD, ML Lifeguard, BFA (XM), Plastimo, and Crewsaver. Owners of rafts are advised to have them serviced by a properly certificated service station as recommended by their manufacturer to ensure validity of guarantees.

Brokerage
Buying or selling, we can help. Come and look through our listings or visit our website for further details of the vessels we have for sale.

Chandlery
We stock a large range of traditional and modern chandlery including nautical publications, books and charts, paints, varnishes and antifouling. A complrehensive selection of ropes, blocks and shackles together with boat fishing tackle enables us to supply boat owners with most of their needs.

Clothing
Fashionable and conventional yachting clothing for adults and children by TBS, Le Glazic, Coude Maille, and Guy Cotton. Extensive leather deck shoe range by TBS, as well as boots, offshore foul weather gear and equipment.

Boat Repairs and Maintenance
Motor & Sailing yacht repairs in GRP and timber, lifting out up to 65 Ton, cleaning and antifouling undertaken. All types of moorings made up and laid from deep water to marina berth.

Rigging Loft
Have your rigging checked, repaired or renewed by experienced staff. Masts, spars and furling gear supplied and fitted. Wire swageing machinery in workshop. Specialists in architectural rigging and wire work.

Sail Loft
All types of sails and covers supplied, valeted and repaired.

Yacht Management
Comprehensive management service ensuring smooth and cost effective running of your vessel. Marine consultancy and guardiennage service for non resident owners. We are a small, owner operated business and pride ourselves in the attention to detail commonly missing in large enterprises to-day. We look forward to meeting you and pledge our commitment to fulfil your boating requirements in connection with the smallest dinghy to the largest yacht.

2007/M&WC58/e

Le Boulevard, St Aubin, Jersey, Channel Islands JE3 8AB
+44 (0) 1534 743819   +44 (0) 1534 745952
sales@jacksonyacht.com • www.jacksonyacht.com

CHANNEL ISLANDS - Guernsey, Jersey & Alderney

ADLARD COLES NAUTICAL
WEATHER FORECASTS

Coastal/Inshore	2-day by Fax	5-day by Phone
Bristol	09065 222 349	09068 969 649
South West	09065 222 348	09068 969 648
Mid Channel	09065 222 347	09068 969 647
Channel Islands	–	09068 969 656
National (3-5 day)	09065 222 340	09068 969 640

Offshore	2-5 day by Fax	2-5 day by Phone
English Channel	09065 222 357	09068 969 657
Southern North Sea	09065 222 358	09068 969 658
Irish Sea	09065 222 359	09068 969 659
Biscay	09065 222 360	09068 969 660

09068 CALLS COST 60P PER MIN. 09065 CALLS COST £1.50 PER MIN.

Key to Marina Plans symbols

Calor Gas		P	Parking
Chandler			Pub/Restaurant
Disabled facilities			Pump out
Electrical supply			Rigging service
Electrical repairs			Sail repairs
Engine repairs			Shipwright
First Aid			Shop/Supermarket
Fresh Water			Showers
Fuel - Diesel			Slipway
Fuel - Petrol		WC	Toilets
Hardstanding/boatyard			Telephone
@ Internet Café			Trolleys
Laundry facilities		V	Visitors berths
Lift-out facilities			Wi-Fi

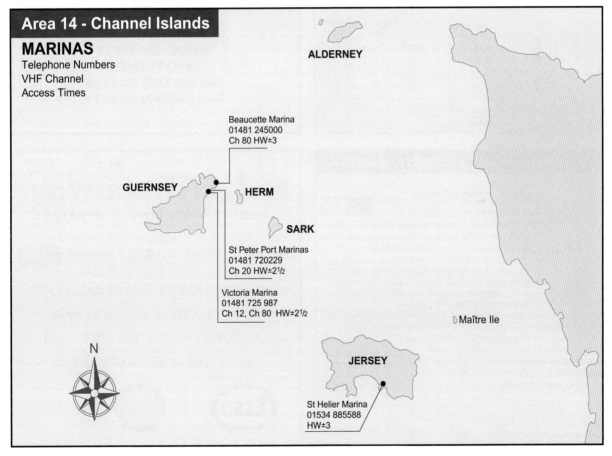

Area 14 - Channel Islands
MARINAS
Telephone Numbers
VHF Channel
Access Times

ALDERNEY

Beaucette Marina
01481 245000
Ch 80 HW±3

GUERNSEY   HERM

SARK

St Peter Port Marinas
01481 720229
Ch 20 HW±2½

Victoria Marina
01481 725 987
Ch 12, Ch 80 HW±2½

Maître Ile

JERSEY

St Helier Marina
01534 885588
HW±3

Adlard Coles Nautical
Instant Wind Forecasting
– 2nd Edition *Alan Watts* **£11.99** 0 7136 6869 5

TO ORDER Tel: **01256 302692** email: **direct@macmillan.co.uk** or **www.adlardcoles.com**

BEAUCETTE MARINA

Beaucette Marina
Vale, Guernsey, GY3 5BQ
Tel: 01481 245000 Fax: 01481 247071
Mobile: 07781 102302
Email: info@beaucettemarina.com

VHF	Ch 80
ACCESS	HW±3

Situated on the north east tip of Guernsey, Beaucette enjoys a peaceful, rural setting in contrast to the more vibrant atmosphere of Victoria Marina. Now owned by a private individual and offering a high standard of service, the site was originally formed from an old quarry.

There is a general store close by, while the bustling town of St Peter Port is only 20 minutes away by bus.

FACILITIES AT A GLANCE

Key
a Harbour office
b Restaurant
c Showers/toilets
d Laundry & telephone
e Manager's cabin
f Boatyard

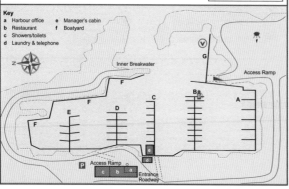

BEAUCETTE MARINA
Vale, Guernsey, Channel Islands GY3 5BQ
Tel: (01481) 245000
Fax: (01481) 247071
e-mail: beaucette@premiermarinas.co.uk
www.permiermarinas.com
A charming deep water marina, situated on the North East coast of Guernsey.

2007/M&WL1/e

Shamrock Chandlery
Shamrock Quay, William Street, Northam, Southampton SO14 5QL

www.shamrock.co.uk

**MAIL ORDER
HOTLINE**
Tel: (02380) 632725
Fax (02380) 225611

2007/M&WC160/z

ST PETER PORT VICTORIA MARINA

Harbour Authority
PO Box 631, St Julian's Emplacement, St Peter Port
Tel: 01481 720229 Fax: 01481 714177
Email: guernsey.harbour@gov.gg

VHF	Ch 12
ACCESS	HW±2.5

Victoria Marina in St Peter Port accommodates approximately 300 visiting yachts. In the height of the season it gets extremely busy, but when the marina is full the overspill can be berthed in other local marinas or moored in the outer harbour. Depending on draught, the marina is accessible approximately two and a half hours either side of HW, with yachts crossing over a sill drying to 4.2m. The marina dory will direct you to a berth on arrival or else will instruct you to moor on one of the waiting pontoons just outside.

Once in the marina, you can benefit from its superb facilities as well as from its central location to St Peter Port's shops and restaurants.

Guernsey is well placed for exploring the rest of the Channel Islands, including the quiet anchorages off Herm and Sark, or making a short hop to one of the French ports such as St Malo, Carteret and Le Dielette.

FACILITIES AT A GLANCE

Key
a Toilets, showers, launderette and shops
b Royal Channel Islands Yacht Club
c Refuse skip
d Marina control, port office
e Dinghy/tender landing pontoon
f Pub/restaurant

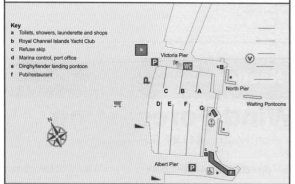

Herm Seaway Marine Ltd
ENGINE SERVICING & REPAIRS

DEALERS FOR:
vetus - Perkins - SABRE - YANMAR - JABSCO

JOHNSON, JABSCO SPARES AND PUMPS

SEAJET & JOTUN, ANTIFOULINGS

CROSLAND FILTERS, RACOR FILTERS

CALOR GAS AND CAMPING GAZ

ESSO and LUBE OILS

MACHINING SERVICES AVAILABLE

2007/M&WC31/j

YOU WILL FIND OUR RETAIL SHOP AND WORKSHOPS AT
MARINE SERVICES, ALBERT MARINA,
CASTLE EMPLACEMENT.
TEL: (01481)726829
FAX: (01481) 714011

ST PETER PORT

Harbour Authority
PO Box 631, St Julian's Emplacement, St Peter Port
Tel: 01481 720229 Fax: 01481 714177
Email: guernsey.harbour@gov.gg

VHF	Ch 12,80
ACCESS	HW±2.5

The harbour of St Peter Port comprises the Queen Elizabeth II Marina to the N and Victoria and Albert Marinas to the S, with visiting yachtsmen usually accommodated in Victoria Marina.

Renowned for being an international financial centre and tax haven, St Peter Port is the capital of Guernsey. Its regency architecture and picturesque cobbled streets filled with restaurants and boutiques help to make it one of the most attractive harbours in Europe. Among the places of interest are Hauteville House, home of the writer Victor Hugo, and Castle Cornet.

FACILITIES AT A GLANCE

Key
a Customs shed
b Tourist Information
c Royal Channel Islands Yacht Club
d Toilets, showers, launderette, shops pub and restaurant
e Guernsey Yacht Club
f Ferry terminal

YACHT CHANDLERS
NORTH PLANTATION, ST. PETER PORT, GUERNSEY
TEL: (01481) 721773 FAX: (01481) 716738

JRC   LOWRANGE   &GARMIN.

All general Chandlery stocked. Large range of Marine Electronics. Admiralty charts and books, water sports equipment, Hanson Fleming flares. We are well stocked for all your boating needs. Oregon weather stations. Yacht brokerage.

NO CHARGE FOR FRIENDLY ADVICE, LOWEST PRICES ON THE ISLAND, GPS SPECIALISTS.

WETLINE INFLATABLES   **QUAYSIDE SHOES**

OREGON SCIENTIFIC   **SILVA**   PEN-DUICK CLOTHING

2007/M&WM16/e

Agents for Bukh Marine Engines.   We specialise in safety and survival equipment, MCA approved service station for liferafts, including RFD, Beaufort/Dunlop, Zodiac, Avon, Plastimo and Lifeguard. Full range of liferafts, dinghies and lifejackets and distress flares.

Telephone: 01481 722378

A B Marine Limited
Castle Walk, St Peter Port, Guernsey, Channel Islands

2007/M&WMD16/e

When responding to adverts please mention Marina & Waypoint Guide 2007

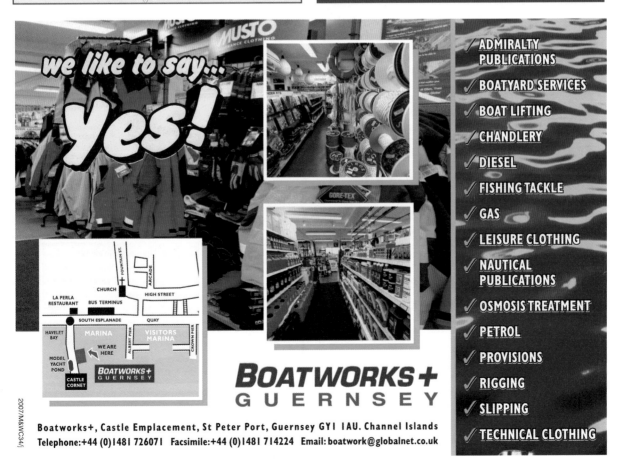

we like to say...
Yes!

✓ ADMIRALTY PUBLICATIONS
✓ BOATYARD SERVICES
✓ BOAT LIFTING
✓ CHANDLERY
✓ DIESEL
✓ FISHING TACKLE
✓ GAS
✓ LEISURE CLOTHING
✓ NAUTICAL PUBLICATIONS
✓ OSMOSIS TREATMENT
✓ PETROL
✓ PROVISIONS
✓ RIGGING
✓ SLIPPING
✓ TECHNICAL CLOTHING

BOATWORKS+
GUERNSEY

Boatworks+, Castle Emplacement, St Peter Port, Guernsey GY1 1AU. Channel Islands
Telephone:+44 (0)1481 726071 Facsimile:+44 (0)1481 714224 Email: boatwork@globalnet.co.uk

2007/M&WC34/j

ST HELIER HARBOUR

St Helier Harbour, Maritime House, La Route du Port Elizabeth
St Helier, Jersey, JE1 1HB
Tel: 01534 885588 Fax: 01534 885599
www.jersey-harbours.com
Email: p.wilson@gov.je

VHF	Ch 14
ACCESS	HW±3

Jersey is the largest of the Channel Islands, attracting the most number of tourists per year. Although St Helier can get very crowded in the height of the summer, if you hire a car and head out to the north coast in particular you will soon find isolated bays and pretty little fishing villages.

All visiting craft are directed to St Helier Marina, which may be enteredthree hours either side of HW via a sill. There is a long holding pontoon to port of the entrance accessible at any state of the tide. La Collette Yacht Basin and Elizabeth Marinas are for craft on long term contracts.

FACILITIES AT A GLANCE

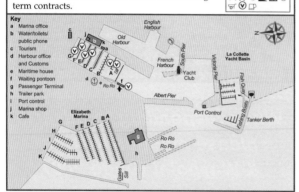

Key
a Marina office
b Water/toilets/public phone
c Tourism
d Harbour office and Customs
e Maritime house
f Waiting pontoon
g Passenger Terminal
h Trailer park
i Port control
j Marina shop
k Cafe

Visit Guernsey's Northern
Marine & Leisure Store

QUAYSIDE MARINE & LEISURE

at St. Sampson's Harbour

Tel: 01481 245881

Chandlery • Electronics • Fishing Tackle
Protective & Leisure Clothing & Shoes
VAT - FREE PRICES

2007/M&WC89/e

Shamrock Chandlery
Shamrock Quay, William Street, Northam, Southampton SO14 5QL

www.shamrock.co.uk

2007/M&WC160/z

75 TON HOIST

VOLVO PENTA

CATERPILLAR®

nannidiesel
energy in blue

FULL ENGINE WORKSHOP, MACHINE SHOP, WELDING SHOP, HULL, PROP & SHAFT REPAIRS
BOAT STORAGE, (V.A.T FREE)

Marine & General
BOATYARD
GUERNSEY

2007/M&WC61/e

TEL: 01481 243048 email: sales@mge.gg

YOUR MARINE & LEISURE CONVENIENCE STORE
Whatever baits your hook, we've got what you're looking for!

Ocean Kayak
Don't miss out on the fun

Fishing equipment
Rods, reels and tackle by
Shakespeare, Fladen, Flashmer,
Pen and Rapala

Boat care
Official suppliers of
Blakes paints

Gift ideas
Birthday, Anniversary,
Christmas or just to say thank you

Apparel & accessories
By Crewsaver

Shoes by
Quayside and
Sebago Dockside

Clothing by
Helly Hansen, Gill
Splashdown, Weird Fish
Wetsuits & diving
equipment by
Marlin
Typhoon
Beuchat

Family Fun
Ocean Kayaks
Bic Kayaks
SportStuff inflatables
Waterskis

Fishing equipment by
Shakespeare
Penn
Rapala

Life saving equipment by
Crewsaver, Typhoon
Eletronics
Navman, Lowrance
General chandlery
Marlow ropes
Charts
Blakes paints
Trailer parts
Boat care products
Inflatable Dinghies

M&WC68/2007/e

15-16 Commercial Buildings
St. Helier.
Telephone: 01534 850090
Facsimile: 01534 850099

Iron Stores

incorporating I.S. Marine

An introduction to Jersey, its harbours and waters

States of Jersey

Tel: 01534 885588
Fax: 01534 885599
Email: jerseyharbours@jersey-harbours.com
www.jersey-harbours.com

This is Jersey - an island with an independent history which has kept many of its ancient traditions alive - an island which has also taken what the world can offer so that it can support a buoyant economy with high employment while seeking to preserve all that is best. An island with its own laws and currency - an island of traditional agriculture and modern finance - an island, above all, at which a welcome is assured whether you stop off for a couple of nights on your passage back from St Malo and the Brittany coast or whether you take several days off to explore Jersey - and why not? It is well worth it.

"You may only want to laze on your boat or you may wish to explore and enjoy what Jersey has to offer, whatever your preference we are here to welcome you and ensure you have a pleasant and enjoyable holiday in Jersey's five gold anchor marinas."

Howard Le Cornu

Captain Howard Le Cornu
Harbour Master
Jersey Harbours

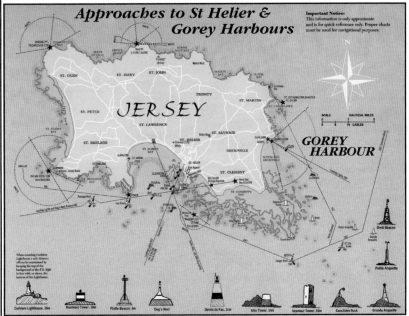

Enjoy the tranquil setting of Jersey's Gorey Harbour en-route to St. Malo or any of the nearby French ports, Portbail, Carteret or Granville.

Fuel prices as @ 10/05/05.
Diesel 39p U/L 48p.

Note: Least deviation for fuel required for U.K. - St. Malo passage.

2007/M&WC42/e

GOREY MARINE FUEL SUPPLIES
TEL: 07797 742384 OPEN: HIGH WATER + OR - 3 HOURS BETWEEN 8AM & 6PM

GOREY HARBOUR

Deep Water Moorings

Fuel Berth

Drying Visitors Moorings

If you are using this Almanac, then you should be a Member or associate of the Royal Institute of Navigation.

Among our 9 Special Interest Groups we have two that are devoted to users of small craft and satellite navigation - but we also have groups covering everything from aircraft to vehicles and walkers. Our membership also spans from the new amateur to the hardened professional.

Associates receive our magazine *Navigation News* and full Members also get *The Journal of Navigation.* As a bonus, all small craft users are also sent our *Fairway* newsletter. all members have their own webpage and can join forums and attend lectures and conferences - most of which are free.

You need no qualifications to join us as a Member or Associate - just an interest in navigation. Contact us at 020 7591 3130 or membership@rin.org.uk or see our website - www.rin.org.uk

'Where would you be without us?'

2007/M&WC153/z

SECTION 2
MARINE SUPPLIES AND SERVICES GUIDE

Mission Critical
TEAM KPM RACING

Www.teamkpmracing.com Tel: 0121-359-6434
Check our website for the best warranty on the market

If this happened to you it would be a bad weekend! But for our Military and Rescue Customers it would be classed as a mission critical failure. All KPM 2006 Run Dry Pumps now incorporate several of the features found on our Mil-spec/ SOLAS approved pumps. To learn more about our full range visit the web sites above.

2007/M&WC113/e

ADHESIVES

Adtech Ltd
Braintree   01376 346511

Bettabond Adhesives
Leeds   0113 278 5088

Casco Products Industrial Adhesives
St Neots   01480 476777

CC Marine (Rubbaweld) Ltd
Chichester   01243 672606

Industrial Self Adhesives Ltd
Nottingham   0115 9681895

Sika Ltd Garden City   01707 394444

Technix Rubber & Plastics Ltd
Southampton   023 8063 5523

Tiflex Liskeard   01579 320808

Trade Grade Products Ltd
Poole   01202 820177

UK Epoxy Resins
Burscough   01704 892364

Wessex Resins & Adhesives Ltd
Romsey   01794 521111

3M United Kingdom plc
Bracknell   01344 858315

ASSOCIATIONS/ AGENCIES

Cruising Association
London   020 7537 2828

Fishermans Mutual Association (Eyemouth) Ltd
Eyemouth   01890 750373

Maritime and Coastguard Agency
Southampton   0870 6006505

Royal Institute of Navigation
London   020 7591 3130

Royal National Lifeboat Institution
Poole   01202 663000

Royal Yachting Association (RYA)
Southampton   0845 345 0400

BERTHS & MOORINGS

ABC Powermarine
Beaumaris   01248 811413

Aqua Bell Ltd Norwich 01603 713013

Ardfern Yacht Centre
Lochgilphead   01852 500247/500636

Ardmair Boat Centre
Ullapool   01854 612054

Arisaig Marine Ltd
Inverness-shire   01687 450224

Bristol Boat Ltd Bristol 01225 872032

British Waterways Argyll
                   01546 603210

Burgh Castle Marine
Norfolk   01493 780331

Cambrian Marine Services Ltd
Cardiff   029 2034 3459

Chelsea Harbour Ltd
London   020 7225 9108

Clapson & Son (Shipbuilders) Ltd
Barton-on-Humber   01652 635620

Crinan Boatyard
Crinan   01546 830232

Dartside Quay Brixham 01803 845445

Douglas Marine Preston
                   01772 812462

Dublin City Moorings
Dublin   +353 1 8183300

Emsworth Yacht Harbour
Emsworth   01243 377727

Exeter Ship Canal   01392 274306

GILLINGHAM MARINA
F. Parham Ltd, 173 Pier Road, Gillingham, Kent, ME7 1UB
Tel: 01634 280022
Fax: 01634 280164
Kent's Five Gold Anchor Marina on the River Medway, eight miles from Sheerness.   M&WL8a/e

HAFAN PWLLHELI
Glan Don, Pwllheli, Gwynedd LL53 5YT
Tel: (01758) 701219
Fax: (01758) 701443 VHF Ch80
Hafan Pwllheli has over 400 pontoon berths and offers access at virtually all states of the tide. Ashore, its modern purpose-built facilities include luxury toilets, showers, launderette, a secure boat park for winter storage, 40-ton travel hoist, mobile crane and plenty of space for car parking. Open 24-hours a day, 7 days a week.   M&WL16

Highway Marine
Sandwich   01304 613925

Iron Wharf Boatyard
Faversham   01795 537122

Jalsea Marine Services Ltd
Northwich   01606 77870

Jersey Harbours
St Helier   01534 885588

Jones (Boatbuilders), David
Chester   01244 390363

KG McColl Oban   01852 200248

Lawrenny Yacht Station
Kilgetty   01646 651212

MacFarlane & Son
Glasgow   01360 870214

Maramarine
Helensburgh   01436 810971

Melfort Pier & Harbour
Kilmelford   01852 200333

NEPTUNE MARINA LTD
Neptune Quay, Ipswich, Suffolk IP4 1AX
Tel: (01473) 215204
Fax: (01473) 215206
e-mail:
enquiries@neptune-marina.com
www.neptune-marina.com
Accessible through continuously operating lockgates (VHF Channel 68) Neptune Marina (VHF Channels 80 or 37) is located on the north side of Ipswich wet dock immediately adjacent to the town centre and integrated into the rapidly regenerating northern quays. M&Wext7

Orkney Marinas Ltd
Kirkwall   01856 872292

PADSTOW HARBOUR COMMISSIONERS
Harbour House, Padstow, Cornwall PL28 8AQ
Tel: (01841) 532239
Fax: (01841) 533346
e-mail:
padstowharbour@compuserve.com
www.padstow-harbour.co.uk
Inner harbour controlled by tidal gate - opens HW±2 hours. Minimum depth 3 metres at all times. Yachtsmen must be friendly as vessels raft together. Services include showers, toilets, diesel, water and ice. Security by CCTV.   2007/M&Wext1/e

Pearn and Co, Norman
Looe   01503 262244

Peterhead Bay Authority
Peterhead   01779 474020

Philip Leisure Group
Dartmouth   01803 833351

Priors Boatyard
Burnham-on-Crouch 01621 782160

Rossiter Yachts Ltd
Christchurch   01202 483250

Sark Moorings
Channel Islands   01481 832260

Surry Boatyard
Shoreham-by-Sea   01273 461491

Sutton Harbour Marina Plymouth
                   01752 204186

Wicor Marine Fareham 01329 237112

Winters Marine Ltd
Salcombe   01548 843580

Yarmouth Marine Service
Yarmouth   01983 760521

Youngboats Faversham 01795 536176

BOAT BUILDERS & REPAIRS

ABC Powermarine
Beaumaris   01248 811413

Aqua-Star Ltd
St Sampsons   01481 244550

Ardoran Marine
Oban   01631 566123

Baumbach Bros Boatbuilders
Hayle   01736 753228

BB Marine Restoration Services Ltd
Southampton   023 8045 4145

Beacon Boatyard
Rochester   01634 841320

Bedwell & Co
Walton on the Naze 01255 675873

Black Dog
Falmouth   01326 318058

Blackwell, Craig
Co Meath   +353 87 677 9605

Bluewater Horizons
Weymouth   01305 782080

Bowman Yachts Penryn 01326 376107

Brennan, John
Dun Laoghaire   +353 1 280 5308

Burghead Boat Centre
Findhorn 01309 690099

Camper & Nicholsons Yachting
Portsmouth 023 9258 0221

Carrick Marine Projects
Co Antrim 02893 355884

Chicks Marine Ltd
Guernsey 01481 724536

Established 1968

CC

PROFESSIONAL REPAIRS
Traditional Boat Builders
Glass Fibre Engineers
*Family-run Business
Modern Workshop
Temperature Controlled*
01389 710070

2007/WMD21/e

Cooks Maritime Craftsmen - Poliglow
Lymington 01590 675521

Creekside Boatyard (Old Mill Creek)
Dartmouth 01803 832649

CTC Marine & Leisure
Middlesbrough 01642 230123

Davies Marine Services
Ramsgate 01843 586172

Dickie & Sons Ltd, AM
Bangor 01248 363400

Dickie & Sons Ltd, AM
Pwllheli 01758 701828

Dudley Marine
Milford Haven 01646 692787

East & Co, Robin
Kingsbridge 01548 531257

East Llanion Marine Ltd
Pembroke Dock 01646 686866

Emblem Enterprises
East Cowes 01983 294243

Exe Leisure Exeter 01392 879055

Fairlie Quay Fairlie 01475 568267

Fairweather Marine
Fareham 01329 283500

Fergulsea Engineering
Ayr 01292 262978

Ferrypoint Boat Co
Youghal +353 24 94232

Floetree Ltd (Loch Lomond Marina)
Balloch 01389 752069

Freshwater Boatyard
Truro 01326 270443

Furniss Boat Building
Falmouth 01326 311766

Gallichan Marine Ltd
Jersey 01534 746387

GILLINGHAM MARINA
F. Parham Ltd, 173 Pier Road,
Gillingham, Kent, ME7 1UB
Tel: 01634 280022
Fax: 01634 280164
Largest repair facilities in the South East
for craft up to 65 tonnes & 26 metres.

M&WL8c/e

Goodchild Marine Services
Great Yarmouth 01493 782301

Gosport Boatyard
Gosport 023 9252 6534

Gweek Quay Boatyard
Helston 01326 221657

Halls
Walton on the Naze 01255 675596

Hardway Marine
Gosport 023 9258 0420

Harris Marine (1984) Ltd, Ray
Barry 01446 740924

Haven Boatyard
Lymington 01590 677073

Hayling Yacht Company
Hayling Island 023 9246 3592

Hoare Ltd, Bob
Poole 01202 736704

Holyhead Marine Services Ltd
Holyhead 01407 760111

International Marine Designs
Aberdyfi 01654 767572

Jackson Marine
Whitehaven 01946 699332

Jackson Yacht Services
Jersey 01534 743819

James Marine Yacht Services
Bristol 0117 966 2291

JEP Marine
Canterbury 01227 710102

Jones (Boatbuilders), David
Chester 01244 390363

JWS Marine Services
Southsea 023 9275 5155

KG McColl Oban 01852 200248

Kimelford Yacht Haven
Oban 01852 200248

Kingfisher Marine
Weymouth 01305 766595

Kingfisher Ultraclean UK Ltd
Tarporley 0800 085 7039

Kippford Slipway Ltd
Dalbeattie 01556 620249

Langley Marine Services Ltd
Eastbourne 01323 470244

Lavis & Son, CH
Exmouth 01395 263095

Lawrenny Yacht Station
Lawrenny 01646 651212

Lencraft Boats Ltd
Dungarvan +353 58 682220

Lifeline Marine Services
Poole 01202 669676

Mackay Boatbuilders
Arbroath 01241 872879

Mannings Marine Ltd
Bootle 0151 933 0820

Marine Services
Norwich 01692 582239

Maritime Workshop
Gosport 023 9252 7805

Mashford Brothers
Torpoint 01752 822232

Mayor & Co Ltd, J
Preston 01772 812250

McKellar's Slipway Ltd
Helensburgh 01436 842334

Mears, HJ Axmouth 01297 23344

Medusa Marina
Woolverstone 01473 780090

Moody Yachts International Ltd
Swanwick 01489 885000

Morrison, A Killyleagh 028 44828215

Moss (Boatbuilders), David
Thornton-Cleveleys 01253 893830

Multi Marine Composites Ltd
Torpoint 01752 823513

Newing, Roy E
Canterbury 01227 860345

Noble and Sons, Alexander
Girvan 01465 712223

Northney Marine Services
Hayling Island 023 9246 9246

Northshore King's Lynn 01485 210236

O'Sullivans Marine Ltd
Tralee +353 66 7124524

Oulton Manufacturing Ltd
Lowestoft 01502 585631

Oyster Marine Ltd
Ipswich 01473 688888

Pachol, Terry Brighton 01273 682724

Partington Marine Ltd, William
Pwllheli 01758 612808

Pasco's Boatyard
Truro 01326 270269

Penrhos Marine
Aberdovey 01654 767478

Penzance Marine Services
Penzance 01736 361081

Pepe Boatyard
Hayling Island 023 9246 1968

PJ Bespoke Boat Fitters Ltd
Crewe 01270 812244

Preston Marine Services Ltd
Preston 01772 733595

McKellars Slipway Ltd

Craft & Gear stored at owners risk

Slipping Wintering Repairs

**SHORE ROAD
HELENSBURGH
EAST DUNBARTONSHIRE
G84 0JL**

Tel: 01436 842334

2007/M&WC100/e

Rampart Yachts
Southampton   023 8023 4777

Red Bay Boats Ltd
Cushendall   028 2177 1331

Reliance Marine
Wirral   0151 625 5219

Retreat Boatyard Ltd
Exeter   01392 874720/875934

Richards, Eddie
East Cowes   01983 299740

Richardson Boatbuilders, Ian
Stromness   01856 850321

Richardson Yacht Services Ltd
Newport   01983 821095

Riley Marine Dover   01304 214544

River Tees Engineering & Welding Ltd
Middlesbrough   01642 226226

Roberts Marine Ltd, S
Liverpool   0151 707 8300

Rustler Yachts Ltd
Penryn   01326 376107

Salterns Boatyard
Poole   01202 707391

Sea & Shore Ship Chandler
Dundee   01382 202666

SEAFIT MARINE SERVICES
**Falmouth Marina, North Parade,
Falmouth, Cornwall TR11 2TD
Tel: (01326) 313713
Fax: (01326) 313713
Mobile: (07971) 196175**
All repair and service work undertaken.

M&Wext3/e **Seamark-Nunn & Co**
Felixstowe 01394 275327

Seaquest Yachts
Penryn   01326 377006

Searanger Yachts
Peterborough   01832 274199

SEAWARD MARINE LTD
**Prospect Road, Cowes,
Isle of Wight PO31 7AD
Tel: 01983 280333
Fax: 01983 295095
e-mail: sales@seawardboat.com
www.seawardboat.com**
Builders of the Seaward brand of Nelson
semi-displacement motor cruisers,
renowned for their good seakeeping and
traditional style. Custom building and
repairs. Used Seaward craft also
available.

2007/M&WEXT2/e

Slipway Cooperative Ltd
Bristol   0117 907 9938

Spencer Sailing Services, Jim
Brightlingsea   01206 302911

Spicer Boatbuilder, Nick
Weymouth Marina   01305 767118

Starlight Yachts Penryn 01326 376107

Stone Pier Yacht Services
Warsash   01489 885400

Storrar Marine Store
Newcastle upon Tyne   0191 266 1037

Tarquin Boat Co
Emsworth   01243 375211

Trio Mouldings Marine
Southampton   01489 787887

TT Marine Eastbourne   01323 472009

WA Simpson Marine Ltd
Dundee   01382 566670

Waterfront Marine
Bangor   01248 352513

Western Marine
Dublin   +353 1 280 0321

Wigmore Wright Marine Services
Penarth   029 2070 9983

Williams, Peter
Fowey   01726 870987

Woodwind Composite Marine
Southampton   023 8033 7722

WQI Ltd
Bournemouth   01202 771292

Yacht Solutions
Portsmouth   023 9220 0670

Yarmouth Marine Service
    01983 760521

Youngboats Faversham 01795 536176

BOATYARD SERVICES & SUPPLIES

A & P Ship Care
Ramsgate   01843 593140

Abersoch Boatyard Services Ltd
Abersoch   01758 713900

Amble Boat Co Ltd
Amble   01665 710267

Amsbrisbeg Ltd
Port Bannatyne   01700 502719

Ardmair Boat Centre
Ullapool   01854 612054

Ardmaleish Boat Building Co
Rothesay   01700 502007

www.ardoran.co.uk
West coast Scotland. All marine facilities.

Ardrishaig Boatyard
Lochgilphead   01546 603280

Arklow Slipway
Arklow   +353 402 33233

Baltic Wharf Boatyard
Totnes   01803 867922

Baltimore Boatyard
Baltimore   +353 28 20444

Battricks Boatyard
St Aubin   01534 743412

Bedwell and Co
Walton-on-the-Naze   01255 675873

Berthon Boat Co
Lymington   01590 673312

Birch Boatbuilders, ER 01268 696094

Birdham Shipyard
Chichester   01243 512310

BJ Marine Ltd Bangor   028 91271434

Blagdon, A Plymouth   01752 561830

Boatworks + Ltd
St Peter Port   01481 726071

Booth W Kelly Ltd
Ramsey   01624 812322

Brennan, John
Dun Laoghaire   +353 1 280 5308

Brightlingsea Boatyard
Brightlingsea   01206 302003/8

Brighton Marina Boatyard
Brighton   01273 819919

Bristol Marina (Yard)
Bristol   0117 921 3198

Buchan & Son Ltd, J
Peterhead   01779 475395

Buckie Shipyard Ltd
Buckie   01542 831245

Bucklers Hard Boat Builders Ltd
Brockenhurst   01590 616214

Bure Marine Ltd
Great Yarmouth   01493 656996

C & J Marine Services
Newcastle Upon Tyne   0191 295 0072

Caley Marina Inverness 01463 236539

Cambrian Boat Centre
Swansea   01792 467263

Cambrian Marine Services Ltd
Cardiff   029 2034 3459

Cantell and Son Ltd
Newhaven   01273 514118

Carroll's Ballyhack Boatyard
New Ross   +353 51 389164

Castlepoint Boatyard
Crosshaven   +353 21 4832154

Chabot, Gary Newhaven 01273 611076

Chapman & Hewitt Boatbuilders
Wadebridge   01208 813487

Chippendale Craft Rye   01797 227707

Clapson & Son (Shipbuilders) Ltd
Barton on Humber   01652 635620

Coastal Marine Boatbuilders
(Berwick upon Tweed)
Eyemouth   01890 750328

Coastcraft Ltd
Cockenzie   01875 812150

Coates Marine Ltd
Whitby   01947 604486

Cook Boatbuilders and Repairers, S
Whitby   01947 820521

Coombes, AA
Bembridge   01983 872296

Corpach Boatbuilding Company
Fort William   01397 772861

Craobh Marina
By Lochgilphead   01852 500222

Creekside Boatyard (Old Mill Creek)
Dartmouth   01803 832649

Crinan Boatyard
By Lochgilphead   01546 830232

Crosshaven Boatyard Co Ltd
Crosshaven   +353 21 831161

Dale Sailing Co Ltd
Neyland 01646 603110

Darthaven Marina
Kingswear 01803 752242

Dartside Quay Brixham 01803 845445

Dauntless Boatyard Ltd
Canvey Island 01268 793782

Davis's Boatyard Poole 01202 674349

Dinas Boat Yard Ltd
Y Felinheli 01248 671642

Dorset Yachts Poole 01202 674531

Douglas Boatyard
Preston 01772 812462

Dover Yacht Co Dover 01304 201073

Dun Laoghaire Marina
Dun Laoghaire +353 1 2020040

Elephant Boatyard
Southampton 023 8040 3268

Elton Boatbuilding Ltd
Kirkcudbright 01557 330177

Fairways Marine Engineers
Maldon 01621 852866

Farrow & Chambers Yacht Builders
Humberston 01472 632424

Felixstowe Ferry Boatyard
Felixstowe 01394 282173

Ferguson Engineering
Wexford +353 6568 66822133

Ferry Marine South
Queensferry 0131 331 1233

Ferrybridge Marine Services Ltd
Weymouth 01305 781518

Findhorn Boatyard
Findhorn 01309 690099

Firmhelm Ltd Pwllheli 01758 612251

Fishbourne Quay Boatyard
Ryde 01983 882200

Fleming Engineering, J
Stornoway 01851 703488

Forrest Marine Ltd
Exeter 08452 308335

Fowey Boatyard Fowey 01726 832194

Fox's Marina Ipswich 01473 689111

Frank Halls & Son
Walton on the Naze 01255 675596

Freeport Marine Jersey 01534 888100

Furniss Boat Building
Falmouth 01326 311766

GILLINGHAM MARINA
**F. Parham Ltd, 173 Pier Road,
Gillingham, Kent, ME7 1UB
Tel: 01634 280022
Fax: 01634 280164**
Largest repair facilities in the South East
for craft up to 65 tonnes & 26 metres.

M&WL8d/e

Goodchild Marine Services
Great Yarmouth 01493 782301

Gosport Boatyard
Gosport 023 9252 6534

Gweek Quay Boatyard
Helston 01326 221657

Haines Boatyard
Chichester 01243 512228

Harbour Marine
Plymouth 01752 204690/1

Harbour Marine Services Ltd
Southwold 01502 724721

Harris Marine Barry 01446 740924

Hartlepool Marine Engineering
Hartlepool 01429 867883

Hayles, Harold Yarmouth 01983 760373

Henderson, J Shiskine 01770 860259

Heron Marine
Whitstable 01227 361255

Hewitt, George Binham 01328 830078

Hillyard, David
Littlehampton 01903 713327

Holyhead Marina & Trinity Marine Ltd
Holyhead 01407 764242

Instow Marine Services
Bideford 01271 861081

Ipswich Haven Marina
Ipswich 01473 236644

Iron Wharf Boatyard
Faversham 01795 537122

Island Boat Services
Port of St Mary 01624 832073

Isle of Skye Yachts
Ardvasar 01471 844216

Jalsea Marine Services Ltd Weaver
Shipyard, Northwich 01606 77870

J B Timber Ltd
North Ferriby 01482 631765

Jersey Harbours Dept
St Helier 01534 885588

Jones & Teague
Saundersfoot 01834 813429

Kilnsale Boatyard
Kinsale +353 21 4774774

Kilrush Marina & Boatyard – Ireland
+353 65 9052072

Kingfisher Ultraclean UK Ltd
Tarporley 0800 085 7039

Lake Yard Poole 01202 674531

Lallow, C Isle of Wight 01983 292112

Latham's Boatyard
Poole 01202 748029

Leonard Marine, Peter
Newhaven 01273 515987

Lincombe Boat Yard
Salcombe 01548 843580

Lomax Boatbuilders
Cliffony +353 71 66124

Lucas Yachting, Mike
Torquay 01803 212840

Lymington Yacht Haven
Lymington 01590 677071

MacDougalls Marine Services
Isle of Mull 01681 700294

Macduff Shipyard Ltd
Macduff 01261 832234

Madog Boatyard
Porthmadog 01766 514205/513435

Mainbrayce Marine
Alderney 01481 822772

Malakoff and Moore
Lerwick 01595 695544

**Mallaig Boat Building and
Engineering** Mallaig 01687 462304

Maramarine
Helensburgh 01436 810971

Marindus Engineering
Kilmore Quay +353 53 29794

Marine Gleam
Lymington 0800 074 4672

Mariners Farm Boatyard
Gillingham 01634 233179

McCallum & Co Boat Builders, A
Tarbert 01880 820209

McCaughty (Boatbuilders), J
Wick 01955 602858

McGruar and Co Ltd
Helensburgh 01436 831313

Mitchell's Boatyard
Poole 01202 747857

Mooney Boats
Killybegs +353 73 31152/31388

Moore & Son, J
St Austell 01726 842964

Morrison, A Killyleagh 028 44828215

Moss (Boatbuilders), David
Thornton-Cleveleys 01253 893830

Noble and Sons, Alexander
Girvan 01465 712223

North Pier (Oban) Oban 01631 562892

North Wales Boat Centre
Conwy 01492 580740

Northshore Yacht Yard
Chichester 01243 512611

Oban Yachts and Marine Services
By Oban 01631 565333

Oulton Manufacturing Ltd
Lowestoft 01502 585631

Parker Yachts and Dinghys Ltd
Nr Boston 01205 722697

Pearn and Co, Norman
Looe 01503 262244

Penrhos Marine
Aberdovey 01654 767478

**Penzance Dry Dock and Engineering
Co Ltd** Penzance 01736 363838

Pepe Boatyard
Hayling Island 023 9246 1968

Philip & Son Dartmouth 01803 833351

Phillips, HJ Rye 01797 223234

Ponsharden Boatyard
Penryn 01326 372215

Powersail and Island Chandlers Ltd
East Cowes Marina 01983 299800

Pratt and Son, VJ
King's Lynn 01553 764058

Priors Boatyard
Burnham-on-Crouch 01621 782160

R K Marine Ltd
Swanwick 01489 583572

Rat Island Sailboat Company (Yard)
St Mary's 01720 423399

Retreat Boatyard Ltd
Exeter 01392 874720/875934

Rice and Cole Ltd
Burnham-on-Crouch 01621 782063

MARINE ENGINEERING
STAINLESS STEEL & ALUMINIUM FABRICATION
STORAGE   REPAIRS   OSMOSIS TREATMENT
SPRAY PAINTING   RIGGING

SILVERS MARINE

SILVERHILLS ROSNEATH
HELENSBURGH G84 0RW

NAUTOR'S
SWAN
AUTHORISED
SERVICE CENTRE

2007/M&WM7/b

Tel (01436) 831222
Fax (01436) 831879

email: enquiries@silversmarine.co.uk www.silversmarine.co.uk

Richardson Boatbuilders, Ian
Stromness   01856 850321

Richardsons Boatbuilders
Binfield   01983 821095

Riverside Yard
Shoreham Beach   01273 592456

RJ Prior (Burnham) Ltd
Burnham-on-Crouch   01621 782160

Robertsons Boatyard
Woodbridge   01394 382305

Rossbrin Boatyard
Schull   +353 28 37352

Rossiter Yachts Ltd
Christchurch   01202 483250

Rossreagh Boatyard
Rathmullan   +353 74 51082

Rudders Boatyard & Moorings
Milford Haven   01646 600288

Ryan & Roberts Marine Services
Askeaton   +353 61 392198

Rye Harbour Marina Rye
                                 01797 227667

Rynn Engineering, Pat
Galway   +353 91 562568

Salterns Boatyard
Poole   01202 707391

Sandbanks Yacht Company
Poole   01202 707500

Sandy Morrison Engineering
Uig   01470 542300

Scarborough Marine Engineering Ltd
Scarborough   01723 375199

Severn Valley Cruisers Ltd (Boatyard)
Stourport-on-Severn   01299 871165

Shepards Wharf Boatyard Ltd
Cowes   01983 297821

Shotley Marina Ltd
Ipswich   01473 788982

Shotley Marine Services Ltd
Ipswich   01473 788913

Silvers Marina Ltd
Helensburgh   01436 831222

Skinners Boat Yard
Baltimore   +353 28 20114

Smith & Gibbs
Eastbourne   01323 734656

South Dock (Seaham Harbour Dock Co) Seaham   0191 581 3877

Sparkes Boatyard
Hayling Island   023 92463572

Spencer Sailing Services, Jim
Brightlingsea   01206 302911

Standard House Boatyard
Wells-next-the-Sea   01328 710593

Storrar Marine Store
Newcastle upon Tyne   0191 266 1037

Strand Shipyard Rye   01797 222070

Stratton Boatyard, Ken
Bembridge   01983 873185

Surry Boatyard
Shoreham-by-Sea   01273 461491

SEA CHEST, THE
Admiralty Chart Agent
Queen Anne's Battery Marina,
Plymouth PL4 0LP
Tel: 01752 222012
Fax: 01752 252679
www.seachest.co.uk
Admiralty and Imray Chart Agent, Huge
stocks of Books and Charts, Rapid
dispatch.   2007/M&WL15/e

Titchmarsh Marina
Walton-on-the-Naze   01255 672185

Tollesbury Marina
Tollesbury   01621 869202

T J Rigging Conwy   07780 972411

Toms and Son Ltd, C
Fowey   01726 870232

Tony's Marine Service
Coleraine   028 7035 6422

Torquay Marina
Torquay   01803 200210

Trinity Marine Holyhead 01407 763855

Trouts Boatyard (River Exe)
Topsham   01392 873044

Upson and Co, RF
Aldeburgh   01728 453047

Versatility Workboats
Rye   01797 224422

Weir Quay Boatyard
Bere Alston   01822 840474

West Solent Boatbuilders
Lymington   01590 642080

Wicor Marine Fareham   01329 237112

Woodrolfe Boatyard
Maldon   01621 869202

BOAT STORAGE

Abersoch Boatyard Services Ltd
Pwllheli   01758 713900

Ambrisbeg Ltd
Port Bannatyne   01700 502719

Arisaig Marine
Inverness-shire   01687 450224

Bedwell and Co
Walton-on-the-Naze   01255 675873

Bembridge Boatyard Marine Works
Bembridge   01983 872911

Berthon Boat Company
Lymington   01590 673312

Bluewater Horizons
Weymouth   01305 782080

Bure Marine Ltd
Great Yarmouth   01493 656996

C & J Marine Services
Newcastle upon Tyne   0191 295 0072

Caley Marine
Inverness   01463 233437

Carrick Marine Projects
Co Antrim   02893 355884

Challenger Marine
Penryn   01326 377222

Coates Marine Ltd
Whitby   01947 604486

Creekside Boatyard (Old Mill Creek)
Dartmouth   01803 832649

Crinan Boatyard Ltd
Crinan   01546 830232

Dale Sailing Co Ltd
Neyland   01646 603110

Dartside Quay
Brixham   01803 845445

Dauntless Boatyard Ltd
Canvey Island   01268 793782

Debbage Yachting
Ipswich   01473 601169

Douglas Marine Preston 01772 812462

East & Co, Robin
Kingsbridge   01548 531257

Emsworth Yacht Harbour
Emsworth   01243 377727

Exeter Ship Canal   01392 274306

Exmouth Marina   01395 2693146

Fairlie Quay Fairlie   01475 568267

Firmhelm Ltd Pwllheli 01758 612244

Fowey Boatyard Fowey   01726 832194

marina

Main Road
Fairlie
North Ayrshire
KA29 0AS

A prime facility just south of the town of Largs
• 80 ton hoist • 64,000sq.ft undercover storage
• 240v power available throughout shed • on-
site contractors for all your maintenance needs •
clean concrete outside storage yard
• call VHF 80 call sign Fairlie Quay.

Visitors are welcome at this developing facility.

Tel: 01475 568267 Fax: 01475 568410
fairliequay@btconnect.com

website: www.fairliequay.co.uk

2007/M&WMD18AVe

Freshwater Boatyard
Truro   01326 270443

Hafan Pwllheli Pwllheli   01758 701219

Gweek Quay Boatyard
Helston   01326 221657

Iron Wharf Boatyard
Faversham   01795 537122

Jalsea Marine Services Ltd
Northwich   01606 77870

KG McColl Oban   01852 200248

Latham's Boatyard
Poole   01202 748029

Lavis & Son, CH
Exmouth   01395 263095

Lincombe Boat Yard
Salcombe   01548 843580

Marine Resource Centre Ltd
Oban   01631 720291

Marine & General Engineers
Guernsey   01481 245808

Milford Marina
Milford Haven   01646 696312/3

Northshore Yachts
Chichester   01243 512611

Oulton Manufacturing Ltd
Lowestoft   01502 585631

Pasco's Boatyard
Truro   01326 270269

Pearn and Co, Norman
Looe   01503 262244

Pepe Boatyard
Hayling Island   023 9246 1968

Philip Leisure Group
Dartmouth   01803 833351

Ponsharden Boatyard
Penryn   01326 372215

Portsmouth Marine Engineering
Fareham   01329 232854

Priors Boatyard
Burnham-on-Crouch   01621 782160

Rossiter Yachts
Christchurch   01202 483250

Shepards Wharf Boatyard Ltd
Cowes   01983 297821

Silvers Marina Ltd
Helensburgh   01436 831222

Waterfront Marine
Bangor   01248 352513

Wicor Marine Fareham   01329 237112

Winters Marine Ltd
Salcombe   01548 843580

Yacht Solutions Ltd
Portsmouth   023 9220 0670

Yarmouth Marine Service
Yarmouth   01983 760521

Youngboats Faversham   01795 536176

BOOKS, CHARTS & PUBLISHERS

Adlard Coles Nautical
London   0207 7580200

Brown Son & Ferguson Ltd
Glasgow   0141 429 1234

Warsash Nautical Bookshop

Books, Charts, Shipping, Yachting.
Callers & Mail Order. Credit cards accepted.
New and Secondhand book catalogues free.

Also on Internet: *http://www.nauticalbooks.co.uk*
6 Dibles Road, Warsash, Southampton SO31 9HZ
Tel: 01489 572384   Fax: 01489 885756
e-mail: orders@nauticalbooks.co.uk   2007/M&WM1/e

Chattan Security Ltd
Edinburgh   0131 555 3155

Cooke & Son Ltd, B Hull 01482 223454

Dubois Phillips & McCallum Ltd
Liverpool   0151 236 2776

Fernhurst Books
Arundel   01903 882277

Imray, Laurie, Norie & Wilson
Huntingdon   01480 462114

Kelvin Hughes
Southampton   023 8063 4911

Lilley & Gillie Ltd, John 0191 257 2217

SAVE 40% or more

on current edition British Admiralty Charts

www.chartsales.co.uk

World-wide stocks, world-wide delivery
Over 10,000 charts and books for sale

Marine Chart Services
Tel UK (07000) 441629
Fax UK (01933) 442662
info@chartsales.co.uk   2007/M&WMD5/e

Marine Chart Services
Wellingborough   01933 441629

Nautical Data
Emsworth   01243 389352

Price & Co Ltd, WF
Bristol   0117 929 2229

Smith AM (Marine) Ltd
London   020 8529 6988

Stanford Charts
West Mersea   01206 381580

BOW THRUSTERS

ARS Anglian Diesels Ltd
Norfolk   01508 520555

Buckler's Hard Boat Builders Ltd
Beaulieu   01590 616214

JS Mouldings International
Bursledon   023 8063 4400

BREAKDOWN

BJ Marine Ltd
Bangor, Ireland   028 9127 1434

Seafit Marine Services
Falmouth   01326 313713

SEA START LIMITED
Unit 13, Hamble Point Marina,
Hamble, Southampton SO31 4JD
Tel: (023) 8045 8000
Fax: (023) 8045 2666
e-mail: sales@seastart.co.uk
www.seastart.co.uk
24 hours a day, 365 days a year - marine
breakdown assistance.   M&WL4

ENGINE STOPS!
SEA START IT.
JOIN NOW
24 HOUR MECHANICAL
BREAKDOWN ASSISTANCE
SEA START
MEMBERSHIP
0800 88 55 00
www.seastart.co.uk   2007/M&WMD7/e

CHANDLERS

ABC Powermarine
Beaumaris   01248 811413

**Acamar Marine Services/Sirius Yacht
Training** Christchurch   01202 488030

Aladdin's Cave Chandlery Ltd
(Deacons) Bursledon   023 8040 2182

Aladdin's Cave Chandlery Ltd
Chichester   01243 773788

Aladdin's Cave Chandlery Ltd (Hamble
Point) Southampton   023 80455 058

Aladdin's Cave Chandlery Ltd
(Mercury) Southampton 023 8045 4849

Aladdin's Cave Chandlery Ltd (Port
Hamble) Southampton   023 8045 4858

Findhorn Marina & Boatyard

Findhorn,
Morayshire IV36 3YE
Tel: 01309 690099
www.findmar.com

Open 7 days a week

- Boat Storage
- Chandlery & Cafe
- Slipway
- Moorings

- Safety Equipment
- Books & Charts
- Mercury, Yamaha Dealers

2007/M&WC16/b

Aladdin's Cave Chandlery Ltd
(Swanwick) Swanwick 01489 555999

Alderney Boating Centre
Alderney 01481 823725

Allgadgets.co.uk
Basingstoke 01256 478000

Alpine Room & Yacht Equipment
Chemsford 01245 223563

Aquatogs Cowes 01493 247890

Arbroath Fishermen's Association
Arbroath 01241 873132

Ardfern Yacht Centre Ltd
Argyll 01852 500247

Ardoran Marine Oban 01631 566123

Arthurs Chandlery
Gosport 023 9252 6522

Arun Aquasports
Littlehampton 01903 713553

Arun Canvas and Rigging Ltd
Littlehampton 01903 732561

Arun Nautique
Littlehampton 01903 730558

Aruncraft Chandlers
Littlehampton 01903 713327

ASAP Supplies – Equipment & Spares Worldwide
Beccles 0845 1300870

Auto Marine Sales
Southsea 023 9281 2263

Bayside Marine
Brixham 01803 856771

Bedwell and Co
Walton on the Naze 01255 675873

BJ Marine Ltd Bangor 028 9127 1434

Bluecastle Chandlers
Portland 01305 822298

Bluewater Horizons
Weymouth 01305 782080

Blue Water Marine Ltd
Pwllheli 01758 614600

Boatshop Chandlery
Brixham 01803 882055

Boatacs
Westcliffe on Sea 01702 475057

Boathouse, The Penryn 01326 374177

Boston Marina 01205 364420

Bosun's Locker, The
Falmouth 01326 312212

Bosun's Locker, The
Milford Haven 01646 697834

Bosun's Locker, The
Ramsgate 01843 597158

Bosuns Locker, The
South Queensferry 0131 331 3875/4496

Brancaster Sailing and Sailboard Centre Kings Lynn 01485 210236

Bridger Marine, John
Exeter 01392 216420

Brigantine Teignmouth 01626 872400

Brighton Chandlery
Brighton 01273 681543

Bristol Boat Ltd Bristol 01225 872032

Brixham Chandlers
Brixham 01803 882055

Brixham Yacht Supplies Ltd
Brixham 01803 882290

Brunel Chandlery Ltd
Neyland 01646 601667

Bucklers Hard Boat Builders
Beaulieu 01590 616214

Burghead Boat Centre
Findhorn 01309 690099

Bussell & Co, WL
Weymouth 01305 785633

Buzzard Marine
Yarmouth 01983 760707

C & M Marine
Bridlington 01262 672212

Cabin Yacht Stores
Rochester 01634 718020

Caley Marina Inverness 01463 236539

Cambrian Boat Centre
Swansea 01792 467263

Cantell & Son Ltd
Newhaven 01273 514118

Carne (Sales) Ltd, David
Falmouth 01326 318314

Carne (Sales) Ltd, David
Penryn 01326 374177

Carrickcraft
Malahide +353 1 845 5438

Caters Carrick Ltd
Carrickfergus 028 93351919

CH Marine (Cork)
Cork +353 21 4315700

CH Marine Skibbereen +353 28 23190

Charity & Taylor Ltd
Lowestoft 01502 581529

Cherry's Chandlery
Bournemouth 01202 517513

Chertsey Marine Ltd
Penton Hook Marina 01932 565195

Chicks Marine Ltd
Guernsey 01481 724536

Christchurch Boat Shop
Christchurch 01202 482751

Churcher Marine
Worthing 01903 230523

Clapson & Son (Shipbuilders) Ltd
South Ferriby Marina 01652 635620

Clarke, Albert
Newtownards 01247 872325

Coastal Marine Boatbuilders Ltd
(Dunbar) Eyemouth 01890 750328

Coates Marine Ltd
Whitby 01947 604486

Collins Marine St Helier 01534 732415

Compass Marine
Lancing 01903 761773

Cosalt International Ltd
Aberdeen 01224 588327

Cosalt International Ltd
Southampton 023 8063 2824

Cotter, Kieran
Baltimore +353 28 20106

Cox Yacht Charter Ltd, Nick
Lymington 01590 673489

www.kipmarina.co.uk
e-mail: dduffield@kipmarina.co.uk

Huge variety of stock covering virtually every aspect of boat maintenance. Yanmar dealers for Scotland with extensive range of maintenance parts and spares available. Open 7 days a week.
Tel: 01475 521485

The Yacht Harbour, Inverkip, Renfrewshire PA16 0AS

2007/M&WC104/e

manx marine
Limited   Yacht Chandlers
Yacht Chandlers
The Tongue Building, The Tongue, Douglas Harbour, Douglas IM1 5AO
The Islands leading and most established Yacht Chandlery. Stockists of quality foul
weather clothing and thermal wear. Large stock holding of s/steel fixtures and fittings
and a comprehensive range of general chandlery including rigging facilities
Telephone: 01624 674842
Web: www.manxmarine.com
E-mail: manxmarine@mcb.net 2007/M&WC102/z

C Q Chandlers Ltd Poole	01202 682095
Crinan Boats Ltd Lochgilphead	01546 830232
CTC Marine & Leisure Middlesbrough	01642 230123
Dale Sailing Co Ltd Milford Haven	01646 603110
Danson Marine Sidcup	0208 304 5678
Dart Chandlers Dartmouth	01803 833772
Dartside Quay Brixham	01803 845445
Dauntless Boatyard Ltd Canvey Island	01268 793782
Davis's Yacht Chandler Littlehampton	01903 722778
Denholm Fishselling Scrabster	01847 896968
Denney & Son, EL Redcar	01642 483507
Deva Marine Conwy	01492 572777
Dickie & Sons Ltd, AM Bangor	01248 363400
Dickie & Sons Ltd, AM Pwllheli	01758 701828
Dinghy Supplies Ltd/Sutton Marine Ltd Sutton	+353 1 832 2312
Diverse Yacht Services Hamble	023 80453399
Dixon Chandlery, Peter Exmouth	01395 273248
DMS Chandlery Noss	01803 833772
Doling & Son, GW Barrow In Furness	01229 823708
Dovey Marine Aberdovey	01654 767581
Down Marine Co Ltd Belfast	028 9048 0247
Douglas Marine Preston	01772 812462
Dubois Phillips & McCallum Ltd Liverpool	0151 236 2776
Duncan Ltd, JS Wick	01955 602689
Duncan Yacht Chandlers Ely	01353 663095
East Anglian Sea School Ipswich	01473 659992

Eastbourne Chandlery Eastbourne	01323 470213
Eccles Marine Co Middlesbrough	01642 230123
Ely Boat Chandlers Hayling Island	023 9246 1968
Emsworth Chandlery Emsworth	01243 375500
Exe Leisure Exeter	01392 879055
Express Marine Services Chichester	01243 773788
Fairways Chandlery Burnham-on-Crouch	01621 782659
Fairweather Marine Fareham	01329 283500
Fal Chandlers Falmouth Marina	01326 212411
Fathom Marine Bridport	01308 420988
Ferrypoint Boat Co Youghal	+353 24 94232
Findhorn Marina & Boatyard Findhorn	01309 690099
Firmhelm Ltd Pwllheli	01758 612244
Fisherman's Mutual Asssociation (Eyemouth) Ltd Eyemouth	01890 750373
Fleetwood Trawlers' Supply Co Ltd, The Fleetwood	01253 873476
Floetree Ltd (Loch Lomond Marina) Balloch	01389 752069
Foc'sle, The Exeter	01392 874105

Freeport Marine Jersey	01534 888100
French Marine Motors Ltd Brightlingsea	01206 302133
Furneaux Riddall & Co Ltd Portsmouth	023 9266 8621
Gallichan Marine Ltd Jersey	01534 746387
Galway Marine Chandlers Ltd Galway	+353 91 566568
GB Attfield & Company Dursley	01453 547185
Gibbons Ship Chandlers Ltd Sunderland	0191 567 2101
Gibbs Chandlery Shepperton	01932 242977

GILLINGHAM MARINA
F. Parham Ltd, 173 Pier Road,
Gillingham, Kent, ME7 1UB
Tel: 01634 280022
Fax: 01634 280164
Large stock of Chandlery & Sailing
clothing. Suzuki, Avon, Bombard, Orkney
dealers; extensive showroom.   M&WL8g/e

Glaslyn Marine Supplies Ltd Porthmadog	01766 513545
Goodwick Marine Fishguard	01348 873955
Gorleston Marine Ltd Great Yarmouth	01493 661883
GP Barnes Ltd Shoreham	01273 591705/596680
Green Marine, Jimmy Fore St Beer	01297 20744
Greenham Marine Emsworth	01243 378314
Gunn Navigation Services, Thomas Aberdeen	01224 595045
Hale Marine, Ron Portsmouth	023 92732985
Harbour Marine Services Ltd (HMS) Southwold	01502 724721
Hardware & Marine Supplies Wexford	+353 53 29791
Hardway Marine Gosport	023 9258 0420
Harris Marine (1984) Ltd, Ray Barry	01446 740924
Hartlepool Marine Supplies Hartlepool	01429 862932

ROWLOCKS CHANDLERY
Tel 01983-299800
Email rowlockschandler@aol.com
Chandlery, Provisions, Gas
"If we don't have it, we can get it"
In East Cowes Marina, 55-57 Britannia Way,
East Cowes, Isle of Wight PO32 6DG
2007/M&WC62/e

MARINE SUPPLIES AND SERVICES GUIDE

CHANDLERS

Harwich Chandlers Ltd	**JNW Services** Aberdoon 01224 594050	**Lencraft Boats Ltd**
Harwich 01255 504061	**JNW Services** Peterhead 01779 477346	Dungarvan +353 58 68220
Harwoods Yarmouth 01983 760258	**Johnston Brothers**	**Lincoln Marina** Lincoln 01522 526896
Hawkins Marine Shipstores, John	Mallaig 01687 462215	**Looe Chandlery**
Rochester 01634 840812	**Johnstons Marine Stores**	West Looe 01503 264355
Hayles, Harold Yarmouth 01983 760373	Lamlash 01770 600333	**Lynch Ltd, PA** Morpeth 01670 512291
Herm Seaway Marine Ltd	**Jones & Teague**	**Mackay Boatbuilders (Arbroath) Ltd**
St Peter Port 01481 726829	Saundersfoot 01834 813429	Aberdeen 01241 872879
Highway Marine	**Kearon Ltd, George**	**Mackay Marine Services**
Sandwich 01304 613925	Arklow +353 402 32319	Aberdeen 01224 575772
Hill Head Chandlers	**Kelpie Boats**	**Mailspeed Marine**
Hill Head 01329 664621	Pembroke Dock 01646 683661	Burnham-on-Crouch 01621 781120
Hoare Ltd, Bob	**Kelvin Hughes Ltd**	**Mailspeed Marine**
Poole 01202 736704	Southampton 023 80634911	Southsea Marina 023 9275 5450
Hornsey (Chandlery) Ltd, Chris	**Kildale Marine** Hull 01482 227464	**Mailspeed Marine**
Southsea 023 9273 4728	**Kingfisher Marine**	Warrington 01925 838858
Hunter & Combes	Weymouth 01305 766595	**Manx Marine Ltd**
Cowes 01983 299599	**Kings Lock Chandlery**	Douglas 01624 674842
Iron Stores Marine	Middlewich 01606 737564	**Marine & Leisure Europe Ltd**
St Helier 01534 877755	**Kip Chandlery Inverkip**	Plymouth 01752 268826
Isles of Scilly Steamship Co	Greenock 01475 521485	**Marine Instruments**
St Mary's 01720 422710	**Kirkcudbright Scallop Gear Ltd**	Falmouth 01326 312414
Jackson Yacht Services	Kirkcudbright 01557 330399	**Marine Scene** Cardiff 029 2070 5780
Jersey 01534 743819	**Kyle Chandlers** Troon 01292 311880	**Marine Services** Jersey 01534 626930
Jamison and Green Ltd	**Lamb & Sons Ltd, JP**	**Marine Store Wyatts**
Belfast 028 9032 2444	Liverpool 0151 709 4861	West Mersea 01206 384745
Jeckells and Son Ltd	**Landon Marine, Reg**	**Marine Store** Maldon 01621 854380
Lowestoft 01502 565007	Truro 01872 272668	**Marine Store**
JF Marine Chandlery	**Largs Chandlers** Largs 01475 686026	Walton on the Naze 01255 679028
Rhu 01436 820584		**Marine Superstore Port Solent**

SETSAIL

Croatia, Turkey, Greece & Majorca
Flotilla sailing, Bareboat yacht charter
RYA Learn to sail courses available

Flights from Gatwick, Stansted, Manchester, Bristol, Birmingham, Newcastle & Glasgow

www.setsail.co.uk   e-mail: boats@setsail.co.uk

tel: 01787 310445

Setsail Holidays is the trading name of Noble Yacht Chartering Ltd.

FULLY BONDED
2007/M&WC96/e

Chandlery Portsmouth   023 9221 9843
MarineCo Looe   01503 265444
Martello Yacht Services
Canvey Island   01268 681970
Maryport Harbour and Marina
Maryport   01900 818447/4431
Matthews Ltd, D
Cork   +353 214 277633
Mayflower Chandlery
Plymouth   01752 500121
McCready Sailboats Ltd
Holywood   028 9042 1821
Moore & Son, J
Mevagissey   01726 842964
Morgan & Sons Marine, LH
Brightlingsea   01206 302003
Mount Batten Boathouse
Plymouth   01752 482666
MR Marine Ltd Brighton 01273 668900
Murphy, Nicholas
Dunmore East   +353 51 383259
Mylor Chandlery & Rigging
Falmouth   01326 375482
Nancy Black Oban   01631 562550
Nautical World Bangor   028 91460330
New World Yacht Care
Helensburgh   01436 820586
Newhaven Chandlery
Newhaven   01273 612612
Nifpo Ardglass   028 4484 2144
Norfolk Marine
Great Yarmouth   01692 670272
Norfolk Marine Chandlery Shop
Norwich   01603 783150
Northshore Sport & Leisure
Brancaster Staithe   01485 210236
Ocean Leisure Ltd
London   020 7930 5050
One Stop Chandlery
Maldon   01621 853558

OUTRIGGERS/UPPER DECK MARINE
Albert Quay, Fowey, Cornwall
PL23 1AQ
Tel: 01726 833233
Fax: 01726 833265
www.fowey.com
'Outriggers' casual and marine clothing, footwear, nautical gifts. Admiralty chart agent and marine books.   M&WL2/e

Partington Marine Ltd, William
Pwllheli   01758 612808
Pascall Atkey & Sons Ltd
Isle of Wight   01983 292381
Paterson, A Macduff   01261 832784
Peculiar's Chandlery
Gosport   023 9258 9953
Pennine Marine Ltd
Skipton   01756 792335
Penrhos Marine
Aberdovey   01654 767478
Penzance Marine Services
Penzance   01736 361081

Perry Marine, Rob
Axminster   01297 631314
Pepe Boatyard
Hayling Island   023 9246 1968
Peterhead Watersports Centre
Peterhead   01779 480888
Peters PLC Chichester   01243 511033
Pinnell & Bax
Northampton   01604 592808
Piplers of Poole Poole   01202 673056
Pirate's Cave, The
Rochester   01634 295233
Powersail Island Chandlers Ltd
East Cowes Marina   01983 299800
Preston Marine Services Ltd
Preston   01772 733595
Price & Co Ltd, WF
Bristol   0117 929 2229
PSM Ltd Alderney   01481 824968
Pumpkin Marine Supplies
Hayling Island   023 9246 8794
Purple Sails & Marine
Walsall   01922 614787
Quay West Chandlers
Poole   01202 742488
Quayside Marine
Salcombe   01548 844300
Racecourse Yacht Basin (Windsor) Ltd Windsor   01753 851501
Rat Rigs Water Sports
Cardiff   029 2062 1309
Reliance Marine Wirral 0151 625 5219
RHP Marine Cowes   01983 290421
Rhu Chandlery Rhu   01436 820584
RNS Marine Northam   01237 474167
Sail Loft Bideford   01271 860001
Sailaway St Anthony   01326 231357
Salcombe Boatstore
Salcombe   01548 843708
Salterns Chandlery
Poole   01202 701556
Sand & Surf Chandlery
Salcombe   01548 844555
Sandrock Marine Rye   01797 222679
Schull Watersports Centre
Schull   +353 28 28554
Sea & Shore Ship Chandler
Dundee   01382 202666
Sea Cruisers of Rye Rye 01797 222070
Sea Span Edinburgh   0131 552 2224
Sea Teach Ltd Emsworth 01243 375774
Seafare Tobermory   01688 302277
Seahog Boats Preston   01772 633016
Seamark-Nunn & Co
Felixstowe   01394 451000
Seaquest Marine Ltd
St Peter Port   01481 721773

Seaware Ltd Penryn   01326 377948
Seaway Marine Macduff 01261 832877
Severn Valley Boat Centre
Stourport-on-Severn   01299 871165
Shamrock Chandlery
Southampton   023 8063 2725
Sharp & Enright Dover   01304 206295
Shearwater Engineering Services Ltd
Dunoon   01369 706666
Shipmates Chandlery
Dartmouth   01803 839292
Shipshape Marine
King's Lynn   01553 764058
Ship Shape
Ramsgate   01843 597000
Shipsides Marine Ltd
Preston   01772 797079
Shorewater Sports
Chichester   01243 672315
Simpson Marine Ltd
Newhaven   01273 612612
Simpson Marine Ltd, WA
Dundee   01382 566670
Sketrick Marine Centre
Killinchy   028 9754 1400
Smith & Gibbs
Eastbourne   01323 723824
Smith AM (Marine) Ltd
London   020 8529 6988
Solent Marine Chandlery Ltd
Gosport   023 9258 4622
South Coast Marine
Christchurch   01202 482695
South Pier Shipyard
St Helier   01534 711000
Southampton Yacht Services Ltd
Southampton   023 803 35266
Southern Masts & Rigging
Brighton   01273 818189
S Roberts Marine Ltd
Liverpool   0151 707 8300
Standard House Chandlery
Wells-next-the-Sea   01328 710593
Stornoway Fishermen's Co-op
Stornoway   01851 702563
Sunset Marine & Watersports
Sligo   +353 71 9162792
Sussex Marine
St Leonards on Sea   01424 425882
Sussex Marine Centre
Shoreham   01273 454737
Sutton Marine (Dublin)
Sutton   +353 1 832 2312
SW Nets Newlyn   01736 360254
Tarbert Ltd, JSB Tarbert 01880 820180
TCS Chandlery Grays   01375 374702
TCS Chandlery
Southend   01702 444423

Thulecraft Ltd Lerwick   01595 693192

Torbay Boating Centre
Paignton   01803 558760

Torquay Chandlers
Torquay   01803 211854

Trafalgar Yacht Services
Fareham   01329 822445

Trident UK N Shields   0191 490 1736

Union Chandlery
Cork   +353 21 4554334

Uphill Boat Services
Weston-Super-Mare   01934 418617

Upper Deck Marine and Outriggers
Fowey   01726 832287

V Ships (Isle of Man)
Douglas   01624 688886

Viking Marine Ltd
Dun Laoghaire   +353 1 280 6654

Waterfront Marine
Bangor   01248 352513

Wayne Maddox Marine
Margate   01843 297157

Western Marine
Dalkey   +353 1280 0321

Whitstable Marine
Whitstable   01227 274168

Williams Ltd, TJ Cardiff 029 20 487676

Worcester Yacht Chandlers Ltd
Barbourne   01905 22522

Work & Leisure
Arbroath   01241 431134

XM Yachting
Southampton   0870 751 4666

Yacht & Boat Chandlery
Faversham   01795 531777

Yacht Parts Plymouth   01752 252489

Yacht Shop, The
Fleetwood   01253 879238

Yachtmail Ltd Lymington 01590 672784

Yare Boatique Norwich 01603 715289

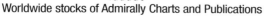

SMALL CRAFT DELIVERIES
International Admiralty Charts Agents &
Marine Suppliers

LTD
Est. 1959

Worldwide stocks of Admiralty Charts and Publications

ARCS & C-Map Electronic
Chart Service

Wide Range of: Imray Charts & Publications, Stanford Charts, Instructional Books, RYA Publications, Chart-Instruments, Safety Equipment, Flags, Binoculars, Bells, GPS, VHF etc.

12 Quay Street, Woodbridge, Suffolk IP12 1BX
Tel: 01394 382655   Fax: 01394 383508
Navigation House, Wilford Bridge Road, Melton, Woodbridge, Suffolk IP12 1RJ
Tel: 01394 382600   Fax: 01394 387672
E-mail: sale@scd-charts.co.uk   www.scd-charts.co.uk

2007/M&WM4/b

CHART AGENTS

Brown Son & Ferguson Ltd
Glasgow   0141 429 1234

Chattan Security Ltd
Edinburgh   0131 554 7527

Cooke & Son Ltd, B
Hull   01482 223454

Dubois Phillips & McCallum Ltd
Liverpool   0151 236 2776

Eland Exeter   01392 255788

Imray Laurie Norie and Wilson Ltd
Huntingdon   01480 462114

Kelvin Hughes
Southampton   023 8063 4911

Lilley & Gillie Ltd, John
North Shields   0191 257 2217

Marine Chart Services
Wellingborough   01933 441629

Price & Co, WF Bristol 0117 929 2229

Sea Chest Nautical Bookshop
Plymouth   01752 222012

Seath Instruments (1992) Ltd
Lowestoft   01502 573811

Small Craft Deliveries
Woodbridge   01394 382655

Smith (Marine) Ltd, AM
London   020 8529 6988

South Bank Marine Charts Ltd
Grimsby   01472 361137

Stanford Charts
Bristol   0117 929 9966

Stanford Charts
London   020 7836 1321

Stanford Charts
Manchester   0161 831 0250

Todd Chart Agency Ltd
County Down   028 9146 6640

UK Hydrographics Office
Taunton   01823 337900

Warsash Nautical Bookshop
Warsash   01489 572384

CLOTHING

Absolute
Gorleston on Sea   01493 442259

Aquatogs Cowes   01493 247890

Chatham Clothing Company Ltd
Chippenham   01249 460770

Compass Watersports
Devizes   01380 813100

Crew Clothing London 020 8875 2300

Crewsaver Gosport   023 9252 8621

Douglas Gill Nottingham 0115 9460844

Fat Face Havant   02392 485555

Gul International Ltd
Bodmin   01208 262400

Guy Cotten UK Ltd
Liskeard   01579 347115

Harwoods Yarmouth   01983 760258

Helly Hansen
Nottingham   0115 9608797

Henri Lloyd Manchester 0161 799 1212

Joules
Market Harborough   01858 461156

Mad Cowes Clothing Co
Cowes   01983 293710

Matthews Ltd, D
Cork   +353 214 277633

Mountain & Marine
Stockport   0800 093 5793

Musto Ltd Laindon   01268 491555

Ocean World Ltd Cowes 01983 291744

Purple Sails & Marine Walsall
01922 614787

Quba Sails Cowes   01983 299004

Quba Sails Lymington 01590 689362

Quba Sails Salcombe 01548 844599

Ravenspring Ltd Totnes 01803 867092

Shorewater Sports
Chichester   01243 672315

Splashdown Leeds   0113 270 7000

Yacht Parts
Plymouth 01752 252489

CODE OF PRACTICE EXAMINERS

Booth Marine Surveys, Graham
Birchington-on-Sea   01843 843793

Cannell & Associates, David M
Wivenhoe   01206 823337

COMPASS ADJUSTERS/ MANUFACTURERS

BPSC Marine Services
Southampton   023 8023 0045

Cleghorn Waring Ltd
Letchworth   01462 480380

Rule - ITT Industries
Hoddesdon   01992 450145

Seath Instruments (1992) Ltd
Lowestoft   01502 573811

Yachting Instruments Ltd
Sturminster Newton   01258 817662

COMPUTERS & SOFTWARE

C-map Ltd Fareham 01329 517777

Dolphin Maritime Software
White Cross 01524 841946

Forum Software Ltd
Nr Haverfordwest 01646 636363

Kelvin Hughes Ltd
Southampton 023 8063 4911

Maptech-Marine
Aldermaston 0870 740 9040

Mariteck Ltd Glasgow 0141 571 9164

PC Maritime Plymouth 01752 254205

Sea Information Systems Ltd
Aberdeen 01224 621326

Square Mile Marlow 0870 1202536

CORPORATE PROMOTIONS

Indulgence Charters
Wendover 01296 696006

407 Racing (Yacht Charter)
Lymington 01590 688407

CORPORATE YACHT OWNERSHIP

407 Racing (Yacht Charter)
Lymington 01590 688407

CUSTOMS

Arklow +353 402 32553
Bantry +353 27 50061
Carlingford Lough +353 42 34248
Cork +353 21 311024
Dingl +353 66 7121480
Dublin +353 1 679 2777
Dun Laoghaire +353 1 280 3992
Dunmore East +353 51 875391
Fenit Harbour +353 66 36115
Galway +353 91 567191
Killybegs +353 73 31070
Kilmore +353 53 33741
Kilrush +353 61 415366
Kinsal +353 21 311044
Lough Swilly +353 74 21611
Malahide +353 1 874 6571
Prest +353 94 21131
Rathmullan +353 74 26324
Rosslare +353 53 33116
Schull +353 27 51562
Shannon +353 61 471076
Shannon Estuary +353 69 415366
Sligo +353 71 61064
UK Customs Nationwide
  0845 0109000
Waterford +353 51 875391
Wexford +353 532 2889
Wicklow +353 404 67222

DECK EQUIPMENT

Aries Van Gear Spares
Penryn 01326 377467

Frederiksen Boat Fittings (UK) Ltd
Gosport 023 9252 5377

Harken UK Lymington 01590 689122

Kearon Ltd George +353 402 32319

Marine Maintenance
Tollesbury 01621 860441

Nauquip Warsash 01489 885336

Pro-Boat Ltd
Burnham-on-Crouch 01621 785455

Ryland, Kenneth
Stanton 01386 584270

Smith, EC & Son Ltd
Luton 01582 729721

Timage & Co Ltd
Braintree 01376 343087

DIESEL MARINE/ FUEL ADDITIVES

Corralls Poole 01202 674551

Cotters Marine & General Supplies
Baltimore +353 28 20106

Diesel Dialysis
St Austelll 0800 389 7874

Expresslube Henfield 01444 881883

Gorey Marine Fuel Supplies
Gorey 07797 742384

Hammond, George
Dover 01304 206809

Iron Wharf Boatyard
Faversham 01795 537122

Lallow, Clare Cowes 01983 760707

Marine Support & Towage
Cowes 01983 200716/07860 297633

Quayside Fuel
Weymouth 07747 182181

Rossiter Yachts
Christchurch 01202 483250

Sleeman & Hawken
Shaldon 01626 872750

DIVERS

Abco Divers Belfast 028 90610492

Andark Diving
Southampton 01489 581755

Aquatech Diving Services
Port of St Mary 01624 833037

Argonaut Marine
Aberdeen 01224 706526

Baltimore Diving and Watersports Centre West Cork +353 28 20300

C & C Marine Services
Largs 01475 687180

Cardiff Commercial Boat Operators Ltd Cardiff 029 2037 7872

C I Diving Services Ltd
Invergordon 01349 852500

Divesafe Sunderland 0191 567 8423

Divetech UK King's Lynn 01485 572323

EC Leisure Craft
North Fambridge 01621 744424

Energy Solutions
Rochester 01634 290772

Enterprise Marine Electronic & Technical Services Ltd
Aberdeen 01224 593281

Eurotex Brighton 01273 818990

Floetree Ltd (Loch Lomond Marina)
Balloch 01389 752069

HNP Engineers (Lerwick) Ltd
Lerwick 01595 692493

Index Marine
Bournemouth 01202 470149

Jackson Yacht Services
Jersey 01534 743819

Jedynak, A Salcombe 01548 843321

Kippford Slipway Ltd
Dalbeattie 01556 620249

Land & Sea Electronics
Aberdeen 01224 593281

Lifeline Marine Services
Dolphin Haven, Poole 01202 669676

Lynch Ltd, PA Morpeth 01670 512291

Mackay Boatbuilders (Arbroath) Ltd
Aberdeen 01241 872879

Marine, AW Gosport 023 9250 1207

Marine Electrical Repair Service
London 020 7228 1336

MES Falmouth Marina,
Falmouth 01326 378497

Mount Batten Boathouse
Plymouth 01752 482666

New World Yacht Care
Rhu 01436 820586

Neyland Marine Services Ltd
Milford Haven 01646 698968

Powell, Martin Shamrock Quay,
Southampton 023 8033 2123

R & J Marine Electricians Suffolk Yacht
Harbour Ltd, Ipswich 01473 659737

Radio & Electronic Services Beaucette
Marina, Guernsey 01481 728837

Redcar Fish Company
Stockton-on-Tees 01642 633638

RHP Marine Cowes 01983 290421

Rothwell, Chris
Torquay Marina 01803 850960

Rutherford, Jeff Largs 01475 568026

Sea Electric Hamble 023 8045 6255

SM International
Plymouth 01752 662129

South Pier Shipyard
St Helier 01534 519700

Sussex Fishing Services
Rye 01797 223895

Ultra Marine Systems
Mayflower International Marina, Plymouth
  07989 941020

Upham, Roger
Chichester 01243 528299

Volspec Woolverstone Marina,
Ipswich 01473 780144

Western Marine Power Ltd
Plymouth 01752 408804

Purcell, D – Crouch Sailing School
Burnham   01621 784140/0585 33

Salvesen UK Ltd
Liverpool   0151 933 6038

Seaguard Marine Engineering Ltd
Goodwick   01348 872976

Sea-Lift Diving Dover   01304 829956

Southern Cylinder Services
Fareham   01329 221125

Stealaway Diving Oban 01631 566349

Sub Aqua Services
North Ormesby   01642 230209

Teign Diving Centre
Teignmouth   01626 773965

Thorpe, Norman Portree 01478 612274

Tuskar Rock Marine
Rosslare   +353 53 33376

Underwater Services
Dyffryn Arbwy   01341 247702

Wilson Alan c/o Portrush Yacht Club
Portrush   028 2076 2225

Woolford, William
Bridlington   01262 671710

ELECTRICAL AND ELECTRONIC ENGINEERS

Allworth Riverside Services, Adrian
Chelsea Harbour Marina   07831 574774

Belson Design Ltd, Nick
Southampton   077 6835 1330

Biggs, John Weymouth Marina,
Weymouth   01305 778445

BJ Marine Ltd Bangor   028 9127 1434

Calibra Marine
Dartmouth   01803 833094

Campbell & McHardy Lossiemouth
Marina, Lossiemouth   01343 812137

CES Sandown Sparkes Marina,
Hayling Island   023 9246 6005

Colin Coady Marine
Malahide   +353 87 265 6496

Contact Electrical
Arbroath   01241 874528

DDZ Marine Clyde Marina,
Ardossan   01294 607077

Diving & Marine Engineering
Barry   01446 721553

Donnelly, R South Shields 07973 119455

DV Diving   028 9146 4671

Falmouth Divers Ltd
Penryn   01326 374736

Fathom Diving (Chislehurst)
Chislehurst   020 8289 8237

Fathoms Ltd Wick   01955 605956

Felixarc Marine Ltd
Felixstowe   01394 676497

Grampian Diving Services
New Deer   01771 644206

Higgins, Noel
Southern Ireland   +353 872027650

Hudson, Dave
Trearddur Bay   01407 860628

Hunt, Kevin Tralee   +353 6671 25979

Inverkip Diving Services
Inverkip   01475 521281

Kaymac Diving Services
Swansea   01792 793316

Keller, Hilary
Buncrana   +353 77 62146

Kilkee Diving Centre
Kilkee   +353 6590 56707

Leask Marine Kirkwall   01856 874725

Looe Divers Hannafore 01503 262727

MacDonald, D Nairn   01667 455661

Medway Diving Contractors Ltd
Gillingham   01634 851902

Mojo Maritime Penzance 01736 762771

Murray, Alex Stornoway 01851 704978

New Dawn Dive Centre
Lymington   01590 675656

New Tec Diving Services
Blackpool   01253 691665

Northern Divers (Engineering) Ltd
Hull   01482 227276

Offshore Marine Services Ltd
Bembridge   01983 873125

Parkinson (Sinbad Marine Services),
J Killybegs   +353 73 31417

Port of London Authority
Gravesend   01474 560311

WESTERN MARINE POWER LTD
Western Hangar, Mount Batten,
Plymouth, Devon PL9 9SJ.
TEL: (01752) 408804 FAX: (01752) 408807
e-mail: info@wmp.co.uk

Suppliers and installers of:-
Watermakers, Air Conditioning,
Generators, Electrical Systems,
Trim tabs, Electronic Engine Controls,
Bow and Stern Thrusters, Teak Decks,
Davits, Passarelles and Cranes,
Galley and Sanitation Equipment.
ISO 9001 Quality Assurance.
Website: www.wmp.co.uk/
2007/M&WMD17/e

Weyland Marine Services
Milford Haven   01646 698968

Wroath, DG Cowes   01983 281467

Yoldings Marine
Eastbourne   01323 470882

ELECTRONIC DEVICES AND EQUIPMENT

Anchorwatch UK
Edinburgh   0131 447 5057

Aquascan International Ltd
Newport   01633 841117

Atlantis Marine Power Ltd
Plymouth   01752 225679

Autosound Marine
Bradford   01274 688990

AW Marine Gosport   023 9250 1207

Brookes & Gatehouse
Maylandsea   01621 743546

Brookes & Gatehouse
Romsey   01794 518448

Boat Electrics & Electronics Ltd
Troon   01292 315355

Cactus Navigation & Communication
London   020 7493 1115

CDL Aberdeen   01224 706655

Charity & Taylor Ltd
Lowestoft   01502 581529

Devtech Plymouth   01752 223388

Diverse Yacht Services
Hamble   023 8045 3399

Dyfed Electronics Ltd
Milford Haven   01646 694572

Echopilot Marine Electronics Ltd
Ringwood   01425 476211

Euronav Ltd Portsmouth 023 9237 3855

Furuno (UK) Ltd
Denmead   023 9223 0303

Garmin (Europe) Ltd
Romsey   01794 579944

Golden Arrow Marine Ltd
Southampton   023 8071 0371

Greenham Regis Marine Electronics
Cowes   01983 293996

Greenham Regis Marine Electronics
Emsworth   01243 378314

Greenham Regis Marine Electronics
Lymington   01590 671144

Greenham Regis Marine Electronics
Southampton   023 8063 6555

Nick Belson **Design** *Ltd.*

Marine Electricians & Custom Electronic Design

From changing a bulb to full boat wiring harnesses

Work by Degree qualified Chartered Engineers
South Coast Based
info@nickbelsondesign.co.uk
Office: 023 8087 9841   Mob: 07768 351330

2007/M&WCB4/k

ICS Electronics Arundel 01903 731101

JG Technologies Ltd
Weymouth 0845 458 9616

KM Electronics
Lowestoft 01502 569079

Kongsberg Simrad Ltd
Aberdeen 01224 226500

Kongsberg Simrad Ltd
Wick 01955 603606

Landau UK Ltd Hamble 01489 881588

Land & Sea Electronics
Aberdeen 01224 593281

Marathon Leisure
Hayling Island 023 9263 7711

Marine Instruments
Falmouth 01326 312414

Marinetrack Ltd
Shoreham-by-Sea 01273 265425

Maritek Ltd Glasgow 0141 571 9164

Microcustom Ltd Ipswich 01473 780724

Nasa Marine Instruments
Stevenage 01438 354033

Navcom Chichester 01243 776625

Navionics UK Plymouth 01752 204735

Navtronics Lowestoft 01502 587696

Ocean Leisure Ltd
London 020 7930 5050

Plymouth Marine Electronics
Plymouth 01752 227711

Radio & Electronic Services Ltd
St Peter Port 01481 728837

Raymarine Ltd
Portsmouth 023 9269 3611

Redfish Car Company
Stockton-on-Tees 01642 633638

Robertson, MK Oban 01631 563836

Safe Marine Ltd
Aberdeen 01224 338338

Satcom Distribution Ltd
Salisbury 01722 410800

Sea Information Systems Ltd
Aberdeen 01224 621326

Seaquest Marine Ltd
Guernsey 01481 721773

Seatronics Aberdeen 01224 853100

Selenia Communications
Aberdeen 01224 585334

Selenia Communications
Brixham 01803 851993

Selenia Communications
Fraserburgh 01346 518187

Selenia Communications
Lowestoft 01502 572365

Selenia Communications
Newlyn 01736 361320

Selenia Communications
Newcastle upon Tyne 0191 265 0374

Selenia Communications
Penryn 01326 378031

Selenia Communications
Southampton 023 8051 1868

Silva Ltd Livingston 01506 419555

Simrad Ltd Gosport 01329 245100

SM International
Plymouth 01752 662129

Sperry Marine Ltd
Peterhead 01779 473475

Sperry Marine Ltd
Ullapool 01854 612024

Stenmar Ltd Aberdeen 01224 827288

STN Atlas Marine UK Ltd
Peterhead 01779 478233

SWALE MARINE
(ELECTRICAL)
The Old Stable, North Road
Queenborough, Kent ME11 5EN
Tel: 01795 580930
Fax: 01795 580238
FOR ALL YOUR ELECTRICAL
AND ELECTRONIC NEEDS
Agents for Furuno, Raymarine, Simrad
and other major manufacturers.
RYA Radios & Radar Courses
E-mail: swalemarin@aol.com
Website: www.swalemarine.com
2007/M&WMD4/e

Tacktick Ltd Emsworth 01243 379331

Transas Nautic
Portsmouth 023 9267 4016

Veripos Precise Navigation
Fraserburgh 01346 511411

Wema (UK) Bristol 01454 316103

Western Battery Service
Mallaig 01687 462044

Wilson & Co Ltd, DB
Glasgow 0141 647 0161

Woodsons of Aberdeen Ltd
Aberdeen 01224 722884

Yeoman Romsey 01794 521079

ENGINES AND ACCESSORIES

Airylea Motors
Aberdeen 01224 872891

Amble Boat Co Ltd
Amble 01665 710267

Anchor Marine Products
Benfleet 01268 566666

Aquafac Ltd Luton 01582 568700

Attfield & Company, GB
Dursley 01453 547185

Barrus Ltd, EP Bicester 01869 363636

Brigantine
Teignmouth 01626 872400

British Polar Engines Ltd
Glasgow 0141 445 2455

Bukh Diesel UK Ltd
Poole 01202 668840

CJ Marine Mechanical
Troon 01292 313400

Cleghorn Waring Ltd
Letchworth 01462 480380

Cook's Diesel Service Ltd
Faversham 01795 538553

Felton Marine Engineering
Brighton 01273 601779

Felton Marine Engineering
Eastbourne 01323 470211

Fender-Fix Maidstone 01622 751518

Fettes & Rankine Engineering
Aberdeen 01224 573343

Fleetwood & Sons Ltd, Henry
Lossiemouth 01343 813015

GILLINGHAM MARINA
F. Parham Ltd, 173 Pier Road,
Gillingham, Kent, ME7 1UB
Tel: 01634 280022
Fax: 01634 280164
Large stock of Chandlery & Sailing
clothing. Suzuki, Avon, Bombard, Orkney
dealers; extensive showroom. M&WL8h/e

Gorleston Marine Ltd
Great Yarmouth 01493 661883

Halyard Salisbury 01722 710922

Interseals (Guernsey) Ltd
Guernsey 01481 246364

Kelpie Boats
Pembroke Dock 01646 683661

Keypart Watford 01923 330570

Lancing Marine
Brighton 01273 410025

Lencraft Boats Ltd
Dungarvan +353 58 68220

Lewmar Ltd Havant 023 9247 1841

Liverpool Power Boats
Bootle 0151 944 1163

Lynch Ltd, PA Morpeth 01670 512291

MacDonald & Co Ltd, JN
Glasgow 0141 334 6171

Marine Maintenance
Tollesbury 01621 860441

Mariners Weigh
Shaldon 01626 873698

Maritime International Ltd
Guernsey 01481 723716

Mooring Mate Ltd
Bournemouth 01202 421199

Mount Batten Boathouse
Plymouth 01752 482666

Nauquip Warsash 01489 885336

Newens Marine, Chas
Putney 020 8788 4587

Ocean Safety
Southampton 023 8072 0800

Outboard Centre
Fareham 01329 234277

Riley Marine Dover 01304 214544

RK Marine Ltd Hamble 01489 583585

RK Marine Ltd Swanwick 01489 583572

Rule – ITT Industries
Hoddesdon 01992 450145

Sillette Sonic Ltd
Sutton 020 8337 7543

Smith & Son Ltd, EC
Luton 01582 729721

Sowester Simpson-Lawrence Ltd
Poole 01202 667700

Timage & Co Ltd
Braintree 01376 343087

MARINE SUPPLIES AND SERVICES GUIDE

DIVERS – ENGINES AND ACCESSORIES

Trident UK Gateshead   0191 259 6797

Vetus Den Ouden Ltd
Totton   023 8086 1033

Western Marine
Dublin   +353 1 280 0321

Whitstable Marine
Whitstable   01227 262525

Yates Marine, Martin
Galgate   01524 751750

Ynys Marine Cardigan   01239 613179

FABRICATION

Sailspar Ltd
Brightlingsea   01206 302679

FIRST AID

Bisham Abbey Sailing & Navigation School Bisham   01628 474960

Coastal Sea School
Weymouth   0870 321 3271

East Coast Offshore Yachting – Les Rant Perry   01480 861381

Hamble School of Yachting
Hamble   023 8045 6687

Hoylake Sailing School
Wirral   0151 632 4664

Plymouth Sailing School
Plymouth   01752 493377

Sail North Wales
Conwy   01492 584208

Southern Sailing
Swanwick   01489 575511

Start Point Sailing
Kingsbridge   01548 810917

Warsash Maritime Centre
Warsash   01489 576161

FOUL-WEATHER GEAR

Aquatogs Cowes   01983 295071

Century Finchampstead   0118 9731616

Crewsaver Gosport   023 9252 8621

Douglas Gill Nottingham 0115 9460844

Gul International Ltd
Bodmin   01208 262400

Helly Hansen
Nottingham   0115 9608797

Henri Lloyd Manchester 0161 799 1212

Musto Ltd Laindon   01268 491555

Pro Rainer Windsor   07752 903882

Splashdown Leeds   0113 270 7000

GENERAL MARINE EQUIPMENT & SPARES

Ampair Ringwood   01425 480780

Aries Vane Gear Spares
Penryn   01326 377467

Arthurs Chandlery, R
Gosport   023 9252 6522

Barden UK Ltd Fareham 01489 570770

Calibra Marine International Ltd
Southampton   08702 400358

CH Marine (Cork)
Cork   +353 21 4315700

Chris Hornsey (Chandlery) Ltd
Southsea   023 9273 4728

Compass Marine (Dartmouth)
Dartmouth   01803 835915

Cox Yacht Charter Ltd, Nick
Lymington   01590 673489

CTC Marine & Leisure
Middlesbrough   01642 230123

Docksafe Ltd
Bangor   028 9147 0453

Frederiksen Boat Fittings (UK) Ltd
Gosport   023 9252 5377

Furneaux Riddall & Co Ltd
Portsmouth   023 9266 8621

Hardware & Marine Supplies
Co Wexford   +353 (53) 29791

GILLINGHAM MARINA
F. Parham Ltd, 173 Pier Road,
Gillingham, Kent, ME7 1UB
Tel: 01634 280022
Fax: 01634 280164
Large stock of Chandlery & Sailing clothing. Suzuki, Avon, Bombard, Orkney dealers; extensive showroom.   M&WL8i/e

Index Marine
Bournemouth   01202 470149

Kearon Ltd, George
Arklow   +353 402 32319

Marathon Leisure
Hayling Island   023 9263 7711

Pro-Boat Ltd
Burnham-on-Crouch   01621 785455

Pump International Ltd
Cornwall   01209 831937

Quay West Chandlers
Poole   01202 742488

Rogers, Angie Bristol   0117 973 8276

Ryland, Kenneth
Stanton   01386 584270

Tiflex Liskeard   01579 320808

Vetus Boating Equipment
Southampton   023 8086 1033

Western Marine Power Ltd
Plymouth   01752 408804

Whitstable Marine
Whitstable   01227 262525

Yacht Parts Plymouth   01752 252489

GENERATORS

Fischer Panda UK Ltd
Verwood   01202 820840

Genacis Poole   01202 624356

Sigma Supplies Ltd
Luton   01582 488110

Wyko Industrial Services
Inverness   01463 224747

HARBOUR MASTERS

Aberaeron HM   01545 571645

Aberdeen HM   01224 597000

Aberdovey HM   01654 767626

Aberystwyth HM   01970 611433

Alderney & Burhou HM 01481 822620

Amble HM   01665 710306

Anstruther HM   01333 310836

Appledore HM   01237 474569

Arbroath HM   01241 872166

Ardglass HM   028 4484 1291

Ardrossan Control Tower HM   01294 463972

Arinagour Piermaster   01879 230347

Arklow HM   +353 402 32466

Baltimore HM   +353 28 22145

Banff HM   01261 815544

Bantry Bay HM   +353 27 53277

Barmouth HM   01341 280671

Barry HM   01446 732665

Beaucette HM   01481 245000

Beaulieu River HM   01590 616200

Belfast Lough HM   028 90 553012

Belfast River Manager 028 90 328507

Bembridge HM   01983 872828

Berwick-upon-Tweed HM   01289 307404

Bideford HM   01237 346131

Blyth HM   01670 352678

Boston HM   01205 362328

Bridlington HM   01262 670148/9

Bridport HM   01308 423222

Brighton HM   01273 819919

Bristol HM   0117 926 4797

Brixham HM   01803 853321

Buckie HM   01542 831700

Bude HM   01288 353111

Burghead HM   01343 835337

Burnham-on-Crouch HM   01621 783602

Burnham-on-Sea HM   01278 782180

Burtonport HM   +353 075 42155

Caernarfon HM   01286 672118

Camber Berthing Offices – Portsmouth   023 92297395

Campbeltown HM   01586 552552

Canal Office (Inverness) HM   01463 233140

Cardiff HM   029 20400500

Carnlough Harbour HM 07703 606763

Castletown Bay HM   01624 823549

Charlestown HM   01726 67526

Chichester Harbour HM 01243 512301

Christchurch HM   01202 495061

Conwy HM   01492 596253

Cork HM   +353 21 4273125

Corpach Canal Sea Lock HM   01397 772249

Courtmacsherry HM   +353 23 46311/46600

Coverack HM   01326 380679

Cowes HM   01983 293952

Crail HM   01333 450820

Craobh Haven HM	01852 502222
Crinan Canal Office HM	01546 603210
Cromarty Firth HM	01381 600479
Crookhaven HM	+353 28 35319
Cullen HM	01261 842477
Dingle HM	+353 66 9151629
Douglas HM	01624 686628
Dover HM	01304 240400 Ext 4520
Dublin HM	+353 1 874871
Dun Laoghaire HM	+353 1 280 1130/8074
Dunbar HM	01368 863206
Dundee HM	01382 224121
Dunmore East HM	+353 51 383166
East Loch Tarbert HM	01859 502444
Eastbourne HM	01323 470099
Eigg Harbour HM	01687 482428
Elie HM	01333 330051
Estuary Control - Dumbarton HM	01389 726211
Exe HM	01392 274306
Eyemouth HM	01890 750223
Falmouth HM	01326 312285
Findochty HM	01542 831466
Fisherrow HM	0131 665 5900
Fishguard (Lower Harbour) HM	01348 874726
Fishguard HM	01348 404425
Fleetwood HM	01253 872323
Flotta HM	01856 701411
Folkestone HM	01303 715354
Fowey HM	01726 832471/2.
Fraserburgh HM	01346 515858
Galway Bay HM	+353 91 561874
Garlieston HM	01988 600274
Glasson Dock HM	01524 751724
Gorey HM	01534 853616
Gourdon HM	01569 762741
Great Yarmouth HM	01493 335501
Grimsby Dockmaster	01472 359181
Groomsport Bay HM	028 91 278040
Hamble River HM	01489 576387
Hayle HM	01736 754043
Helford River HM	01326 250749
Helmsdale HM	01431 821692
Holy Island HM	01289 389217
Holyhead HM	01407 763071
Hopeman HM	01343 835337
Howth HM	+353 1 832 2252
Ilfracombe HM	01271 862108
Inverness HM	01463 715715
Irvine HM	01294 487286
Johnshaven HM	01561 362262
Kettletoft Bay HM	01857 600227
Killybegs HM	+353 73 31032
Kilmore Quay HM	+353 53 29955
Kinlochbervie HM	01971 521235
Kinsale HM	+353 21 4772503
Kirkcudbright HM	01557 331135
Kirkwall HM	01856 872292
Langstone Harbour HM	023 9246 3419
Larne HM	02828 872100
Lerwick HM	01595 692991
Littlehampton HM	01903 721215
Liverpool HM	0151 949 6134/5
Loch Gairloch HM	01445 712140
Loch Inver HM	01571 844265
Looe HM	01503 262839
Lossiemouth HM	01343 813066
Lough Foyle HM	028 7186 0555
Lowestoft HM	01502 572286
Lyme Regis HM	01297 442137
Lymington HM	01590 672014
Lyness HM	01856 791387
Macduff HM	01261 832236
Maryport HM	01900 814431
Menai Strait HM	01248 712312
Methil HM	01333 462725
Mevagissey HM	01726 843305
Milford Haven HM	01646 696100
Minehead HM	01643 702566
Montrose HM	01674 672302
Mousehole HM	01736 731511
Mullion Cove HM	01326 240222
Newhaven HM	01273 612868
Newlyn HM	01736 362523
Newquay HM	01637 872809
Newport Harbour Office	01983 525994
Oban HM	01631 562892
Padstow HM	01841 532239
Par HM	01726 818337
Peel HM	01624 842338
Penrhyn Bangor HM	01248 352525
Penzance HM	01736 366113
Peterhead HM	01779 483630
Pierowall HM	01857 677216
Pittenweem HM	01333 312591
Plockton HM	01599 534589
Polperro HM	01503 272809
Poole HM	01202 440233
Port St Mary HM	01624 833205
Porth Dinllaen HM	01758 720276
Porthleven HM	01326 574207
Porthmadog HM	01766 512927
Portknockie HM	01542 840833
Portland HM	01305 824044
Portpatrick HM	01776 810355
Portree HM	01478 612926
Portrush HM	028 70822307
Portsmouth Harbour Commercial Docks HM	023 92297395
Portsmouth Harbour Control	023 92723694
Portsmouth Harbour HM	023 92723124
Preston HM	01772 726711
Pwllheli HM	01758 704081
Queenborough HM	01795 662051
Queens Gareloch/Rhu HM	01436 674321
Ramsey HM	01624 812245
Ramsgate HM	01843 572100
River Bann & Coleraine HM	028 7034 2012
River Blackwater HM	01621 856487
River Colne (Brightlingsea) HM	01206 302200
River Dart HM	01803 832337
River Deben HM	01394 270106
River Exe Dockmaster	01392 274306
River Humber HM	01482 327171
River Medway HM	01795 596593
River Orwell HM	01473 231010
River Roach HM	01621 783602
River Stour HM	01255 243000
River Tyne/North Shields HM	0191 257 2080
River Yealm HM	01752 872533
Rivers Alde & Ore HM	01473 450481
Rosslare Harbour HM	+353 53 57921
Rothesay HM	01700 503842
Ryde HM	01983 613879
Salcombe HM	01548 843791
Sark HM	01481 832323
Scalloway HM	01595 880574
Scarborough HM	01723 373530
Scrabster HM	01847 892779
Seaham HM	0191 581 3246
Sharpness HM	01453 811862/64
Shoreham HM	01273 598100
Silloth HM	016973 31358
Sligo HM	+353 71 61197
Southampton HM	023 8033 9733
Southend-on-Sea HM	01702 611889
Southwold HM	01502 724712
St Helier HM	01534 885588
St Ives HM	01736 795018
St Margaret's Hope HM	01856 831454
St Mary's HM	01720 422768
St Monans HM	01333 350055
St Peter Port HM	01481 720229
Stonehaven HM	01569 762741
Stornoway HM	01851 702688
Strangford Lough HM	028 44 881637
Stromness HM	01856 850744
Stronsay HM	01857 616317
Sullom Voe HM	01806 242551
Sunderland HM	0191 567 2626
Swale HM	01795 561234
Swansea HM	01792 653787
Tees & Hartlepool Port Authority	01429 277205

Teignmouth HM	01626 773165
Tenby HM	01834 842717
Thames Estuary HM	01474 562200
Tobermory Port Manager HM	01688 302017
Torquay HM	01803 292429
Troon HM	01292 281687
Truro HM	01872 272130
Ullapool HM	01854 612091
Walton-on-the-Naze HM	01255 851899
Watchet HM	01984 631264
Waterford HM	+353 51 874907
Wells-next-the-Sea HM	01328 711646
Weymouth HM	01305 206423
Whitby HM	01947 602354
Whitehaven HM	01946 692435
Whitehills HM	01261 861291
Whitstable HM	01227 274086
Wick HM	01955 602030
Wicklow HM	+353 404 67455
Workington HM	01900 602301
Yarmouth HM	01983 760321
Youghal HM	+353 24 92626

HARBOURS

Bristol Harbour Bristol 0117 922 2000

Clyde Marina – Ardrossan
01294 607077

Jersey Harbours
St Helier 01534 885588

Maryport Harbour and Marina
Maryport 01900 818447/4431

PADSTOW HARBOUR COMMISSIONERS
Harbour House, Padstow,
Cornwall PL28 8AQ
Tel: (01841) 532239
Fax: (01841) 533346
e-mail:
padstowharbour@compuserve.com
www.padstow-harbour.co.uk
Inner harbour controlled by tidal gate - opens HW±2 hours. Minimum depth 3 metres at all times. Yachtsmen must be friendly as vessels raft together. Services include showers, toilets, diesel, water and ice. Security by CCTV. 2007/M&Wext1/e

Peterhead Bay Authority
Peterhead 01779 474020

QUAY MARINAS
Avon House, Newbrick Road,
Stokegifford, Bristol BS34 8RA
Tel: (01179) 236466
Fax: (01179) 236508
e-mail: sriggs@quaymarinas.com
A wholly owned subsidary of Quay Marinas, operate comprehensive yachting facilities at 5 locations in the UK and are marketing agents for Malahide Marina in Dublin Bay. 2007/M&WEXT9/e

Sark Moorings – Channel Islands
01481 832260

INSTRUMENTATION & POSITION FIXING

Belson Design Ltd, Nick
Southampton 077 6835 1330

Cooke & Son Ltd, B
Hull 01482 223454

Diverse Yacht Services
Hamble 023 8045 3399

Dolphin Maritime Software Ltd
Lancaster 01624 673965

Geonav UK Ltd Poole 0870 240 4575

Lilley & Gillie Ltd, John
North Shields 0191 257 2217

Precision Navigation
Romsey 01794 521079

Smith AM (Marine) Ltd
London 020 8529 6988

Yachting Instruments Ltd
Sturminster Newton 01258 817662

INSURANCE/FINANCE

Admiral Marine Ltd
Salisbury 01722 416106

Bigfish London 020 8651 4096

Bishop Skinner Boat Insurance
London 0800 7838057

Bristol Channel Marine
Cardiff 029 2063 1163

Carter Boat Insurance, RA
0800 174061

Castlemain Ltd
St Peter Port 01481 721319

Clark Insurance, Graham
Tyneside 0191 455 8089

Craftinsure.com
Orpington 01689 889507

Craven Hodgson Associates
Leeds 0113 243 8443

Curtis & Partners, Colin
Plymouth 01752 664649

Giles Insurance Brokers
Irvine 01294 315481

GJW Direct Liverpool 0151 473 8000

Haven Knox-Johnston
West Malling 01732 223600

Lombard Southampton 023 8024 2171

Mardon Insurance
Shrewsbury 0800 515629

Marine & General Insurance Services Ltd Maidstone 01622 201106

Mercia Marine Malvern 01684 564457

Nautical Insurance Services Ltd
Leigh-on-Sea 01702 470811

Navigators & General
Brighton 01273 863400

Pantaenius UK Ltd
Plymouth 01752 223656

Porthcawl Insurance Consultants
Porthcawl 01656 784866

Saga Boat Insurance Folkestone
01303 771135

St Margarets Insurances
London 020 8778 6161

Weysure Ltd Weymouth 07000 939787

LIFERAFTS & INFLATABLES

A B MARINE LTD
Castle Walk, St Peter Port,
Guernsey, Channel Islands
GY1 1AU.
Tel: (01481) 722378
Fax: (01481) 711080
We specialise in safety and survival equipment and are a M.C.A. approved service station for liferafts including R.F.D., Beaufort/Dunlop, Zodiac, Avon, Plastimo and Lifeguard. We also carry a full range of new liferafts, dinghies and lifejackets and distress flares. M&WL48

AB Marine Ltd Guernsey 01481 722378

Adec Marine Ltd
Croydon 020 8686 9717

Avon Inflatables Llanelli 01554 882000

Cosalt International Ltd
Aberdeen 01224 588327

Glaslyn Marine Supplies Ltd
Porthmadog 01766 513545

Hale Marine, Ron
Portsmouth 023 9273 2985

Herm Seaway Marine Ltd
St Peter Port 01481 722838

For Expert, Helpful & Friendly Independent Marine Insurance Advice Call:

Porthcawl Insurance Consultants Ltd.

Open 7 days, Established 1967

Tel: 01656 784866   Fax: 01656 784872
Email: quotes@porthcawl-insurance.co.uk
or why not log for a quote on our website
www.porthcawl-insurance.co.uk

2007/M&WC32/e

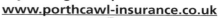

Member
British Marine Federation

"P.I.C (UK) Ltd is authorised and regulated by the Financial Services Authority"

IBS Boats South Woodham Ferrers
01245 323211/425551

KTS Seasafety Kilkeel   028 918 28405

Nationwide Marine Hire
Warrington   01925 245788

Norwest Marine Ltd
Liverpool   0151 207 2860

Ocean Safety
Southampton   023 8072 0800

Polymarine Ltd Conwy   01492 583322

Premium Liferaft Services
Burnham-on-Crouch   0800 243673

Ribeye Dartmouth   01803 832060

Secumar Swansea   01792 280545

South Eastern Marine Services Ltd
Basildon   01268 534427

Suffolk Sailing Ipswich 01473 833010

Whitstable Marine
Whitstable   01227 262525

MAIL ORDER

**ASAP Supplies – Equipment &
Spares Worldwide**
Suffolk   0845 1300 870

Bridger Marine, John
Exeter   01392 216420

Compass Watersports
Devizes   01380 813100

Duncan Yacht Chandlers
Glasgow   0141 429 6044

Inspirations Everything
Clacton-on-Sea   01255 428113

Mailspeed Marine
Warrington   01925 838858

Marine Store Chandlers
Maldon   01621 854380

Pinnell & Bax
Northampton   01604 592808

Purple Sails & Marine
Walsall   01922 614787

Reed's Nautical
Bradford-on-Avon   01225 868821

MARINAS

Aberystwyth Marina   01970 611422

Amble Marina   01665 712168

Arbroath Harbour   01241 872166

Ardfern Yacht Centre Ltd
01852 500247

Ardglass Marina   028 44842332

Arklow Marina   +353 402 39901

Ballycastle Marina   028 2076 8525

Bangor Marina   028 91 453297

Beaucette Marina   01481 245000

Bembridge Harbour   01983 872828

Berthon Lymington Marina
01590 647405

Birdham Pool Marina   01243 512310

Blackwater Marina   01621 740264

Boston Marina   01205 364420

Bradwell Marina   01621 776235

HASLAR MARINA

Only minutes from open water in The Solent. Annual berths £402 per metre including VAT
Tel: 023 9260 1201

EAST COWES MARINA

Sheltered pontoon berths with all the Isle of Wight has to offer. Annual berths £342 per metre including VAT
Tel: 01983 293983

WEYMOUTH MARINA

Ideal stop off whilst cruising the South Coast. Annual berths £365 per metre including VAT
Tel: 01305 767576

DEAN & REDDYHOFF
MARINAS

See our full page colour advert at the end of Area 1

2007/M&WC49/b

Bray Marina   01628 623654

Brentford Dock Marina 020 8232 8941

Bridgemarsh Marine   01621 740414

Brighton Marina   01273 819919

Bristol Marina   0117 9213198

Brixham Marina   01803 882929

Bucklers Hard Marina   01590 616200

Burnham Yacht Harbour Marina Ltd
01621 782150

Cahersiveen Marina+353 66 947 2777

Caley Marina   01463 236539

Carlingford Marina   +353 42 9373073

Carrickfergus Marina   028 9336 6666

Castlepark Marina   +353 21 477 4959

Chatham Maritime Marina
01634 899200

Chelsea Harbour Marina
020 7225 9157

Chichester Marina   01243 512731

Clyde Marina Ltd   01294 607077

Cobbs Quay Marina   01202 674299

Coleraine Marina   028 703 44768

Conwy Marina   01492 593000

Cowes Yacht Haven   01983 299975

Craobh Marina   01852 500222

Crosshaven Boatyard Marina
+353 21 483 1161

Dart Marina Yacht Harbour
01803 833351

Darthaven Marina   01803 752242

Dartside Quay   01803 845445

Deganwy Quay   01492 583984

Dingle Marina   +353 66 915 1629

Dover Marina   01304 241663

DUN LAOGHAIRE MARINA
Harbour Road, Dun Laoghaire,
Co. Dublin
Tel: ++353 1 2020040
Fax: ++353 1 2020043
e-mail: dlmarina@indigo.ie
www.dlharbour.ie
Located within Dun Laoghaire Harbour -
8 miles from Dublin City centre adjacent
suburban rail station and all amenities.
Facilities include shore power, potable
water, showers/toilet incl. disabled,
laundry, fuel - petrol & diesel, gaz, pump
out, boatyard, hoist.   2007/M&WL9/z

Dun Laoghaire Marina
+353 1 202 0040

Dunstaffnage Marina Ltd
01631 566555

East Cowes Marina   01983 293983

East Ferry Marina   +353 21 483 1342

Emsworth Yacht Harbour
01243 377727

Essex Marina   01702 258531

Falmouth Marina   01326 316620

Falmouth Yacht Haven 01326 312285

Fambridge Yacht Haven01621 740370

Fenit Harbour Marina
+353 66 7136231

Fleetwood Harbour Village Marina
01253 872323

Fox's Marina Ipswich Ltd
01473 689111

Gallions Point Marina 0207 476 7054

GILLINGHAM MARINA
F. Parham Ltd, 173 Pier Road,
Gillingham, Kent, ME7 1UB
Tel: 01634 280022
Fax: 01634 280164
Kent's Five Gold Anchor Marina on the
River Medway, eight miles from
Sheerness.   M&WL8a/e

Gillingham Marina   01634 280022

Glasson Dock Marina   01524 751491

Gosport Marina   023 9252 4811

Gunwharf Quays   02392 836732

Hafan Pwllheli   01758 701219

Hamble Point Marina 023 8045 2464

Harbour of Rye   01797 225225

Hartlepool Marina   01429 865744

Haslar Marina   023 9260 1201

Heybridge Basin   01621 853506

Hillyards   01903 713327

Holy Loch Marina   01369 701800

Holyhead Marina   01407 764242

Hoo Marina   01634 250311

Howth Marina   +353 1839 2777

Hull Marina   01482 330505

Hythe Marina   023 8020 7073

Ipswich Haven Marina   01473 236644

Island Harbour Marina 01983 822999

MARINE SUPPLIES AND SERVICES GUIDE

HARBOUR MASTERS – MARINAS

Kemps Quay Marina	023 8063 2323	
Kilmore Quay Marina	+353 53 29955	
Kilrush Creek Marina	+353 65 9052072	
Kinsale Yacht Club Marina	+353 21 477 2196	
Kip Marina	01475 521485	
Kirkwall Marina	01856 872292	
La Collette Yacht Basin	01534 885588	
Lady Bee Marina	01273 593801	
Lake Yard Marina	01202 674531	
Largs Yacht Haven	01475 675333	
Lawrence Cove Marina	+353 27 75044	
Limehouse Marina	020 7308 9930	
Littlehampton Marina	01903 713553	
Liverpool Marina	0151 707 6777	
Lossiemouth Marina	01343 813066	
Lowestoft Haven Marina	01502 580300	
Lymington Yacht Haven	01590 677071	
Malahide Marina	+353 1 845 4129	
Marina - Esbjerg		
Maryport Harbour and Marina	01900 814431	
Mayflower International Marina	01752 556633	
Melfort Pier & Harbour	01852 200333	
Mercury Yacht Harbour	023 8045 5994	

Meridian Quay Marina	01472 268424
Milford Marina	01646 696312
Millbay Marina Village	01752 226785
Mylor Yacht Harbour	01326 372121
Nairn Marina	01667 456008

NEPTUNE MARINA LTD
Neptune Quay, Ipswich, Suffolk
IP4 1AX
Tel: (01473) 215204
Fax: (01473) 215206
e-mail:
enquiries@neptune-marina.com
www.neptune-marina.com
Accessible through continuously operating lockgates (VHF Channel 68) Neptune Marina (VHF Channels 80 or 37) is located on the north side of Ipswich wet dock immediately adjacent to the town centre and integrated into the rapidly regenerating northern quays. M&Wext7

Neptune Marina Ltd	01473 215204
Newhaven Marina	01273 513881
Neyland Yacht Haven	01646 601601
Northney Marina	023 9246 6321
Noss-on-Dart Marina	01803 834582
Ocean Village Marina	023 8022 9385
Parkstone Yacht Haven	01202 738824
Penarth Quays Marina	02920 705021
Penton Hook	01932 568681

Peterhead Bay Marina	01779 483600
Plymouth Yacht Haven	01752 404231
Poole Quay Boat Haven	01202 649488
Poplar Dock Marina	020 7517 5550
Port Edgar Marina & Sailing School	0131 331 3330
Port Ellen Marina	01496 302441
Port Hamble Marina	023 8045 2741
Port Pendennis Marina	01326 211211
Port Solent Marina	023 9221 0765
Portaferry Marina	028 4272 9598
Portishead Quays Marina	01275 841941
Preston Marina	01772 733595

QUAY MARINAS
Avon House, Newbrick Road,
Stokegifford, Bristol BS34 8RA
Tel: (01179) 236466
Fax: (01179) 236508
e-mail: sriggs@quaymarinas.com
A wholly owned subsidary of Quay Marinas, operate comprehensive yachting facilities at 5 locations in the UK and are marketing agents for Malahide Marina in Dublin Bay. 2007/M&WEXT9/e

SOVEREIGN
HARBOUR
EASTBOURNE

FIRST CLASS SERVICE • 24HR ACCESS

Sovereign Harbour's award-winning marina is committed to providing first class facilities – 860 berths (up to 22m) with electricity and fresh water – 24 hour staffing and security 365 days per year – showers, toilets, car parking, restaurants and shops, all at convenient locations.

Tel: 01323 470099 (24 hours) • Email: fpoinboeuf@carillionplc.com
www.sovereignharbour.co.uk

2007/M&WC62/e

PLOT A COURSE FOR...
QUAY MARINAS

With their unique blend of superb yachting facilities and residential development, Quay Marinas are internationally recognised as among the finest anywhere. All marinas offer a friendly welcome to yachtsmen and cater for every boating requirement.

HEAD OFFICE:
A & W Building
The Docks
Portishead
N. Somerset
BF20 7DF
Tel: 01275 841188

BANGOR MARINA ....Belfast Lough Tel: 028 9145 3297
CONWY MARINA ....North Wales Tel: 028 9145 3297
PENARTH MARINA...Cardiff Bay Tel: 029 2070 5021
PORTISHEAD QUAYS MARINA ....Bristol Channel Tel: 01275 841941
ROYAL QUAYS MARINA ....North Sheilds Tel: 0191 272 8282

*Marketing agents   2007/M&WM20/e

Queen Anne's Battery Marina
01752 671142

Ramsgate Royal Harbour Marina
01843 572100

Rhu Marina Ltd   01436 820238

Ridge Wharf Yacht Centre
01929 552650

Royal Clarence Marina 02392 523810

Royal Cork Yacht Club Marina
+353 21 483 1023

Royal Norfolk and Suffolk Yacht Club
01502 566726

Royal Northumberland Yacht Club
01670 353636

Royal Quays Marina   0191 272 8282

Ryde Leisure Harbour   01983 613879

Salterns Marina Boatyard & Hotel
01202 709971

Salve Engineering Marina
+353 21 483 1145

Sandpoint Marina (Dumbarton)
01389 762396

Saxon Wharf Marina   023 8033 9490

Seaport Marina   01463 725500

Seaton's Marina   028 703 832086

Shamrock Quay Marina
023 8022 9461

Sharpness Marina   01453 811476

Shepherds Wharf Boatyard Ltd
01983 297821

Shotley Marina   01473 788982

South Dock Marina   020 7252 2244

South Ferriby Marina   01652 635620

Southdown Marina   01752 823084

Southsea Marina   023 9282 2719

Sovereign Harbour Marina
01323 470099

Sparkes Marina   023 92463572

St Helier Marina   01534 885588

St Katharine Marina Ltd
0207 264 5312

St Peter Port Marinas 01481 720229

St Peter's Marina   0191 265 4472

Stromness Marina   01856 850744

Suffolk Yacht Harbour Ltd
01473 659240

Sunderland Marina   0191 514 4721

Sunseeker International Marina
01202 381111

Sutton Harbour   01752 204702

Swansea Marina   01792 470310

Swanwick Marina   01489 884081

Titchmarsh Marina   01255 672185

Tollesbury Marina   01621 869204

Torpoint Yacht Harbour 01752 813658

Torquay Marina   01803 200210

Troon Yacht Haven   01292 315553

Victoria Marina   01481 725987

Walton Yacht Basin   01255 675873

Waterford City Marina
+353 51 309900

Weymouth Harbour   01305 838423

Weymouth Marina   01305 767576

Whitby Marina   01947 602354

Whitehaven Harbour Marina
01946 692435

Whitehills Marina   01261 861291

Windsor Marina   01753 853911

Wisbech Yacht Harbour 01945 588059

Woolverstone Marina   01473 780206

Yarmouth Harbour   01983 760321

MARINE ACTIVITY CENTRES

Cowes Yacht Haven
Cowes   01983 299975

Doune Marine
Mallaig   01687 462667

Tollesbury Marina
Tollesbury   01621 869202

MARINE ARTISTS

Farrow Marine Artist, Steve
Cleethorpes   01472 311994

Lynch, Mari Godalming 01483 201085

Taylor Marine Artist, Neil
Newcastle   01782 251194

Wright Marine Artist, Colin
Poole   01202 687947

MARINE CONSULTANTS AND SURVEYORS

Amble Boat Company Ltd
Amble   01665 710267

Ark Surveys East Anglia/South Coast
01621 857065/01794 521957

Atkin and Associates
Lymington   01590 688633

Barbican Yacht Agency Ltd
Plymouth   01752 228855

Booth Marine Surveys, Graham
Birchington-on-Sea   01843 843793

Bureau Maritime Ltd
Maldon   01621 859181

Byrde & Associates
Kimmeridge   01929 480064

Cannell & Associates, David M
Wivenhoe   01206 823337

Clarke Designs LLP, Owen
Dartmouth   01803 770495

Davies, Peter N
Wivenhoe   01206 823289

Down Marine Co Ltd
Belfast   028 90480247

Green, James Plymouth 01752 660516

Greening Yacht Design Ltd, David
Chichester   023 9263 1806

Hansing & Associates
North Wales/Midlands   01248 671291

JP Services – Marine Safety & Training Chichester 01243 537552

Marintec Lymington   01590 683414

Norwood Marine
Margate   01843 835711

Quay Consultants Ltd
West Wittering   01243 673056

Scott Marine Surveyors & Consultants Conwy 01248 680759

Staton-Bevan, Tony
Lymington   01590 645755

Swanwick Yacht Surveyors
Southampton   01489 564822

Thomas, Stephen
Southampton   023 8048 6273

Victoria Yacht Surveys
Cornwall   0800 093 2113

Ward & McKenzie
Woodbridge   01394 383222

Ward & McKenzie (North East)
Pocklington   01759 304322

Yacht Designers & Surveyors Association Bordon 0845 0900 162

MARINE ENGINEERS

Allerton Engineering
Lowestoft   01502 537870

APAS Engineering Ltd
Southampton   023 8063 2558

Ardmair Boat Centre
Ullapool   01854 612054

4 Branches on the East Coast

Brightlingsea (Head Office)
61 - 63 Waterside, Brightlingsea, Essex, CO7 0AX
Tel: 01206 302133 / 01206 305233 Fax: 01206 305601
Email: info@frenchmarine.com

Walton-on-the-Naze (Essex)
Titchmarsh Marina, Coles Lane, Walton-on-the-naze, Essex, CO14 8SL
Tel/Fax: 01255 850303
Email: walton@frenchmarine.com

Levington (Suffolk)
Suffolk Yacht Harbour (Stratton Hall), Levington, Ipswich, IP10 0LN
Tel/Fax: 01473 659882
Email: suffolk@frenchmarine.com

Rackheath (Norfolk)
Unit 19, Wendover Road, Rackheath, Norfolk, NR13 6LR
Tel: 01603 722079 Fax: 01603 721311
Email: norfolk@frenchmarine.com

Specialists in:
• Marine engine repair
• Marine engine maintenance
• Prop shaft fabrication
• Stern gear fabrication
• Propeller repair - Fast turn around
• Engine Spares - all manufacturers supported
• Full Marine Chandlery

Suppliers of:
New and Second-hand engines and gearboxes,
marine installation equipment, propellers, stern tubes,
seacocks, exhaust hose, mufflers and fuel systems
Full range of chandlery stocked, ropes, paints, etc.

www.frenchmarine.com

2007/M&WM22/e

Arisaig Marine
Inverness-shire   01687 450224

Arun Craft Littlehampton 01903 723667

Attrill & Sons, H
Bembridge   01983 872319

Auto & Marine Services
Botley   01489 785009

Auto Marine Southsea 023 9282 5601

BJ Marine Ltd
Bangor, Ireland   028 9127 1434

Bristol Boat Ltd Bristol 01225 872032

Buzzard Marine Engineering
Yarmouth   01983 760707

C & B Marine Ltd
Chichester Marina   01243 511273

Caddy, Simon Falmouth Marina,
Falmouth   01326 372682

Caledonian Marine
Rhu Marina   01436 821184

Cambrian Engineering (Cymru) Ltd
Bangor   01248 370248

Cardigan Outboards
Cardigan   01239 613966

Channel Islands Marine Ltd
Guernsey   01481 716880

Channel Islands Marine Ltd
Jersey   01534 767595

Clarence Marine Engineering
Gosport   023 9251 1555

Cook's Diesel Service Ltd
Faversham   01795 538553

Cragie Engineering
Kirkwall   01856 874680

Crane Marine, John
Havant   023 9240 0121

Crinan Boatyard Ltd
Crinan   01546 830232

Cutler Marine Engineering, John
Emsworth   01243 375014

Dale Sailing Co Ltd
Milford Haven   01646 603110

Davis Marine Services
Ramsgate   01843 586172

Denney & Son, EL
Redcar   01642 483507

DH Marine (Shetland) Ltd
Shetland   01595 690618

Emark Marine Ltd
Emsworth   01243 375383

Evans Marine Engineering, Tony
Pwllheli   01758 613219

Fairways Marine Engineers
Maldon   01376 572866

Felton Marine Engineering
Brighton   01273 601779

Felton Marine Engineering
Eastbourne   01323 470211

Ferrypoint Boat Co
Youghal   +353 24 94232

Fettes & Rankine Engineering
Aberdeen   01224 573343

Fleetwood & Sons Ltd, Henry
Lossiemouth   01343 813015

Fleming Engineering, J
Stornoway   01851 703488

Floetree Ltd (Loch Lomond Marina)
Balloch   01389 752069

Fowey Harbour Marine Engineers
Fowey   01726 832806

Fox Marine Services Ltd
Jersey   01534 721312

Freeport Marine Jersey 01534 888100

French Marine Motors Ltd
Colchester   01206 302133

GH Douglas Marine Services
Fleetwood Harbour Village Marina,
Fleetwood   01253 877200

GILLINGHAM MARINA
F. Parham Ltd, 173 Pier Road,
Gillingham, Kent, ME7 1UB
Tel: 01634 280022
Fax: 01634 280164
Largest repair facilities in the South East
for craft up to 65 tonnes & 26 metres.

M&WL8d/e

Golden Arrow Marine
Southampton   023 8071 0371

Goodchild Marine Services
Great Yarmouth   01493 782301

Goodwick Marine
Fishguard   01348 873955

Gosport Boat Yard
Gosport   023 9252 4811

Griffins Garage Dingle Marina,
Co Kerry   +353 66 91 51178

Hale Marine, Ron
Portsmouth   023 9273 2985

Hamnavoe Engineering
Stromness   01856 850576

Hampshire Marine Ltd
Stubbington   01329 665561

Harbour Engineering
Itchenor   01243 513454

Hardway Marine Store
Gosport   023 9258 0420

Hartlepool Marine Engineering
Hartlepool   01429 867883

Hayles, Harold
Yarmouth   01983 760373

Herm Seaway Marine Ltd
St Peter Port   01481 726829

HNP Engineers (Lerwick Ltd)
Lerwick   01595 692493

Home Marine Emsworth Yacht Harbour,
Emsworth   01243 374125

Hook Marine Ltd
Troon   01292 679500

Hooper Marine
Littlehampton   01903 731195

Humphrey, Chris
Teignmouth   01626 772324

Instow Marine Services
Bideford   01271 861081

Jones (Boatbuilders), David
Chester   01244 390363

Keating Marine Engineering Ltd, Bill
Jersey   01534 733977

Kingston Marine Services
Cowes   01983 299385

Kippford Slipway Ltd
Dalbeattie   01556 620249

Lansdale Pannell Marine
Chichester   01243 512374

Lencraft Boats Ltd
Dungarvan   +353 58 68220

Lifeline Marine Services
Dolphin Haven, Poole   01202 669676

Llyn Marine Services
Pwllheli   01758 612606

Lynx Engineering
St Helens, Isle of Wight 01983 873711

M&G Marine Services
Mayflower International Marina, Plymouth
          01752 563345

MacDonald & Co Ltd, JN
Glasgow   0141 334 6171

Mackay Marine Services
Aberdeen   01224 575772

Mainbrayce Marine
Alderney   01481 822772

Malakoff and Moore
Lerwick   01595 695544

Mallaig Boat Building and Engineering Mallaig   01687 462304

Marindus Engineering
Kilmore Quay   +353 53 29794

Marine Engineering Looe
Brixham   01803 844777

Marine Engineering Looe
Looe   01503 263009

Marine General Engineers Beaucette
Marina, Guernsey   01481 245808

Marine Maintenance
Portsmouth   023 9260 2344

Marine Maintenance
Tollesbury   01621 860441

Marine Propulsion
Hayling Island   023 9246 1694

Marine & General Engineers
St. Sampsons Harbour, Guernsey
                              01481 245808

Marine-Trak Engineering Mylor Yacht
Harbour, Falmouth   01326 376588

Marlec Marine
Ramsgate   01843 592176

Martin (Marine) Ltd, Alec
Birkenhead   0151 652 1663

Medusa Marine Ipswich 01473 780090

Mobile Marine Engineering Liverpool
Marina, Liverpool   01565 733553

Motortech Marine Engineering
Portsmouth   023 9251 3200

Mount's Bay Engineering
Newlyn   01736 363095

MP Marine Maryport   01900 810299

New World Yacht Care
Helensburgh   01436 820586

North Western Automarine Engineers
Largs   01475 687139

Noss Marine Services
Dart Marina, Dartmouth 01803 833343

Owen Marine, Robert
Porthmadog   01766 513435

Pace, Andy Newhaven   01273 516010

Penzance Dry Dock and Engineering Co Ltd Penzance   01736 363838

Pirie & Co, John S
Fraserburgh   01346 513314

Portavon Marine
Keynsham   0117 986 1626

Power Afloat, Elkins Boatyard
Christchurch   01202 489555

Powerplus Marine Cowes Yacht Haven,
Cowes   01983 200036

Pro-Marine Queen Anne's Battery
Marina, Plymouth   01752 267984

PT Marine Engineering
Hayling Island   023 9246 9332

R & M Marine
Portsmouth   023 9273 7555

R & S Engineering Dingle Marina,
Ireland   +353 66 915 1189

Reddish Marine
Salcombe   01548 844094

Reynolds, Cliff
Hartlepool   01429 272049

RHP Marine
Cowes   01983 290421

River Tees Engineering & Welding Ltd
Middlesbrough   01642 226226

RK Marine Ltd Hamble   01489 583585

RK Marine Ltd
Swanwick   01489 583572

Rossiter Yachts Ltd
Christchurch   01202 483250

Ryan & Roberts Marine Services
Askeaton   +353 61 392198

Salve Marine Ltd
Crosshaven   +353 21 4831145

Scarborough Marine Engineering Ltd
Scarborough   01723 375199

Seaguard Marine Engineering Ltd
Goodwick   01348 872976

Seamark-Nunn & Co
Felixstowe   01394 275327

Seaward Engineering
Glasgow   0141 632 4910

Seaway Marine
Gosport   023 9260 2722

Shearwater Engineering Services Ltd
Dunoon   01369 706666

Silvers Marina Ltd
Helensburgh   01436 831222

Starey Marine
Salcombe   01548 843655

Stratton Boatyard, Ken
Bembridge   01983 873185

Strickland Marine Engineering, Brian
Chichester   01243 513454

Tarbert Marine Arbroath 01241 872879

Tollesbury Marine Engineering
Tollesbury Marina,
Tollesbury   01621 869919

Troon Marine Services Ltd
Troon   01292 316180

Vasey Marine Engineering, Gordon
Fareham   07798 638625

Volspec Ltd Ipswich Marina,
Ipswich   01473 219651

Wallis, Peter Torquay Marina,
Torquay   01803 844777

WB Marine Chichester   01243 512857

West, Mick Brighton   01273 626656

West Point Marine Services
Fareham   01329 232881

Western Marine Power Ltd
Plymouth   01752 408804

Weymouth Marina Mechanical Services Weymouth   01305 779379

Whittington, G Lady Bee Marine,
Shoreham   01273 593801

Whitewater Marine
Malahide   +353 1 816 8473

Wigmore Wright Marine Services
Penarth Marina   029 2070 9983

Wright, M Manaccan   01326 231502

Wyko Industrial Services
Inverness   01463 224747

Yates Marine, Martin
Galgate   01524 751750

Ynys Marine
Cardigan   01239 613179

Yoldings Marine
Eastbourne   01323 470882

Youngboats
Faversham   01795 536176

1° West Marine Ltd
Portsmouth   023 9283 8335

MASTS, SPARS & RIGGING

A2 Rigging
Falmouth   01326 312209

Allspars Plymouth   01752 266766

Amble Boat Co Ltd
Morpeth   01665 710267

ATLANTIC SPARS LTD
Brixham   01803 843322
                              2007/M&WL17/e

Arun Canvas & Rigging
Littlehampton   1903 732561

Buchanan, Keith
St Mary's   01720 422037

Bussell & Co, WL
Weymouth   01305 785633

Carbospars Ltd Hamble 023 8045 6736

Cable & Rope Works
Pevensey   01323 763019

Coates Marine Ltd
Whitby   01947 604486

Composite Rigging
Southampton   023 8023 4488

Dauntless Boatyard Ltd
Canvey Island   01268 793782

Davies Marine Services
Ramsgate   01843 586172

Eurospars Ltd Plymouth 01752 550550

Exe Leisure Exeter   01392 879055

Fox's Marine Ipswich Ltd
Ipswich   01473 689111

Freeland Yacht Spars Ltd
Dorchester on Thames 01865 341277

Gordon, AD Portland   01305 821569

Harris Rigging
Totnes   01803 840160

Heyn Engineering
Belfast   028 9035 0022

MARINE ENGINEERS – MASTS, SPARS & RIGGING

MARINE SUPPLIES AND SERVICES GUIDE

Irish Spars and Rigging
Malahide   +353 86 209 5996

Lowestoft Yacht Services
Lowestoft   01502 585535

Marine Resource Centre
Oban   01631 720291

MP Marine Maryport   01900 810299

Ocean Rigging
Lymington   01590 676292

Owen Sails Oban   01631 720485

Premier Spars Poole   01202 677717

Pro Rig S Ireland   +353 87 298 3333

Rig Magic Ipswich   01473 655089

Rig Shop, The
Southampton   023 8033 8341

Roberts Marine Ltd, S
Liverpool   0151 707 8300

Sailspar Ltd
Brightlingsea   01206 302679

Salcombe Boatstore
Salcombe   01548 843708

Seldén Mast Ltd
Southampton   01489 484000

Silvers Marina Ltd
Helensburgh   01436 831222

Silverwood Yacht Services Ltd
Portsmouth   023 9232 7067

Southern Spar Services
Northam   023 8033 1714

Southern Masts & Rigging
Brighton   01273 668902

Storrar Marine Store
Newcastle upon Tyne   0191 266 1037

Tedfords Rigging & Rafts
Belfast   028 9032 6763

TJ Rigging Conwy   07780 972411

TS Rigging Malden   01621 874861

Windjammer Marine
Milford Marina   01646 699070

Yacht Rigging Services
Plymouth   01752 226609

Yacht Shop, The
Fleetwood   01253 879238

Yacht Solutions Ltd
Portsmouth   023 9220 0670

XW Rigging Gosport   023 9251 3553

Z Spars UK Hadleigh   01473 822130

1° West Marine Ltd
Portsmouth   023 9283 8335

NAVIGATION
EQUIPMENT – GENERAL

Belson Design Ltd, Nick
Southampton   077 6835 1330

B & G UK Romsey   01794 510010

Brown Son & Ferguson Ltd
Glasgow   0141 429 1234

Chattan Security Ltd
Edinburgh   0131 555 3155

Cooke & Son Ltd, B Hull 01482 223454

Diverse Yacht Services
Hamble   023 8045 3399

Dolphin Maritime Software Ltd
Lancaster   01524 841946

Dubois Phillips & McCallum Ltd
Liverpool   0151 236 2776

Eland Exeter   01392 255788

Garmin Romsey   01794 519944

Geonav UK Ltd Poole   0870 240 4575

Imray Laurie Norie and Wilson Ltd
St Ives, Cambs   01480 462114

Kelvin Hughes
Southampton   023 8063 4911

Lilley & Gillie Ltd, John
North Shields   0191 257 2217

Marine Chart Services
Wellingborough   01933 441629

PC Maritime Plymouth   01752 254205

Navimo UK Ltd
Hedge End   01489 778850

Precision Navigation
Romsey   01794 521079

Price & Co, WF Bristol   0117 929 2229

Raymarine Ltd
Portsmouth   023 9269 3611

Robbins Marine Electronics
Liverpool   0151 709 5431

Royal Institute of Navigation
London   020 7591 3130

ROYAL INSTITUTE OF NAVIGATION
1 Kensington Gore, London
SW1 2AT
Tel: 0207 591 3130
Fax: 0207 591 3131
www.rin.org.uk
If you are using this Almanac then you should be a member or associate of the Royal Institute of Navigation. Call the number above.   M&WL13

Sea Chest Nautical Bookshop
Plymouth   01752 222012

Seath Instruments (1992) Ltd
Lowestoft   01502 573811

Smith (Marine) Ltd, AM
London   020 8529 6988

South Bank Marine Charts Ltd
Grimsby   01472 361137

Southcoasting Navigators
Devon   01626 335626

Stanford Charts
Bristol   0117 929 9966

Stanford Charts
London   020 7836 1321

Stanford Charts
Manchester   0161 831 0250

Todd Chart Agency Ltd
County Down   028 9146 6640

UK Hydrographic Office
Taunton   01823 337900

Warsash Nautical Bookshop
Warsash   01489 572384

Yachting Instruments Ltd
Sturminster Newton   01258 817662

PAINT & OSMOSIS

Advanced Blast Cleaning Paint
Tavistock 01822 617192/07970 407911

Blakes Paints
Southampton   01489 864440

GILLINGHAM MARINA
F. Parham Ltd, 173 Pier Road,
Gillingham, Kent, ME7 1UB
Tel: 01634 280022
Fax: 01634 280164
Spraying up to 26 metre craft.
International Paint centre and osmosis centre.   M&WL8f/e

Herm Seaway Marine Ltd
St Peter Port   01481 726829

International Coatings Ltd
Southampton   023 8022 6722

Marineware Ltd
Southampton   023 8033 0208

New Guard Coatings Ltd
Wetherby   01937 568311

NLB Marine Ardrossan 01563 521509

Pro-Boat Ltd
Burnham on Crouch   01621 785455

Rustbuster Ltd
Peterborough   0870 9090093

Smith & Son Ltd, EC
Luton   01582 729721

SP Systems
Isle of Wight   01983 828000

Teal & Mackrill Ltd Hull 01482 320194

Troon Marine Services Ltd
Troon   01292 316180

POLICE

Aberdeen	01224 386000
Aberdovey	01286 673333
Abersoch	01286 673333
Aberystwyth	01970 612791
Alderney and Burhou	01481 725111
Anstruther	01333 592100
Appledore	08705 777444
Arbroath	01241 872222
Ardglass	028 4461501
Ardrishaig	01546 603233
Ardrossan	01294 468236
Arklow	+353 402 32304/5

Baltimore	+353 28 20102	Glandore	+353 23 48162	Nairn	01667 452222
Bantry Bay	+353 27 50045	Great Yarmouth	01493 336200	Newhaven	01273 515801
Barmouth	01286 673333	Grimsby	01482 210031	Newtown Creek	08705 777444
Barry	01446 734451	Guernsey	01481 725111	Oban	01631 562213
Beaulieu River	023 80335444	Hamble River	023 80335444	Padstow	08705 777444
Belfast Lough	028 91 454444	Hartlepool	01429 221151	Peel	01624 631212
Berwick-upon-Tweed	01289 307111	Herm	01481 722377	Penzance	08705 777444
Blyth	01661 872555	Helmsdale	01431 821222	Peterhead	01779 472571
Boston	01205 366222	Holyhead	01286 673333	Plymouth	0990 777444
Bridlington	01262 672222	Hopeman	01343 830222	Poole Harbour	01202 223954
Bridport	01305 768970	Howth	+353 1 6664900	Port St Mary	01624 631212
Brighton	01273 606744	Hull	01482 210031	Porthmadog	01286 673333
Bristol	0117 9277777	Ilfracombe	08705 777444	Portishead	01934 638272
Brixham	0990 777444	Inverkip	01475 521222	Portland	01305 768970
Buckie	01542 832222	Inverness	01463 715555	Portpatrick	01776 702112
Burnham-on-Crouch	01621 782121	Isles of Scilly	01721 422444	Portree	01478 612888
Burnham-on-Sea	01823 337911	Kenmare River	+353 64 41177	Portrush	028 70344122
Burry Port	01554 772222	Keyhaven	01590 615101	Preston	01772 203203
Caernarfon	01286 673333	Killybegs	+353 73 31002	Pwllheli	01286 673333
Campbeltown	01586 552253	Kilmore Quay	+353 53 29642	Queenborough	01795 477055
Cardiff	01446 734451	Kilrush	+353 65 51057	Ramsey	01624 631212
Carlingford Lough	042 9373102	Kinlochbervie	01971 521222	Ramsgate	01843 231055
Castle Haven	+353 28 36144	Kinsale	+353 21 4772302	Rhu	01436 672141
Christchurch	01202 486333	Kirkcudbright	01557 330600	River Bann and Coleraine	
Colchester	01206 762212	Kirkwall	01856 872241		028 70344122
Conwy	01492 517171	Lamlash	01770 302573	River Colne	01255 221312
Corpach	01397 702361	Largs	01475 674651	River Deben	01394 383377
Courtmacsherry	+353 23 46122	Larne	02828 272266	River Humber	01482 359171
Crinan Canal	01546 602222	Lerwick	01595 692110	River Stour	01255 241312
Dartmouth	08452 777444	Littlehampton	01903 731733	River Tyne	0191 232 3451
Dingle	+353 66 9151522	Liverpool	0151 709 6010	River Yealm	0990 777444
Douglas	01624 631212	Loch Melfort	01852 562213	Rivers Alde and Ore	01394 613500
Dover	01304 216084	Looe	08705 777444	Rothesay	01700 502121
Dover	01304 240055	Lossiemouth	01343 812022	Rye	01797 222112
Dublin	+353 1 6665000	Lough Foyle	028 77766797	S Queensferry	0131 331 1798
Dunbar	01368 862718	Lough Swilly	+353 72 51102	St Mary's	08705 777444
Dunmore East	+353 51 383112	Lowestoft	01986 855321	Salcombe	01548 842107
East Loch Tarbert	01880 820200	Lyme Regis	01305 768970	Sarky	01481 725111
Eastbourne	01323 722522	Macduff and Banff	01261 812555	Scarborough	01723 500300
Exeter	08705 777444	Malahide	+353 1 6664600	Schull	+353 28 28111
Eyemouth	01890 750217	Mallaig	01687 462177	Scrabster	01847 893222
Falmouth	08705 777444	Maryport	01900 602422	Seaham	0191 581 2255
Findhorn	01309 672224	Medway	01634 811281	Sharpness	01452 521201
Fishguard	01437 763355	Menai Strait	01286 673333	Shoreham	01273 454521
Fleetwood	01524 63333	Methil	01592 418888	Sligo	+353 71 57000
Folkestone	01303 850055	Mevagissey	0990 555999	Southampton	023 80845511
Fowey	08452 777444	Milford Haven	01437 763355	Southend-on-Sea	01702 341212
Fraserburgh	01346 513121	Minehead	01823 337911	Southwold	01986 855321
Galway Bay	+353 91 538000	Montrose	01674 672222	St Helier	01534 612612

Stonehaven	01569 762963
Stornoway	01851 702222
Strangford Lough	028 44615011
Stromness	01856 850222
Stronsay	01857 872241
Sunderland	0191 4547555
Swanage	01929 422004
Swansea	01792 456999
Teignmouth	08705 777444
Tenby	01834 842303
Thames Estuary	020 7 754421
The Swale	01795 536639
Tobermory	01688 302016
Torquay	0990 777444
Troon	01292 313100
Ullapool	01854 612017
Walton Backwaters	01255 241312
Wells-next-the-Sea	01493 336200
West Mersea	01206 382930
Westport	+353 98 25555
Wexford	+353 404 67107
Weymouth	01305 768970
Whitby	01947 603443
Whitehaven	01946 692616
Whitstable	01227 770055
Wick	01955 603551
Wicklow	+353 404 67107
Workington	01900 602422
Yarmouth	01983 528000
Youghal	+353 24 92200

PROPELLERS & STERNGEAR/REPAIRS

CJR Propulsion Ltd
Southampton   023 8063 9366

Darglow Engineering Ltd
Wareham   01929 556512

Gori Propellers Poole   01202 621631

Propeller Revolutions
Poole   01202 671226

Sillette – Sonic Ltd
Sutton   020 8337 7543

Vetus Den Ouden Ltd
Southampton   023 8086 1033

RADIO COURSES/SCHOOLS

Bisham Abbey Sailing & Navigation School Bisham   01628 474960

East Coast Offshore Yachting – Les Rant Perry   01480 861381

Hamble School of Yachting
Hamble   023 8045 6687

Pembrokeshire Cruising
Neyland   01646 602500

Plymouth Sailing School
Plymouth   01752 493377

Sail East Ipswich   01206 734319

Sail North Wales
Conwy   01492 584208

Southern Sailing
Swanwick   01489 575511

Start Point Sailing
Kingsbridge   01548 810917

REEFING SYSTEMS

Atlantic Spars Ltd
Brixham   01803 843322

Calibra Marine International Ltd
Southampton   08702 400358

Eurospars Ltd Plymouth 01752 550550

Holman Rigging
Chichester   01243 514000

Navimo UK Ltd
Hedge End   01489 778850

Sea Teach Ltd Emsworth 01243 375774

Southern Spar Services
Northam   023 8033 1714

Wragg, Chris Lymington 01590 677052

Z Spars UK Hadleigh   01473 822130

REPAIR MATERIALS AND ACCESSORIES

Akeron Ltd
Southend on Sea   01702 297101

Howells & Son, KJ
Poole   01202 665724

JB Timber Ltd
North Ferriby   01482 631765

Robbins Timber Bristol 0117 9633136

Sika Ltd
Welwyn Garden City   01707 394444

SP Systems Newport,
Isle of Wight   01983 828000

Technix Rubber & Plastics Ltd
Southampton   01489 789944

Tiflex Liskeard   01579 320808

Timage & Co Ltd
Braintree   01376 343087

Trade Grade Products Ltd
Poole   01202 820177

Wessex Resins & Adhesives Ltd
Romsey   01794 521111

ROPE AND WIRE

Cable & Rope Works
Pevensey   01323 763019

Euro Rope Ltd
Scunthorpe   01724 280480

Marlow Ropes
Hailsham   01323 444444

Mr Splice Leicester   0800 1697178

Spinlock Ltd Cowes   01983 295555

TJ Rigging Conwy   07780 972411

SAFETY EQUIPMENT

AB Marine Ltd
St Peter Port   01481 722378

Adec Marine Ltd
Croydon   020 8686 9717

ADEC MARINE LIMITED
4 Mason Avenue, Croydon,
Surrey, CR0 9XS
Tel: 020 8686 9717
Fax: 020 8680 9912
Approved liferaft services station for
South East.   M&WL12

ADEC Marine Limited
Approved liferaft service station for South East.
Buy or hire new rafts. Complete range of safety
equipment for yachts including pyrotechnics.
Fire extinguishers – Lifejackets – Buoyancy aids
4 Masons Avenue, Croydon,
Surrey CR0 9XS
Tel: 020 8686 9717
Fax: 020 8680 9912
E-mail: sales@adecmarine.co.uk
Website: www.adecmarine.co.uk
2007/M&WMD14/e

Anchorwatch UK
Edinburgh   0131 447 5057

Avon Inflatables
Llanelli   01554 882000

Cosalt International Ltd
Aberdeen   01224 588327

Crewsaver Gosport   023 9252 8621

Glaslyn Marine Supplies Ltd
Porthmadog   01766 513545

Guardian Fire Ltd
Norwich   01603 787679

Hale Marine, Ron
Portsmouth   023 9273 2985

Herm Seaway Marine Ltd
St Peter Port   01481 722838

IBS Boats South Woodham Ferrers
01245 323211/425551

KTS Seasafety Kilkeel   028 41762655

McMurdo Pains Wessex
Portsmouth   023 9262 3900

Met Office Bracknell   0845 300 0300

Nationwide Marine Hire
Warrington   01925 245788

Norwest Marine Ltd
Liverpool   0151 207 2860

Ocean Safety
Southampton   023 8072 0800

Navimo UK Ltd
Hedge End · 01489 778850

Polymarine Ltd Conwy · 01492 583322

Premium Liferaft Services
Burnham-on-Crouch · 0800 243673

Ribeye Dartmouth · 01803 832060

Secumar Swansea · 01792 280545

South Eastern Marine Services Ltd
Basildon · 01268 534427

Suffolk Sailing
Ipswich · 01473 833010

Whitstable Marine
Whitstable · 01227 262525

Winters Marine Ltd
Salcombe · 01548 843580

SAILMAKERS & REPAIRS

Allison-Gray Dundee · 01382 505888

Alsop Sailmakers, John
Salcombe · 01548 843702

Arun Canvas & Rigging
Littlehampton · 01903 732561

Arun Sails Chichester · 01243 573185

Bank Sails, Bruce
Southampton · 01489 582444

Bissett and Ross
Aberdeen · 01224 580659

Breaksea Sails Barry · 01446 730785

Bristol Sails Bristol · 0117 922 5080

Buchanan, Keith
St Mary's · 01720 422037

C&J Marine Textiles
Chichester · 01243 782629

Calibra Sails Dartmouth · 01803 833094

Canard Sails Swansea · 01792 367838

Coastal Covers
Portsmouth · 023 9252 0200

Covercare Fareham · 01329 311878

Crawford, Margaret
Kirkwall · 01856 875692

Crusader Sails Poole · 01202 670580

Cullen Sailmakers
Galway · +353 91 771991

Dawson (Sails), J
Port Dinorwic · 01248 670103

Dolphin Sails Harwich · 01255 243366

Doyle Sails Southampton · 023 8033 2622

Downer International Sails & Chandlery
Dun Laoghaire · +353 1 280 0231

Duthie Marine Safety, Arthur
Glasgow · 0141 429 4553

East Coast Sails
Walton-on-the-Naze · 01255 678353

Flew Sailmakers
Portchester · 01329 822676

Fylde Coast Sailmaking Co
Fleetwood · 01253 873476

Garland Sails Bristol · 0117 935 3233

Goldfinch Sails
Whitstable · 01227 272295

Gowen Ocean Sailmakers
West Mersea · 01206 384412

Green Sailmakers, Paul
Plymouth · 01752 660317

Henderson Sails & Covers
Southsea · 023 9229 4700

Hood Sailmakers
Lymington · 01590 675011

Hooper, A Plymouth · 01752 830411

Hyde Sails (Benfleet)
Benfleet · 01268 756254

Irish Sea Yachts
Maryport · 01900 816881

Jackson Yacht Services
Jersey · 01534 743819

Jeckells and Son Ltd (Wroxham)
Wroxham · 01603 782223

Jessail Ardrossan · 01294 467311

JKA Sailmakers
Pwllheli · 01758 613266

Kemp Sails Ltd
Wareham · 01929 554308/554378

Lawrence Sailmakers, J
Brightlingsea · 01206 302863

Leith UK
Berwick on Tweed · 01289 307264

Lodey Sails Newlyn · 01736 719359

Lossie Sails
Lossiemouth · 07989 956698

Lucas Sails Portchester · 023 9237 3699

Malakoff and Moore
Lerwick · 01595 695544

Malcolm Sails Fairlie · 01475 568500

McCready and Co Ltd, J
Belfast · 028 90232842

McKillop Sails, John
Kingsbridge · 01548 852343

McKillop Sails (Sail Locker)
Ipswich · 01255 678353

McNamara Sails, Michael
Great Yarmouth · 01692 584186

McWilliam Sailmaker (Crosshaven)
Crosshaven · +353 21 4831505

Mitchell Sails Fowey · 01726 833731

Montrose Rope and Sails
Montrose · 01674 672657

Mountfield Sails
Hayling Island · 023 9246 3720

Mouse Sails Holyhead · 01407 763636

Nicholson Hughes Sails
Rosneath · 01436 831356

North Sea Sails
Tollesbury · 01621 869367

North West Sails
Keighley · 01535 652949

Northrop Sails
Ramsgate · 01843 851665

Ocean Sails Plymouth · 01752 563666

Ösen Sails Ltd
Plymouth · 01752 563666

Owen Sails (Gourock)
Gourock · 01475 636196

Owen Sails By Oban · 01631 720485

Parker & Kay Sailmakers –
East Ipswich · 01473 659878

Parker & Kay Sailmakers –
South Hamble · 023 8045 8213

Penrose Sailmakers
Falmouth · 01326 312705

Pinnell & Bax
Northampton · 01604 592808

Pollard Marine
Port St Mary · 01624 835831

Quantum Sails
Ipswich Haven Marina · 01473 659878

Quantum-Parker & Kay Sailmakers
Hamble · 023 8045 8213

Quay Sails (Poole) Ltd
Poole · 01202 681128

Ratsey & Lapthorn
Isle of Wight · 01983 294051

Ratsey Sailmakers, Stephen
Milford Haven · 01646 601561

Relling One Design
Portland · 01305 826555

Richardson Sails
Southampton · 023 8040 3914

Rig Shop, The
Southampton · 023 8033 8341

Rockall Sails
Chichester · 01243 573185

Sail Locker
Woolverstone Marina · 01473 780206

Sail Style Hayling Is · 023 9246 3720

Sails & Canvas Exeter · 01392 877527

Saltern Sail Co
West Cowes · 01983 280014

Saltern Sail Company
Yarmouth · 01983 760120

Sanders Sails
Lymington · 01590 673981

Saturn Sails Largs · 01475 689933

Scott & Co, Graham
St Peter Port · 01481 259380

Shore Sailmakers
Swanwick · 01489 589450

SKB Sails Falmouth · 01326 372107

Sketrick Sailmakers Ltd
Killinchy · 028 9754 1400

South West Sails
Penryn · 01326 375291

Southern Sails Poole · 01202 309129

Stanley Sail & Cover Makers, G
Hull · 01482 225590

Storrar Marine Store
Newcastle upon Tyne   0191 266 1037

Suffolk Sails
Woodbridge   01394 386323

Sunset Sails
Sligo   +353 71 62792

Teltale Sails Prestwick   01355 500001

Torquay Marina Sails and Canvas
Exeter   01392 877527

Trident UK Gateshead   0191 490 1736

UK McWilliam Cowes   01983 281100

Underwood Sails Queen Anne's
Battery, Plymouth   01752 229661

W Sails Leigh-on-Sea   01702 714550

Watson Sails
Dublin 13   +353 1 846 2206

WB Leitch and Son
Tarbert   01880 820287

Westaway Sails
Plymouth Yacht Haven   01752 892560

Wilkinson, Ursula
Brighton   01273 677758

Wilkinson Sails
Burnham-on-Crouch   01621 786770

Wilkinson Sails
Teynham   01795 521503

Yacht Shop, The
Fleetwood   01253 879238

SLIPWAYS

Aberystwyth Marina
Aberystwyth   01970 611422

Amble Marina Amble   01665 712168

Ardfern Yacht Centre Ltd
by Lochgilphead   01852 500247

Ardglass Marina
Ardglass   028 448 42332

Arklow Marina
Arklow   +353 402 39901

Bangor Marina
Bangor, Ireland   028 91 453297

Beaucette Marina
Vale, Guernsey   01481 245000

Birdham Pool Marina
Chichester   01243 512310

Blackwater Marina
Maylandsea   01621 740264

Bradwell Marina
Bradwell-on-Sea   01621 776235

Bristol Marina Bristol   0117 9213198

Buckler's Hard Marina
Beaulieu   01590 616200

Cahersiveen Marina
Cahersiveen   +353 669 473214

Caley Marina
Inverness   01463 233437

Carlingford Marina – Ireland
Carlingford   +353 42 9373073

Carrickfergus Marina
Carrickfergus   028 93 366666

Castlepark Marina
Kinsale   +353 21 4774959

Chichester Marina
Chichester   01243 512731

Coleraine Marina
Coleraine   028 7034 4768

Craobh Marina
By Lochgilphead   01852 500222

Crosshaven Boatyard Marina –
Ireland Crosshaven   +353 21 48 31161

Darthaven Marina
Kingswear   01803 752242

Dingle Marina – Ireland
Co Kerry   +353 66 91 51629

Dover Marina Dover   01304 241663

Dunstaffnage Marina Ltd
By Oban   01631 566555

Duver Boatyard
St Helens, Isle of Wight   01983 873711

East Ferry Marina
Cobh   +353 21 481 1342

Emsworth Yacht Harbour
    01243 377727

Falmouth Yacht Haven
Falmouth   01326 312285

Fleetwood Harbour Village Marina
Fleetwood   01253 872323

Glasson Dock Marina
Lancaster   01524 751491

Gosport Marina
Gosport   023 9252 4811

Hafan Pwllheli Pwllheli   01758 701219

Hamble Point Marina
Hamble   023 8045 2464

Hartlepool Marina
Hartlepool   01429 865744

Haslar Marina
Gosport   023 9260 1201

Holy Loch Marina
Dunoon   01369 701800

Holyhead Marina
Holyhead   01407 764242

Howth Marina – Ireland
Howth   +353 1 839 2777

Hythe Marina Village
Southampton   023 8020 7073

Island Harbour Marina
Newport, Isle of Wight   01983 822999

Kilmore Quay Marina – Ireland
Co Wexford   +353 53 29 955

Kilrush Marina & Boatyard – Ireland
Co Clare   +353 65 9052072

Kinsale Yacht Club Marina
Kinsale   +353 21 4772196

Lady Bee Marina
Shoreham   01273 593801

Largs Yacht Haven
Largs   01475 675333

Lawrence Cove Marina – Ireland
Bantry Bay   +353 27 75 044

Littlehampton Marina
Littlehampton   01903 713553

Liverpool Marina
Liverpool   0151 708 5228

Lossiemouth Marina
Lossiemouth   01343 813066

Lymington Marina
Lymington   01590 673312

Malahide Marina – Ireland
Malahide   +353 1 8454129

Marine & General Engineers
Guernsey   01481 245808

Maryport Harbour and Marina
Maryport   01900 814431

Mayflower International Marina
Plymouth   01752 556633

Melfort Pier & Harbour
Kilmelford   01852 200333

Mercury Yacht Harbour
Hamble   023 8045 5994

Milford Marina
Milford Haven   01646 696312/3

Mylor Yacht Harbour Ltd
Falmouth   01326 372121

Newhaven Marina Ltd
Newhaven   01273 513881

Northney Marina
Hayling Island   023 9246 6321

Noss-on-Dart Marina
Dartmouth   01803 834582

Ocean Village Marina
Southampton   023 8022 9385

Parkstone YC (Haven) Ltd
Poole   01202 743610

Penarth Marina
Penarth   029 2070 5021

Penton Hook Marina
Chertsey   01932 568681

Peterhead Bay Marina
Peterhead   01779 474020

Plymouth Yacht Haven
Plymouth   01752 404231

Port Edgar Marina & Sailing School
South Queensferry   0131 331 3330

Portaferry Marina
Portaferry   07703 209780

Portishead Quays Marina
Bristol   01275 841941

Queen Anne's Battery
Plymouth   01752 671142

Ramsgate Royal Harbour Marina
Ramsgate   01843 592277

Ridge Wharf Yacht Centre
Wareham   01929 552650

Royal Cork Yacht Club Marina
Crosshaven   +353 21 4831023

Royal Norfolk and Suffolk Yacht Club
Lowestoft   01502 566726

Ryde Leisure Harbour
Ryde 01983 613879

Salterns Marina Boatyard & Hotel
Poole 01202 707321

Sandpoint Marina (Dumbarton)
Dumbarton 01389 762396

Saxon Wharf Marina
Southampton 023 8033 9490

Seaport Marina
Inverness 01463 233140

Seatons Marina
Coleraine 028 703 832086

Shamrock Quay Marina
Southampton 023 8022 9461

Shepards Wharf Boatyard Ltd
Cowes 01983 297821

St Helier Marina (La Collette)
St Helier 01534 885588

St Peter Port Marinas
St Peter Port 01481 720229

Stromness Marina
Stromness 01856 850744

Suffolk Yacht Harbour
Ipswich 01473 659240

Sunderland Marina
Sunderland 0191 5144721

Sutton Harbour Marina
Sutton 01752 204186

Swanwick Premier Marina
Hamble 01489 885000

Titchmarsh Marina
Walton-on-the-Naze 01255 672185

Tollesbury Marina
Maldon 01621 869202

Torpoint Yacht Harbour
Plymouth 01752 813658

Torquay Marina (Paignton Harbour
Master**)** 01803 557812

Town Quay Marina
Southampton 023 8023 4397

Troon Yacht Haven
Troon 01292 315553

Victoria Marina
St Peter Port 01481 725987

West Wick Marina Ltd
Nr Chelmsford 01245 741268

Weymouth Marina
Weymouth 01305 767576

Whitby Marina
Whitby 01947 602354

Whitehaven Harbour Marina
Whitehaven 01946 692435

Windsor Marina
Windsor 01753 853911

Winters Marine Ltd
Salcombe 01548 843580

Wisbech Yacht Harbour
Wisbech 01945 588059

Woolverstone Marina
Ipswich 01473 780206

SOLAR POWER

Ampair Ringwood 01425 480780

Barden UK Ltd Fareham 01489 570770

Marlec Engineering Co Ltd
Corby 01536 201588

SPRAYHOODS & DODGERS

A & B Textiles
Gillingham 01634 579686

Allison-Gray Dundee 01382 505888

Arton, Charles
Milford-on-Sea 01590 644682

Arun Canvas and Rigging Ltd
Littlehampton 01903 732561

Buchanan, Keith
St Mary's 01720 422037

C & J Marine Textiles
Chichester 01243 785485

Covercare Fareham 01329 311878

Covercraft Southampton 023 8033 8286

Crawford, Margaret
Kirkwall 01856 875692

Flexicovers Poole 01202 721309

Jasper Covers Fareham 01329 845353

JB Yacht Services
Southampton 01489 572487

Jeckells and Son Ltd
Lowestoft 01502 565007

Jeckells and Son Ltd
Wroxham 01603 782223

Jessail Ardrossan 01294 467311

Lomond Boat Covers
Alexandria 01389 602734

Lucas Sails
Portchester 023 9237 3699

Poole Canvas Co Ltd
Poole 01202 677477

Saundersfoot Auto Marine
Saundersfoot 01834 812115

Teltale Sails Prestwick 01292 475125

Trident UK Gateshead 0191 490 1736

SURVEYORS AND NAVAL ARCHITECTS

Amble Boat Company Ltd
Amble 01665 710267

Ark Surveys East Anglia/South Coast
01621 857065/01794 521957

Atkin & Associates
Lymington 01590 688633

Barbican Yacht Agency Ltd
Plymouth 01752 228855

Battick, Lee
St Helier 01534 611143

Booth Marine Surveys, Graham
Birchington-on-Sea 01843 843793

Byrde & Associates
Kimmeridge 01929 480064

Bureau Maritime Ltd
Maldon 01621 859181

Cannell & Associates, David M
Wivenhoe 01206 823337

**Cardiff Commercial Boat Operators
Ltd** Cardiff 029 2037 7872

CE Proof Hamble 023 8045 3245

Clarke Designs LLP, Owen
Dartmouth 01803 770495

Cox, David Penryn 01326 340808

Davies, Peter N
Wivenhoe 01206 823289

Down Marine Co Ltd
Belfast 028 90480247

Evans, Martin
Kirby le Soken 01255 677883

Goodall, JL
Whitby 01947 604791

Green, James
Plymouth 01752 660516

Greening Yacht Design Ltd, David
Chichester 023 9263 1806

Hansing & Associates
North Wales/Midlands 01248 671291

**JP Services – Marine Safety &
Training** Chichester 01243 537552

Levy, Derek
Brighton 01273 721095

MacGregor, WA
Felixstowe 01394 676034

Mahoney & Co, KPO
Co Cork +353 21 477 6150

Marintec
Lymington 01590 683414

McGarry, Mark
Port Dinorwic 01248 671023

Norwood Marine
Margate 01843 835711

Pritchard, Jim
Southampton 023 8045 5544

Quay Consultants Ltd
West Wittering 01243 673056

**Scott Marine Surveyors &
Consultants** Conwy 01492 573001

S Roberts Marine Ltd
Liverpool 0151 707 8300

Staton-Bevan, Tony
Lymington 01590 645755/07850 315744

Swanwick Yacht Surveyors
Southampton 01489 564822

Temple, Chris
Yarmouth 01983 760947

Thomas, Stephen
Southampton 023 8048 6273

Victoria Yacht Surveys
Cornwall 0800 093 2113

Ward & McKenzie
Woodbridge 01394 383222

Ward & McKenzie (North East)
Pocklington   01759 304322

**YDSA Yacht Designers & Surveyors
Association** Bordon   0845 0900162

TAPE TECHNOLOGY

Adhesive Technologies
Braintree   01376 346511

CC Marine (Rubbaweld) Ltd
Chichester   01243 672606

Trade Grade Products Ltd
Poole   01202 820177

UK Epoxy Resins
Burscough   01704 892364

3M United Kingdom plc
Bracknell   01344 858315

TRANSPORT/YACHT DELIVERIES

Anglo European Boat Transport
Devon   01803 868691

Boat Shifters
          07733 344018/01326 210548

**CONVOI EXCEPTIONNEL LTD
10 Mitchell Point, Ensign Way,
Hamble, Southampton
SO31 4RF
Tel: (023) 8045 3045
Fax: (023) 8045 4551
Email: info@convoi.co.uk**
International marine haulage and abnormal
load consultants. European abnormal load
permits obtained and escort car service.
Capacity for loads up to 100 tons.

M&WEXT5/e

Convoi Exceptionnel Ltd
Hamble   023 8045 3045

Debbage Yachting
Ipswich   01473 601169

East Coast Offshore Yachting
                       01480 861381

Forrest Marine Ltd
Exeter   08452 308335

Hainsworth's UK and Continental
Bingley   01274 565925

Houghton Boat Transport
Tewkesbury   07831 486710

Moonfleet Sailing
Poole   01202 682269

Ocean Yacht Deliveries
Mold   01352 740962

Performance Yachting
Plymouth   01752 565023

Peters & May Ltd
Southampton   023 8048 0480

Reeder School of Seamanship, Mike
Lymington   01590 674560

Sail North Wales
Conwy   01492 584208

Sealand Boat Deliveries Ltd

Nationwide and worldwide
yacht transport, for 32
years. Storage, salvage
and lifting 24/7 ops room
01254 705225 fax 776582
ros@poptel.org
www.btx.co.uk

2006/M&WMD2/e

Seafix Boat Transfer
North Wales   01766 514507

Sealand Boat Deliveries Ltd
Liverpool   01254 705225

Shearwater Sailing
Southampton   01962 775213

Southcoasting Navigators
Devon   01626 335626

West Country Boat Transport
                       01566 785651

Wolff, David   07659 550131

TUITION/SAILING SCHOOLS

**Association of Scottish Yacht
Charterers** Argyll   01880 820012

**Bisham Abbey Sailing & Navigation
School** Bisham   01628 474960

Blue Baker Yachts
Ipswich   01473 780008

Britannia Sailing (East Coast)
Ipswich   01473 787019

British Offshore Sailing School
Hamble   023 8045 7733

Coastal Sea School
Weymouth   0870 321 3271

Conwy School of Yachting
Conwy   01492 572999

Corsair Sailing
Banstead   01737 211466

Dart Sailing School
Dartmouth   01803 833973

Dartmouth Sailing
Dartmouth   01803 833399

Drake Sailing School
Plymouth   01635 253009

East Anglian Sea School
Ipswich   01473 659992

**East Coast Offshore Yachting – Les
Rant** Perry   01480 861381

Five Star Sailing
Southampton   01489 885599

Fowey Cruising School
Fowey   01726 832129

Gibraltar Sailing Centre
Gibraltar   00350 78554

Go Sail Ltd East
Cowes   01983 280220

Hamble School of Yachting
Hamble   023 8045 6687

Haslar Sea School
Gosport   023 9252 0099

Hobo Yachting
Southampton   023 8033 4574

Hoylake Sailing School
Wirral   0151 632 4664

Ibiza Sailing School   07092 235 853

International Yachtmaster Academy
Southampton   0800 515439

Island Sea School
Port Dinorwic   01248 352330

**JP Services – Marine Safety &
Training** Chichester   01243 537552

Lymington Cruising School
Lymington   01590 677478

Menorca Cruising School
                       01995 679240

Moncur Sailing School, Bob
Newcastle upon Tyne   0191 265 4472

Moonfleet Sailing Poole 01202 682269

**National Federation of Sea Schools,
The** Woodlands   023 8029 3822

**National Marine Correspondence
School** Birkenhead   0151 647 6777

Northshore King's Lynn 01485 210236

On Deck Sailing
Southampton   023 8033 3887

Pembrokeshire Cruising
Neyland   01646 602500

Performance Yachting
Plymouth   01752 565023

Plain Sailing
Dartmouth   01803 853843

Plymouth Sailing School
Plymouth   01752 493377

Port Edgar Marina & Sailing School
Port Edgar   0131 331 3330

Portsmouth Outdoor Centre
Portsmouth   023 9266 3873

Portugal Sail & Power   01473 833001

Rainbow Sailing School
Swansea   01792 467813

Reeder School of Seamanship, Mike
Lymington   01590 674560

Safe Water Training Sea School Ltd
Wirral   0151 630 0466

Sail East Harwich   01473 689344

Sally Water Training
East Cowes   01983 299033

Sea 'N' Ski Portsmouth 023 9246 6041

Seafever 01342 316293

Solaris Mediterranean Sea School
01925 642909

Solent School of Yachting
Southampton 023 8045 7733

Southcoasting Navigators
Devon 01626 335626

Southern Sailing
Southampton 01489 575511

Start Point Sailing
Dartmouth 01548 810917

Sunsail
Port Solent/Largs 0870 770 6314

Team Sailing Gosport 023 9252 4370

The Dream Or Two Experience of
Yachting Portsmouth 0800 970 7845

Tiller School of Navigation
Banstead 01737 211466

Workman Marine School
Portishead 01275 845844

Wride School of Sailing, Bob
North Ferriby 01482 635623

WATERSIDE ACCOMMODATION & RESTAURANTS

Abbey, The Penzance 01736 330680

Arun View Inn, The
Littlehampton 01903 722335

Baywatch on the Beach
Bembridge 01983 873259

Baywatch on the Harbour
Yarmouth 01983 760054

Beaucette Marina Restaurant
Guernsey 01481 247066

Bella Napoli
Brighton Marina 01273 818577

Bembridge Coast Hotel
Bembridge 01983 873931

Budock Vean Hotel
Porth Navas Creek 01326 252100

Café Mozart Cowes 01983 293681

Caffé Uno Port Solent 023 9237 5227

Chandlers Bar & Bistro Queen Anne's
Battery Marina, Plymouth 01752 257772

Chiquito Port Solent 023 9220 1181

Critchards Seafood Restaurant
Porthleven 01326 562407

Cruzzo Malahide Marina, Co Dublin
+353 1 845 0599

Cullins Yard Bistro
Dover 01304 211666

Custom House, The
Poole 01202 676767

Dart Marina River Lounge
Dartmouth 01803 832580

Deer Leap, The Exmouth 01395 265030

Doghouse Swanwick Marina,
Hamble 01489 571602

Dolphin Restaurant
Gorey 01534 853370

Doune Knoydart 01687 462667

El Puertos
Penarth Marina 029 2070 5551

Falmouth Marina Marine Bar and
Restaurant Falmouth 01326 313481

Ferry Boat Inn West Wick Marina,
Nr Chelmsford 01621 740208

Ferry Inn, The (restaurant)
Pembroke Dock 01646 682947

First and Last, The Braye,
Alderney 01481 823162

Fisherman's Wharf
Sandwich 01304 613636

Folly Inn Cowes 01983 297171

Gaffs Restaurant Fenit Harbour Marina,
County Kerry +353 66 71 36666

Godleys Hotel Fenit,
County Kerry +353 66 71 36108

Harbour Lights Restaurant
Walton on the Naze 01255 851887

Haven Bar and Bistro, The
Lymington Yacht Haven 01590 679971

Haven Hotel Poole 01202 707333

HMS Ganges Restaurant
Mylor Yacht Harbour 01326 374320

Jolly Sailor, The
Bursledon 023 8040 5557

Kames Hotel Argyll 01700 811489

Ketch Rigger, The Hamble Point Marina
Hamble 023 8045 5601

La Cala Lady Bee Marina,
Shoreham 01273 597422

Le Nautique
St Peter Port 01481 721714

Lighter Inn, The
Topsham 01392 875439

Mariners Bistro Sparkes Marina,
Hayling Island 023 9246 9459

Mary Mouse II Haslar Marina,
Gosport 023 9252 5200

Martha's Vineyard
Milford Haven 01646 697083

Master Builder's House Hotel
Buckler's Hard 01590 616253

Millstream Hotel
Bosham 01243 573234

Montagu Arms Hotel
Beaulieu 01590 612324

Olivo Port Solent 023 9220 1473

Oyster Quay Mercury Yacht Harbour,
Hamble 023 8045 7220

Paris Hotel Coverack 01326 280258

Pebble Beach, The
Gosport 023 9251 0789

Petit Champ Sark 01481 832046

Philip Leisure Group
Dartmouth 01803 833351

Priory Bay Hotel Seaview,
Isle of Wight 01983 613146

Quayside Hotel Brixham 01803 855751

Queen's Hotel Kirkwall 01856 872200

Sails Dartmouth 01803 839281

Sharksfin Waterside
Mevagissey 01726 843241

Shell Bay Seafood Restaurant
Poole Harbour 01929 450363

Simply Italian Sovereign Harbour,
Eastbourne 01323 470911

Slackwater Jacques
Port Solent 023 9278 0777

Spinnaker, The
Chichester Marina 01243 511032

Spit Sand Fort
The Solent 01329 242077

Smugglers, The Newlyn 01736 331501

Square Rigger, The Port Hamble Marina
Hamble 023 8045 3446

Steamboat Inn Lossiemouth Marina,
Lossiemouth 01343 812066

Taps Shamrock Quay,
Southampton 023 8022 8621

Tayvallich Inn, The
Argyll 01546 870282

Thai Marina Sovereign Harbour,
Eastbourne 01323 470414

TIGH AN EILEAN HOTEL AND SHIELDAIG BAR
**Shieldaig, on Loch Torridon,
Ross-shire IV54 8XN
Tel: (01520) 755251
Fax: (01520) 755321**
Dramatic mountain surrounded seaside
village with friendly family-run hotel/bar.
Renowned for serving excellent fresh local
produce (speciality seafood). Great drying
room for wet clothes! Lochside courtyard.
Passing seafarers welcome for baths
(towels provided). M&Wext10

Villa Adriana Newhaven Marina
Newhaven 01903 722335

Warehouse Brasserie, The
Poole 01202 677238

Windrose Bar & Restaurant
Carrickfergus Marina,
Carrickfergus 028 9335 1164

36 on the Quay
Emsworth 01243 375592

Coastal/Inshore	2-day by Fax	5-day by Phone
National (3-5 day)	09065 222 340	09068 969 640
Scotland North	09065 222 341	09068 969 641
Scotland East	09065 222 342	09068 969 642
North East	09065 222 343	09068 969 643
East	09065 222 344	09068 969 644
Anglia	09065 222 345	09068 969 645
Channel East	09065 222 346	09068 969 646

Coastal/Inshore	2-day by Fax	5-day by Phone
Mid Channel	09065 222 347	09068 969 647
South West	09065 222 348	09068 969 648
Bristol	09065 222 349	09068 969 649
Wales	09065 222 350	09068 969 650
North West	09065 222 351	09068 969 651
Clyde	09065 222 352	09068 969 652
Caledonia	09065 222 353	09068 969 653
Minch	09065 222 354	09068 969 654
Northern Ireland	09065 222 355	09068 969 655
Channel Islands	—	09068 969 656

Offshore	2-5 day by Fax	2-5 day by Phone
English Channel	09065 222 357	09068 969 657
S North Sea	09065 222 358	09068 969 658
Irish Sea	09065 222 359	09068 969 659
Biscay	09065 222 360	09068 969 660
NW Scotland	09065 222 361	09068 969 661
N North Sea	09065 222 362	09068 969 662

09066 CALLS COST 60P PER MIN. 09061 CALLS COST £1.50 PER MIN.

WEATHER INFORMATION/ METEOROLOGICAL

Met Office Exeter   0870 900 0100

WIND POWER

Ampair Ringwood   01425 480780
LVM Limited Arlesey   01462 733336

WOOD FITTINGS

Howells & Son, KJ
Poole   01202 665724

Onward Trading Co Ltd
Southampton   01489 885250

Robbins Timber
Bristol   0117 963 3136

Sheraton Marine Cabinet
Witney   01993 868275

YACHT BROKERS

ABC Powermarine
Beaumaris   01248 811413

ABYA Association of Brokers & Yacht Agents Bordon   0845 0900162

Adur Boat Sales
Southwick   01273 596680

Ancasta International Boat Sales
Southampton   023 8045 0000

Anglia Yacht Brokerage
Bury St Edmunds   01359 271747

Ardmair Boat Centre
Ullapool   01854 612054

Assured Boating Egham 01784 473300

Barbican Yacht Agency, The
Plymouth   01752 228855

Bates Wharf Marine Sales Ltd
    01932 571141

BJ Marine
Bangor   028 9127 1434

Bluewater Horizons
Weymouth   01305 782080

Boatworks + Ltd
St Peter Port   01481 726071

Caley Marina Inverness   01463 236539

Calibra Marine International Ltd
Southampton   08702 400358

Carrick Marine Projects
Co Antrim   02893 355884

Carroll's Ballyhack Boatyard
New Ross   +353 51 389164

Chichester Harbour Brokerage
Emsworth   0845 345 1473

CJ Marine Mechanical
Troon   01292 313400

Clarke & Carter Interyacht Ltd
Ipswich/Burnham on Crouch
    01473 659681/01621 785600

Coastal Leisure Ltd
Southampton   023 8033 2222

Dale Sailing Brokerage
Neyland   01646 603105

Deacons
Southampton   023 8040 2253

Exe Leisure
Essex Marina   01702 258190

Ferrypoint Boat Co
Youghal   +353 24 94232

GILLINGHAM MARINA
F. Parham Ltd, 173 Pier Road, Gillingham, Kent, ME7 1UB
Tel: 01634 280022
Fax: 01634 280164
30 years of local, friendly service, with 200 plus listed boats. North Kent's agent for Jeanneau.   M&WL8j/e

Gweek Quay Boatyard
Helston   01326 221657

International Barge & Yacht Brokers
Southampton   023 8045 5205

Iron Wharf Boatyard
Faversham   01795 537122

Jackson Yacht Services
Jersey   01534 743819

Kings Yacht Agency
Beaulieu/Southampton
    01590 616316/023 8033 1533

Kippford Slipway Ltd
Dalbeattie   01556 620249

Knox-Johnston, Paul
Southsea   023 9286 4524

Lencraft Boats Ltd
Dungarvan   +353 58 68220

Liberty Yachts Ltd
Plymouth   01752 227911

Lucas Yachting, Mike
Torquay   01803 212840

Network Yacht Brokers
Dartmouth   01803 834864

Network Yacht Brokers
Plymouth   01752 605377

New Horizon Yacht Agency
Guernsey   01481 726335

Oyster Brokerage Ltd
Ipswich   01473 602263

Pearn and Co, Norman
(Looe Boatyard) Looe   01503 262244

Performance Boat Company
Maidenhead   07768 464717

Peters Chandlery
Chichester   01243 511033

Portavon Marina
Keynsham   0117 986 1626

Prosser Marine Sales Ltd
Glasgow   0141 552 2005

Retreat Boatyard
Topsham   01392 874720

Scanyachts
Southampton   023 8045 5608

SD Marine Ltd
Southampton   023 8045 7278

Sea & Shore Ship Chandler
Dundee   01382 202666

South Pier Shipyard
St Helier   01534 519700

South West Yacht Brokers Group
Plymouth   01752 551991

Sunbird Marine Services
Fareham   01329 842613

Trafalgar Yacht Services
Fareham   01329 823577

Transworld Yachts
Hamble   023 8045 7704

WA Simpson Marine Ltd
Dundee   01382 566670

Walton Marine Sales
Brighton   01273 670707

Walton Marine Sales
Portishead   01275 840132

Walton Marine Sales
Wroxham   01603 781178

Watson Marine, Charles
Hamble   023 8045 6505

Western Marine
Dublin   +353 1280 0321

Westways of Plymouth Ltd
Plymouth   01752 670770

Woodrolfe Brokerage
Maldon   01621 868494

Youngboats Faversham   01795 536176

YACHT CHARTERS & HOLIDAYS

Ardmair Boat Centre
Ullapool   01854 612054

Association of Scottish Yacht
Charterers Argyll   01880 820012

Blue Baker Yachts
Ipswich   01473 780111/780008

Coastal Leisure Ltd
Southampton   023 8033 2222

Crusader Yachting
Turkey   01732 867321

Dart Sailing Charters
Dartmouth   01803 833973

Dartmouth Sailing
Dartmouth   01803 833399

Dartmouth Yacht Charters
Dartmouth   01803 883718

Doune Marine Mallaig   01687 462667

Elizabethan Charters (Dartmouth)
Bristol   0117 9615739

Four Seasons Yacht Charter
Gosport   023 9251 1789

Golden Black Sailing
Cornwall   01209 715757

Hamble Point Yacht Charters
Hamble   023 8045 7110

Haslar Marina & Victory Yacht
Charters Gosport   023 9252 0099

OCEAN LEISURE

☎ 0207 930 5050 (EMBANKMENT)
0208 741 4994 (CHISWICK)
✉ INFO@OCEANLEISURE.CO.UK
🌐 WWW.OCEANLEISURE.CO.UK

○ TWO BRANCHES IN CENTRAL LONDON
○ THE CAPITALS LARGEST CHANDLER
○ TECHNICAL AND CASUAL SAILING WEAR
○ HARDWARE AND MARINE ELECTRONICS
○ ONLINE SHOPPING
○ WATERSPORTS EQUIPMENT AND CLOTHING
   FOR...
   SAILING
   SCUBA DIVING
   SURFING
   SWIMMING AND MORE

London's premier
watersports store

2007/NC39/e

Indulgence Charters
Wendover   01296 696006

Liberty Yachts West Country, Greece,
Mallorca & Italy   01752 227911

Nautilus Yachting Mediterranean &
Caribbean   01732 867445

Patriot Charters & Sail School
Milford Haven   01437 741202

Plain Sailing Yacht Charters
Dartmouth   01803 853843

Portway Yacht Charters
Plymouth/Falmouth
            01752 606999/01326 212320

Puffin Yachts
Port Solent   01483 420728

Rainbow Sailing School
Swansea   01792 467813

Sailing Holidays Ltd
Mediterranean   020 8459 8787

Sailing Holidays in Ireland
Kinsale   +353 21 477 2927

Setsail Holidays Greece, Turkey,
Croatia, Majorca   01787 310445

Shannon Sailing Ltd
Tipperary   +353 67 24499

Sleat Marine Services
Isle of Skye   01471 844216

Smart Yachts
Mediterranean   01425 614804

Sunsail Worldwide   0870 770 0102

Templecraft Yacht Charters
Lewes   01273 812333

Top Yacht Charter Ltd
Worldwide   01243 520950

Victory Yacht Charters
Gosport   023 9252 0099

West Wales Yacht Charter
Pwllheli   07748 634869

Westward Ho Sailing Ltd
UK and Greece   01633 760970

Westways of Plymouth Ltd
Plymouth   01752 481200

39 North (Mediterranean)
Kingskerwell   07071 393939

407 Racing (Yacht Charter)
Lymington   01590 688407

YACHT CLUBS

Aberaeron YC
Aberdovey   01545 570077

Aberdeen and Stonehaven SC
Nr Inverurie   01569 764006

Aberdour BC Aberdour   01383 860632

Abersoch Power BC
Abersoch   01758 712027

Aberystwyth BC
Aberystwyth   01970 624575

Aldeburgh YC Aldeburgh 01728 452562

Alderney SC Alderney   01481 822959

Alexandra YC
Southend-on-Sea   01702 340363

Arklow SC Arklow   +353 402 33100

Arun YC Littlehampton 01903 716016

Axe YC Axemouth   01297 20043

Ayr Yacht and CC Ayr   01292 476034

Ballyholme YC Bangor   028 91271467

Baltimore SC
Baltimore   +353 28 20426

Banff SC Banff   01464 820308

MARINE SUPPLIES AND SERVICES GUIDE

YACHT CLUBS · METEOROLOGICAL · WEATHER INFORMATION/METEOROLOGICAL – YACHT CLUBS

Bantry Bay SC Bantry +353 27 50081

Barry YC Barry 01446 735511

Beaulieu River SC
Brockenhurst 01590 616273

Bembridge SC
Isle of Wight 01983 872237

Benfleet YC
Canvey Island 01268 792278

**Blackpool and
Fleetwood YC** 01253 884205

Blackwater SC Maldon 01621 853923

Blundellsands SC 0151 929 2101

Bosham SC Chichester 01243 572341

Brading Haven YC
Isle of Wight 01983 872289

Bradwell CC Bradwell 01621 892970

Bradwell Quay YC
Wickford 01268 776539

Brancaster Staithe SC 01485 210249

Brandy Hole YC
Hullbridge 01702 230320

Brightlingsea SC
Colchester 01206 303275

Brighton Marina YC
Peacehaven 01273 818711

Bristol Avon SC Bristol 01225 873472

Bristol Channel YC
Swansea 01792 366000

Bristol Corinthian YC
Axbridge 01934 732033

Brixham YC Brixham 01803 853332

**Burnham Overy
Staithe SC** 01328 730961

Burnham-on-Crouch SC
Burnham-on-Crouch 01621 782812

Burnham-on-Sea SC
Bridgwater 01278 792911

Burry Port YC
Burry Port 01554 833635

Cabot CC 01275 855207

Caernarfon SC (Menai Strait)
Caernarfon 01286 672861

Campbeltown SC
Campbeltown 01586 552488

Cardiff YC Cardiff 029 2046 3697

Cardiff Bay YC Cardiff 029 20226575

Carlingford Lough YC
Rostrevor 028 4173 8604

Carrickfergus SC
Whitehead 028 93 351402

Castle Cove SC
Weymouth 01305 783708

Castlegate Marine Club
Stockton on Tees 01642 583299

Chanonry SC Fortrose 01463 221415

Chichester Cruiser and Racing Club
01483 770391

Chichester YC
Chichester 01243 512918

Christchurch SC
Christchurch 01202 483150

Clyde CC Glasgow 0141 221 2774

Co Antrim YC
Carrickfergus 028 9337 2322

Cobnor Activities Centre Trust
01243 572791

Coleraine YC Coleraine 028 703 44503

Colne YC Brightlingsea 01206 302594

Conwy YC Deganwy 01492 583690

Coquet YC 01665 711179

Corrib Rowing & YC
Galway City +353 91 564560

Cowes Combined Clubs
01983 295744

Cowes Corinthian YC
Isle of Wight 01983 296333

Cowes Yachting 01983 280770

Cramond BC 0131 336 1356

Creeksea SC
Burnham-on-Crouch 01245 320578

Crookhaven SC
Crookhaven 087 2379997 mobile

Crouch YC
Burnham-on-Crouch 01621 782252

Dale YC Dale 01646 636362

Dartmouth YC
Dartmouth 01803 832305

Deben YC Woodbridge 01394 386504

Dell Quay SC Chichester 01243 785080

Dingle SC Dingle +353 66 51984

Douglas Bay YC
Douglas 01624 673965

Dovey YC Aberdovey 01213 600008

Dun Laoghaire MYC +353 1 288 938

Dunbar SC
Cockburnspath 01368 86287

East Antrim BC Antrim 028 28 277204

East Belfast YC Belfast 028 9065 6283

East Cowes SC
Isle of Wight 01983 531687

East Dorset SC Poole 01202 706111

East Lothian YC 01620 892698

Eastney Cruising Association
Portsmouth 023 92734103

Eling SC 023 80863987

Emsworth SC Emsworth 01243 372850

Emsworth Slipper SC
Emsworth 01243 378881

Essex YC Southend 01702 478404

Exe SC (River Exe)
Exmouth 01395 264607

Eyott SC Mayland 01245 320703

Fairlie YC 01294 213940

Falmouth Town SC
Falmouth 01326 373915

Falmouth Watersports Association
Falmouth 01326 211223

Fareham Sailing & Motor BC
Fareham 01329 280738

Felixstowe Ferry SC
Felixstowe 01394 283785

Findhorn YC Findhorn 01309 690247

Fishguard Bay YC
Lower Fishguard 01348 872866

Flushing SC Falmouth 01326 374043

Folkestone Yacht and Motor BC
Folkestone 01303 251574

Forth Corinthian YC
Haddington 0131 552 5939

Forth YCs Association
Edinburgh 0131 552 3006

Fowey Gallants SC
Fowey 01726 832335

Foynes YC Foynes +353 69 91201

Galway Bay SC +353 91 794527

Glasson SC Lancaster 01524 751089

Glenans Irish Sailing School
+353 1 6611481

Glenans Irish SC (Westport)
+353 98 26046

Gosport CC Gosport 02392 586838

Gravesend SC
Gravesend 01474 533974

Greenwich YC London 020 8858 7339

Grimsby and Cleethorpes YC
Grimsby 01472 356678

Guernsey YC
St Peter Port 01481 722838

Halfway YC 01702 582025

Hamble River SC
Southampton 023 80452070

Hampton Pier YC
Herne Bay 01227 364749

Hardway SC Gosport 023 9258 1875

Hartlepool YC
Hartlepool 01429 233423

Harwich Town SC
Harwich 01255 503200

Hastings and St Leonards YC
Hastings 01424 420656

Haven Ports YC
Woodbridge   01394 659658

Hayling Ferry SC; Locks SC
Hayling Island   023 80829833

Hayling Island SC
Hayling Island   023 92463768

Helensburgh SC Rhu   01436 672778

Helensburgh   01436 821234

Helford River SC
Helston   01326 231006

Herne Bay SC
Herne Bay   01227 375650

Highcliffe SC
Christchurch   01425 274874

Holyhead SC Holyhead 01407 762526

Holywood YC Holywood 028 90423355

Hoo Ness YC Sidcup   01634 250052

Hornet SC Gosport   023 9258 0403

Howth YC Howth   +353 1 832 2141

Hoylake SC Wirral   0151 632 2616

Hullbridge YC   01702 231797

Humber Yawl Club   01482 667224

Hurlingham YC London 020 8788 5547

Hurst Castle SC   01590 645589

Hythe SC Southampton 02380 846563

Ilfracombe YC
Ilfracombe   01271 863969

Iniscealtra SC
Limerick   +353 61 338347

Invergordon BC   01349 852265

Irish CC   +353 214870031

Island CC Salcombe   01548 531176

Island SC Isle of Wight 01983 296621

Island YC Canvey Island 01268 510360

Isle of Bute SC
Rothesay   01700 502819

Isle of Man YC
Port St Mary   01624 832088

Itchenor SC Chichester 01243 512400

Keyhaven YC Keyhaven 01590 642165

Killyleagh YC
Killyleagh   028 4482 8250

Kircubbin SC
Kirkcubbin   028 4273 8422

Kirkcudbright SC
Kirkcudbright   01557 331727

Langstone SC Havant   023 9248 4577

Largs SC Largs   01475 670000

Larne Rowing & SC
Larne   028 2827 4573

Lawrenny YC   01646 651212

Leigh-on-Sea SC   01702 476788

Lerwick BC Lerwick   01595 696954

Lilliput SC Poole   01202 740319

Littlehampton Sailing and Motor Club Littlehampton   01903 715859

Loch Ryan SC Stranraer 01776 706322

Lochaber YC Fort William 01397 772361

Locks SC Portsmouth   023 9282 9833

Looe SC Looe   01503 262559

Lossiemouth CC
Fochabers   01348 812121

Lough Swilly YC Fahn +353 74 22377

Lowestoft CC
Lowestoft   01502 574376

Lyme Regis Power BC
Lyme Regis   01297 443788

Lyme Regis SC
Lyme Regis   01297 442373

Lymington Town SC
Lymington   0159 674514

Lympstone SC Exeter   01395 278792

Madoc YC Porthmadog   01766 512976

Malahide YC
Malahide   +353 1 845 3372

Maldon Little Ship Club
                          01621 854139

Manx Sailing & CC
Ramsey   01624 813494

Marchwood YC
Marchwood   023 80666141

Margate YC Margate   01227 292602

Marina BC Pwllheli   01758 612271

Maryport YC   01228 560865

Mayflower SC Plymouth 01752 662526

Mayo SC (Rosmoney)
Rosmoney   +353 98 27772

Medway YC Rochester   01634 718399

Menai Bridge BC
Beaumaris   01248 810583

Mengham Rythe SC
Hayling Island   023 92463337

Merioneth YC
Barmouth   01341 280000

Monkstone Cruising and SC
Swansea   01792 812229

Montrose SC Montrose 01674 672554

Mumbles YC Swansea   01792 369321

Mylor YC Falmouth   01326 374391

Nairn SC Nairn   01667 453897

National YC
Dun Laoghaire   +353 1 280 5725

Netley SC Netley   023 80454272

New Quay YC
Aberdovey   01545 560516

Newhaven & Seaford SC
Seaford   01323 890077

Newport and Uskmouth SC
Cardiff   01633 271417

Newtownards SC
Newtownards   028 9181 3426

Neyland YC Neyland   01646 600267

North Devon YC
Bideford   01271 861390

North Fambridge Yacht Centre
                          01621 740370

North Haven YC Poole   01202 708830

North of England Yachting Association Kirkwall   01856 872331

North Sunderland Marine Club
Sunderland   01665 721231

North Wales CC
Conwy   01492 593481

North West Venturers YC (Beaumaris) Beaumaris 0161 2921943

Oban SC Ledaig by Oban
                          01631 563999

Orford SC Woodbridge 01394 450997

Orkney SC Kirkwall   01856 872331

Orwell YC Ipswich   01473 602288

Oulton Broad Yacht Station
                          01502 574946

Ouse Amateur SC
Kings Lynn   01553 772239

Paignton SC Paignton 01803 525817

Parkstone YC Poole   01202 743610

Peel Sailing and CC
Peel   01624 842390

Pembroke Haven YC   01646 684403

Pembrokeshire YC
Milford Haven   01646 692799

Penarth YC Penarth   029 20708196

Pentland Firth YC
Thurso   01847 891803

Penzance YC Penzance 01736 364989

Peterhead SC Ellon   01779 75527

Pin Mill SC Woodbridge 01394 780271

Plym YC Plymouth   01752 404991

Poolbeg YC   +353 1 660 4681

Poole YC Poole   01202 672687

Porlock Weir SC
Watchet   01643 862702

Port Edgar YC Penicuik 01968 674210

Port Navas YC
Falmouth   01326 340065

Port of Falmouth Sailing Association
Falmouth   01326 372927

Portchester SC
Portchester   023 9237 6375

Porthcawl Harbour BC
Swansea   01656 655935

Porthmadog SC
Porthmadog   01766 513546

Portrush YC Portrush   028 7082 3932

Portsmouth SC
Portsmouth   02392 820596

Prestwick SC Prestwick   01292 671117

Pwllheli SC Pwllheli   01758 613343

Queenborough YC
Queenborough   01795 663955

Quoile YC
Downpatrick   028 44 612266

R Towy BC Tenby   01267 241755

RAFYC   023 80452208

Redclyffe YC Poole   01929 557227

Restronguet SC
Falmouth   01326 374536

Ribble CC
Lytham St Anne's   01253 739983

River Wyre YC   01253 811948

RNSA (Plymouth)
Plymouth   01752 55123/83

Rochester CC
Rochester   01634 841350

Rock Sailing and Water Ski Club
Wadebridge   01208 862431

Royal Dart YC
Dartmouth   01803 752496

Royal Motor YC Poole   01202 707227

Royal Anglesey YC (Beaumaris)
Anglesey   01248 810295

Royal Burnham YC
Burnham-on-Crouch   01621 782044

Royal Channel Islands YC (Jersey)
St Aubin   01534 745783

Royal Cinque Ports YC
Dover   01304 206262

Royal Corinthian YC (Burnham-on-Crouch)
Burnham-on-Crouch   01621 782105

Royal Corinthian YC (Cowes)
Cowes   01983 292608

Royal Cork YC
Crosshaven   +353 21 831023

Royal Cornwall YC (RCYC)
Falmouth   01326 317190

Royal Dorset YC
Weymouth   01305 786258

Royal Forth YC
Edinburgh   0131 552 3006

Royal Fowey YC Fowey   01726 833573

Royal Gourock YC
Gourock   01475 632983

Royal Highland YC
Connel   01546 510261

Royal Irish YC
Dun Laoghaire   +353 1 280 9452

Royal London YC
Isle of Wight   019 83299727

Royal Lymington YC
Lymington   01590 672677

Royal Mersey YC
Birkenhead   0151 645 3204

Royal Motor YC Poole   01202 707227

Royal Naval Club and Royal Albert YC Portsmouth   023 9282 5924

Royal Naval Sailing Association
Gosport   023 9252 1100

Royal Norfolk & Suffolk YC
Lowestoft   01502 566726

Royal North of Ireland YC
                        028 90 428041

Royal Northern and Clyde YC
Rhu   01436 820322

Royal Northumberland YC
Blyth   01670 353636

Royal Plymouth Corinthian YC
Plymouth   01752 664327

Royal Scottish Motor YC
                        0141 881 1024

Royal Solent YC
Yarmouth   01983 760256

Royal Southampton YC
Southampton   023 8022 3352

Royal Southern YC
Southampton   023 8045 0300

Royal St George YC
Dun Laoghaire   +353 1 280 1811

Royal Tay YC Dundee   01382 477133

Royal Temple YC
Ramsgate   01843 591766

Royal Torbay YC
Torquay   01803 292006

Royal Ulster YC
Bangor   028 91 270568

Royal Victoria YC
Fishbourne   01983 882325

Royal Welsh YC (Caernarfon)
Caernarfon   01286 672599

Royal Welsh YC
Aernarfon   01286 672599

Royal Western YC
Plymouth   01752 660077

Royal Yacht Squadron
Isle of Wight   01983 292191

Royal Yorkshire YC
Bridlington   01262 672041

Rye Harbour SC Rye   01797 223136

Salcombe YC Salcombe   01548 842593

Saltash SC Saltash   01752 845988

Scalloway BC Lerwick   01595 880409

Scarborough YC
Scarborough   01723 373821

Schull SC Schull   +353 28 37352

Scillonian Sailing and BC
St Mary's   01720 277229

Seasalter SC
Whitstable   01227 264784

Seaview YC
Isle of Wight   01983 613268

Shoreham SC Henfield   01273 453078

Skerries SC
Carlingford Lough   +353 1 849 1233

Slaughden SC Duxford   01728 689036

Sligo YC Sligo   +353 71 77168

Solva Boat Owners Association
Fishguard   01437 721538

Solway YC
Kirkdudbright   01556 620312

South Caernavonshire YC
Abersoch   01758 712338

South Cork SC   +353 28 36383

South Devon Sailing School
Newton Abbot   01626 52352

South Gare Marine Club - Sail Section Middlesbrough 01642 505630

South Shields SC
South Shields   0191 456 5821

South Woodham Ferrers YC
Chelmsford   01245 325391

Southampton SC
Southampton   023 8044 6575

Southwold SC   01986 784225

Sovereign Harbour YC
Eastbourne   01323 470888

St Helier YC
St Helier   01534 721307/32229

St Mawes SC
St Mawes   01326 270686

Starcross Fishing & CC (River Exe)
Starcross   01626 891996

Starcross YC Exeter   01626 890470

Stoke SC Ipswich   01473 624989

Stornoway SC
Stornoway   01851 705412

Stour SC   01206 393924

Strangford Lough YC
Newtownards   028 97 541202

Strangford SC
Downpatrick   028 4488 1404

Strood YC Aylesford   01634 718261

Sunderland YC
Sunderland   0191 567 5133

Sunsail Portsmouth   023 92222224

Sussex YC
Shoreham-by-Sea   01273 464868

Swanage SC
Swanage   01929 422987

Swansea Yacht & Sub-Aqua Club
Swansea   01792 469096

Tamar River SC
Plymouth   01752 362741

Tarbert Lochfyne YC
Tarbert   01880 820376

Tay Corinthian BC
Dundee   01382 553534

Tay YCs Association   01738 621860

Tees & Hartlepool YC   01429 262249

Tees SC
Aycliffe Village   01429 265400

Teifi BC - Cardigan Bay
Fishguard   01239 613846

Teign Corinthian YC
Teignmouth   01626 777699

Tenby SC
Tenby   01834 842762

Tenby YC   01834 842762

Thames Estuary YC   01702 345967

Thorney Island SC
Thorney Island   01243 371731

Thorpe Bay YC   01702 587563

Thurrock YC
Grays   01375 373720

Tollesbury CC
Tollesbury   01621 869561

Topsham SC
Topsham   01392 877524

Torpoint Mosquito SC -
Plymouth   01752 812508

Tralee SC
Tralee   +353 66 36119

Troon CC
Troon   01292 311190

Troon YC
Troon   01292 315315

Tudor SC
Portsmouth   023 92662002

Tynemouth SC
Newcastle upon Tyne   0191 2572167

Up River YC
Hullbridge   01702 231654

Upnor SC
Upnor   01634 718043

Wakering YC
Rochford   01702 530926

Waldringfield SC
Woodbridge   01394 283347

Walls Regatta Club
Lerwick   01595 809273

Walton & Frinton YC
Walton-on-the-Naze   01255 675526

Warrenpoint BC
Warrenpoint   028 4175 2137

Warsash SC
Southampton   023 80583575

Watchet Boat Owner Association
Watchet   01984 633736

Waterford Harbour SC
Dunmore East   +353 51 383230

Watermouth YC
Watchet   01271 865048

Wear Boating Association
                            0191 567 5313

Wells SC
Wells-next-the-sea   01328 711190

West Kirby SC
West Kirby   0151 625 5579

West Mersea YC
Colchester   01206 382947

Western Isles YC   01688 302371

Western YC
Kilrush   +353 87 2262885

Weston Bay YC
Portishead   01275 620772

Weston CC
Southampton   07905 557298

Weston SC
Southampton   023 80452527

Wexford HBC
Wexford   +353 53 22039

Weymouth SC
Weymouth   01305 785481

Whitby YC
Whitby   01947 603623

Whitstable YC
Whitstable   01227 272343

Wicklow SC
Wicklow   +353 404 67526

Witham SC
Boston   01205 363598

Wivenhoe SC
Colchester   01206 822132

Woodbridge CC
Woodbridge   01394 386737

Wormit BC   01382 553878

Yarmouth SC
Yarmouth   01983 760270

Yealm YC
Newton Ferrers   01752 872291

Youghal Sailing Club
Youghal   +353 24 92447

YACHT DESIGNERS

Cannell & Associates, David M
Wivenhoe   01206 823337

Clarke Designs LLP, Owen
Dartmouth   01803 770495

Giles Naval Architects, Laurent
Lymington   01590 641777

Greening Yacht Design Ltd
Chichester   023 9263 1806

Harvey Design, Ray
Barton on Sea   01425 613492

Jones Yacht Design, Stephen
Warsash   01489 576439

Wharram Designs, James
Truro   01872 864792

Wolstenholme Yacht Design
Coltishall   01603 737024

YACHT MANAGEMENT

Barbican Yacht Agency Ltd
Plymouth   01752 228855

Coastal Leisure Ltd
Southampton   023 8033 2222

O'Sullivan Boat Management
Dun Laoghaire   +353 86 829 6625

Swanwick Yacht Surveyors
Swanwick   01489 564822

407 Racing (Yacht Charter)
Lymington   01590 688407

YACHT VALETING

Blackwell, Craig
Co Meath   +353 87 677 9605

Bright 'N' Clean
South Coast   07789 494430

BoatScrubber International
Haslar Marina, Gosport   023 9251 0567

Clean It All
Nr Brixham   01803 844564

Kip Marina Inverkip   01475 521485

Mainstay Yacht Maintenance
Dartmouth   01803 839076

Marine Gleam
Lymington   0800 074 4672

Mobile Yacht Maintenance
                            07900 148806

Shipshape Hayling Is   023 9246 6277

Smith Boat Care, Paul
Isle of Wight   01983 754726